The Sociolinguistics of Globalization

Human language has changed in the age of globalization: no longer tied to stable and resident communities, it moves across the globe, and it changes in the process. The world has become a complex 'web' of villages, towns, neighbourhoods and settlements connected by material and symbolic ties in often unpredictable ways. This phenomenon requires us to revise our understanding of linguistic communication. In *The Sociolinguistics of Globalization* Jan Blommaert constructs a theory of changing language in a changing society, reconsidering locality, repertoires, competence, history and sociolinguistic inequality.

JAN BLOMMAERT is Professor of Language, Culture and Globalization in the Department of Language and Culture Studies at Tilburg University, The Netherlands.

Cambridge Approaches to Language Contact

General Editor
Salikoko S. Mufwene, *University of Chicago*

Editorial Board
Robert Chaudenson, *Université d'Aix-en-Provence*
Braj Kachru, *University of Illinois at Urbana*
Raj Mesthrie, *University of Cape Town*
Lesley Milroy, *University of Michigan*
Shana Poplack, *University of Ottawa*
Michael Silverstein, *University of Chicago*

Cambridge Approaches to Language Contact is an interdisciplinary series bringing together work on language contact from a diverse range of research areas. The series focuses on key topics in the study of contact between languages or dialects, including the development of pidgins and creoles, language evolution and change, world Englishes, code-switching and code-mixing, bilingualism and second language acquisition, borrowing, interference, and convergence phenomena.

Published titles

Salikoko Mufwene, *The Ecology of Language Evolution*
Michael Clyne, *Dynamics of Language Contact*
Bernd Heine and Tania Kuteva, *Language Contact and Grammatical Change*
Edgar W. Schneider, *Postcolonial English*
Virginia Yip and Stephen Matthews, *The Bilingual Child*
Bernd Heine and Derek Nurse (eds), *A Linguistic Geography of Africa*
J. Clancy Clements, *The Linguistic Legacy of Spanish and Portuguese*
Umberto Ansaldo, *Contact Languages*
Jan Blommaert, *The Sociolinguistics of Globalization*

Further titles planned for the series

Guy Bailey and Patricia Cukor-Avila, *African–American English*
Maarten Mous, *Controlling Language*
Bridget Drinka, *Language Contact in Diachronic Perspective*

The Sociolinguistics
of Globalization

Jan Blommaert

Tilburg University

CAMBRIDGE UNIVERSITY PRESS
Cambridge, New York, Melbourne, Madrid, Cape Town, Singapore,
São Paulo, Delhi, Tokyo, Mexico City

Cambridge University Press
The Edinburgh Building, Cambridge CB2 8RU, UK

Published in the United States of America by Cambridge University Press, New York

www.cambridge.org
Information on this title: www.cambridge.org/9780521710237

First published 2010
3rd printing 2011

Printed in the United Kingdom at the University Press, Cambridge

A catalogue record for this publication is available from the British Library

Library of Congress Cataloguing in Publication data
Blommaert, Jan.
The sociolinguistics of globalization / Jan Blommaert.
  p. cm. – (Cambridge approaches to language contact)
ISBN 978-0-521-88406-8 (hardback) – ISBN 978-0-521-71023-7 (pbk.)
1. Language and languages – Globalization. 2. Languages in contact.
3. Linguistic change. 4. Sociolinguistics. I. Title. II. Series.
P130.5.B58 2010
306.44–dc22

                                                                2009050366

ISBN 978-0-521-88406-8 Hardback
ISBN 978-0-521-71023-7 Paperback

For Michael S. and Sali M., loyal Kepketarians

Contents

Illustrations

Series editor's foreword

The series *Cambridge Approaches to Language Contact* (CALC) was set up to publish outstanding monographs on language contact, especially by authors who approach their specific subject matter from a diachronic or developmental perspective. Our goal is to integrate the ever-growing scholarship on language diversification (including the development of creoles, pidgins, and indigenized varieties of colonial European languages), bilingual language development, code-switching, and language endangerment. We hope to provide a select forum to scholars who contribute insightfully to understanding language evolution from an interdisciplinary perspective. We favour approaches that highlight the role of ecology and draw inspiration both from the authors' own fields of specialization and from related research areas in linguistics or other disciplines. Eclecticism is one of our mottoes, as we endeavour to comprehend the complexity of evolutionary processes associated with contact.

We are very happy to add to our list Jan Blommaert's *The Sociolinguistics of Globalization*, an authoritative invitation to rethink linguistic communication in a world that has become increasingly interconnected, is marked by more and more mobility of both people and commodities (including language) as well as by socio-economic inequities, and is undeniably polycentric. Some hegemonic languages, chiefly English, have spread world-wide but have not only become 'global' but also indigenized, both adapted to new communicative habits and subjected to local norms. Consequently, their market values are not universally identical across national borders; in fact, not even within the same borders. It is more and more a question of whose English it is and where it is spoken. These factors determine not only whether a speaker is (fully) integrated or marginalized by the host population, especially in the metropoles of former colonies, but also what social representations their communication in English conjures up of the speaker or writer.

The increasing population mobility brought about by European colonization and associated especially with today's patterns of economic globalization and war refugeeism have also produced non-hegemonic diasporas, in which languages of the politically and/or economically underprivileged have spread (far) beyond their homelands, making traditional, static geolinguistics clearly out of date. While some linguists have blamed the globalization of today's world for language endangerment, little attention has been paid to the new forms of individual and societal multilingualism that it has produced and to the need to conceive of speakers' repertoires dynamically and no longer as complete but as 'truncated'. Blommaert proposes a 'sociolinguistics of mobile resources', which should acknowledge not only the variable communicative capacities and functions of the different languages spoken by individual speakers but also differences between purely communicative and emblematic uses of a language, such that the same phrases from the same language (say, English or Japanese) used in different settings (say, London or Tokyo) may not have the same ethnographic values.

The Sociolinguistics of Globalization highlights the ways in which heterogeneity in language practice and inequities in the authorities that dictate normative standards reflect new forms of socio-economic inequities created by the recent colonization of the world by Europe and by the way world-wide economic globalization is now practised. They also reflect the particularly uneven ways in which national and world economies have developed world-wide, especially increasing the gap between the economic North and South as well as between the rural and urban communities in the economic South. They have likewise created enormous gaps between urban centres and urban peripheries, between national centres and national peripheries, and of course between world centres and world peripheries. As people travel across their residential boundaries, the market values of the language varieties they practise change as much as their own, as their socio-economic positions are constantly being redefined. It is becoming obviously inadequate to practise a sociolinguistics of Saussurean synchrony. Blommaert argues for one that can capture the historical trajectories of speakers and their linguistic communities as they move across social and geographical spaces, i.e. a sociolinguistics in which both speakers and language varieties are treated as historical entities. Linguistic communities can thus be treated as emergent ones, constantly being reshaped by the interactive dynamics of their members. This is a stimulating and thought-provoking book that CALC is proud to be associated with.

SALIKOKO S. MUFWENE
University of Chicago

Preface

I see this book as the third one of a trilogy in which I try to formulate some of the consequences of globalization for the study of language in society. The first book of the series, *Discourse: A Critical Introduction* (2005) attempted to sketch these consequences for our understanding of discourse, as well as for our ethos of analysing it. The same approach was applied to literacy in *Grassroots Literacy* (2008), and I am here bringing the same exercise to the field of sociolinguistics. Each of the books is an attempt, an *essai* in the classical and original sense of the term, in which I try my best to describe the problem and offer some conceptual and analytical tools for addressing it. And I make this effort because I believe that globalization forces us – whether we like it or not – to an *aggiornamento* of our theoretical and methodological toolkit. Much as modernism defined most of the current widespread tools of our trade, the transition towards a different kind of social system forces us to redefine them. Such an exercise, however iconoclastic it may seem at first, cannot be avoided or postponed.

The tone of this book, like the previous two, is consequently critical and paradigmatic. I deliberately try to push myself to explore the limits of the present sociolinguistic instrumentarium in an attempt to demonstrate its short-comings and the need to revise its ingredients. It is a conscious attempt to think outside the box, and at times it will suffer from its own radicalism. There will be passages in this book where I will probably overstate my case while trying to be as clear as possible, and there will be places where I produce theoretical over-kill. I hope, however, that I will nowhere create a caricature of sociolinguistic globalization processes. I have in this book tried to be outspokenly empirical in the theoretical effort I make. The theoretical issues will be addressed by providing long and detailed empirical analyses, partly to enhance the clarity of my argument and partly to provide baseline descriptions of globalization phenomena of a particular kind. I hope that, even in the event that the theoretical effort will be judged to be worthless, the empirical effort will be appreciated. Behind the job of theoretical development lies the work of description, and being an ethnographer I tend to take that job quite seriously. I also believe that this job of description is the most important contribution that sociolinguistic work can make. We possess (if we use it well) a descriptive apparatus of unparalleled precision, capable of reading infinitely big features of society from infinitely small details of communicative behaviour. Our most persuasive discourse is empirical and descriptive: we are at our best when we provide theoretically grounded and sophisticated descriptions of language problems in the world. The theoretical challenges of globalization may make some scholars inclined to produce more theory than description; in my view this would mean that we thereby sacrifice some of our best and most powerful tools.

The three books have one large theoretical theme in common – a theme which will emerge here towards the end of this book. It is a critique of the Saussurean synchrony – a view of sociolinguistic reality in which language is undressed, so to speak, and robbed of the spatial and temporal features that define its occurrence, meaning and function in real social life. It is my view that this Saussurean synchrony has no real existence, and cannot remain intact even as a hypothetical theoretical construct. We need to replace it with a view of language as something intrinsically and perpetually mobile, through space as well as time, and *made for* mobility. The finality of language is mobility, not immobility. I share this insight with several other scholars and cannot claim to be original in this respect. Michael Silverstein, for one, has done a lot in questioning this old paradigm, and the book is dedicated to him and to Salikoko Mufwene, another scholar with a unique sense of history (and the man who offered me an opportunity to write this book). But the attack started as soon as people such as John Gumperz, Dell Hymes, Erving Goffman and Aaron Cicourel rediscovered the theoretical and paradigmatic value of ethnography, and Pierre Bourdieu, Michel Foucault and others launched their critiques on structuralism. Needless to say, Gunther Kress's development of multimodal analysis was also instrumental in the critique of the static and totalizing features of synchronicity. In my view, synchrony is a feature of a modernist epistemology, one that reflected its times. Now that times have changed and we are looking at a world that can no longer be neatly divided into clear and transparent categories, the theoretical paradigms need to be revised as well. My effort is, in that sense, deeply historical.

Even if the direct origins of the book are a series of seminars I taught at the University of Chicago in 2003, this book is a synthesis of a decade of research, and I cannot possibly thank everyone who has influenced its sound and shape. But I must thank the original co-authors of certain parts of it for allowing me to re-use our joint work here: Tope Omoniyi, Charlyn Dyers, Nathalie Muyllaert, Marieke Huysmans, Evita Willaert, Lies Creve and Lieselotte Van der Donck. Stef Slembrouck and Jim Collins were essential in formulating some of the key concepts and insights that drive this book. I am also grateful to Dong Jie, April Huang, Sjaak Kroon, Max Spotti, Sari Pietikäinen and Rob Moore, my partners during fieldwork adventures over the past few years, who have helped me shape my thoughts on numerous issues (and sometimes also helped me in formulating them). My wife Pika gave me advice on the Japanese examples and read the whole manuscript a couple of times, providing me with tons of helpful comments and suggestions for clarification. And some of my interlocutors of the past few years – Gunther Kress, Ben Rampton, Roxy Harris, Brian Street, Constant Leung, David Block, Sirpa Leppänen and Päivi Pahta – constantly fed me with a supply of thoughts, reflections and criticisms of my radical views.

One final word about the series in which this book is appearing. I consider it a great privilege to become an author in the *Cambridge Approaches to Language Contact*. The series has consistently produced books of the highest quality, and I can only be flattered and humbled by the association with the outstanding group of authors in that series. The consistent quality of the series is to a large extent the result of the rigorous and meticulous editorial work of Sali Mufwene, who thus deserves another accolade here. In my own case, Sali provided me with hundreds of thoughtful and constructive comments and questions on the first draft of this book. The revisions prompted by them greatly improved the book.

All of these people deserve my thanks, and if the book is judged to be good, it is in no small measure due to them. On the other hand, if it is judged to be bad, I alone naturally take the blame for it.

JAN BLOMMAERT
ANTWERP AND JYVÄSKYLÄ

Acknowledgements

Different parts of this book are based on materials that were previously published. Section 2.2 is based on 'Sociolinguistic scales' (*Intercultural Pragmatics* 4/1: 1–19, 2007). The sections 2.3 and 2.4 have their origins in 'Sociolinguistics and discourse analysis: orders of indexicality and polycentricity' (*Journal of Multicultural Discourses* 2/2: 115–130, 2007). Section 3.1 is a revised version of 'Writing locality in globalized Swahili: Semiotizing space in a Tanzanian novel' (In Cécile B. Vigouroux and Salikoko S. Mufwene, eds., *Globalization and Language Vitality: Perspectives from Africa:* 210–228. London: Continuum, 2008). Section 3.3 is based on 'Peripheral normativity: literacy and the production of locality in a South African Township school (*Linguistics and Education* 16: 378–403, 2005), a paper co-authored with Nathalie Muyllaert, Marieke Huysmans and Charlyn Dyers. Section 4.2 has its origins in a paper, co-authored with Tope Omoniyi and titled 'Email fraud: language, technology, and the indexicals of globalisation' (*Social Semiotics* 16/4: 573–605, 2006). Section 6.2 appeared as 'Language, asylum and the national order' in *Current Anthropology* 50/4: 415–441. Section 7.2, finally, is an adapted version of 'Situating language rights: English and Swahili in Tanzania revisited' (*Journal of Sociolinguistics* 9/3: 390–417, 2005). I am grateful to Mouton de Gruyter, Routledge, Continuum, Elsevier and Wiley-Blackwell for permission to use these materials for inclusion in the book.

1 A critical sociolinguistics of globalization

1.1   The challenge

Sociolinguistically, the world has not become a village. That well-matured metaphor of globalization does not work, and that is a pity for sociolinguistics – a science traditionally more at ease when studying a village than when studying the world. Globalization is the catchword for a particular historical phase (the capitalist present, so to speak) and even if the processes we call *globalization* are not new in substance, they are new in intensity, scope and scale. The novelty transpires in the labels we use for them: one of the main features of globalization is that it has spawned its own discourses-on-globalization, thus making it into a self-conscious and seemingly autonomous political, economic, cultural and intellectual project. I will have a word or two to say about the self-consciousness and autonomy, but for now I can restrict myself to accepting the challenge of globalization, that is, to rethink our conceptual and analytic apparatus. The world has not become a village, but rather a tremendously complex web of villages, towns, neighbourhoods, settlements connected by material and symbolic ties in often unpredictable ways. That complexity needs to be examined and understood.

I consider this state of affairs a positive effect of globalization, because it forces us to think about phenomena as located in and distributed across different scales, from the global to the local, and to examine the connections between these various levels in ways that do not reduce phenomena and events to their strict context of occurrence. In other words, globalization forces sociolinguistics to unthink its classic distinctions and biases and to rethink itself as a sociolinguistics of mobile resources, framed in terms of trans-contextual networks, flows and movements. This unthinking and rethinking is long overdue (Wallerstein 2001 reminds us of that), and sociolinguistics still bears many marks of its own peculiar history, as it has focused on static variation, on local distribution of varieties, on stratified language contact, and so on. It shares this problem with many other branches of the language sciences – a point I tried to make elsewhere with respect to discourse analysis and literacy studies (Blommaert 2005, 2008). What is needed is a new vocabulary to describe events, phenomena and processes, new metaphors for representing them, new arguments to explain them – those elements of scientific imagination we call theory. This book is theoretical in ambition, formulating proposals for a different theoretical approach to sociolinguistic issues in globalization. More directly, it describes globalization as a sociolinguistic subject matter, and language as something intrinsically connected to processes of globalization. At the same time, the book is empirically grounded; my hypotheses are based on extensive analyses of various kinds of data that instantiate, in my view, processes of globalization.

My own attempt joins an emerging tradition in sociolinguistics and related disciplines in which scholars engage with globalization (e.g. Heller 1999; de Swaan 2001; Block and Cameron 2001; Coupland 2003; Block 2005; Rampton 2006; Harris 2006; Calvet 2006; Fairclough 2006; Pennycook 2007). The engagement is not always successful, as we shall see shortly; nor does it always result in elegant pieces of intellectual work – the aspect of unthinking is sometimes left aside and replaced by a quick patch-up of current theoretical and methodological complexes. Many people still believe that the issue can be formulated as 'language *and* globalization', in precisely the same way as one would speak of 'language *and* culture', 'language *and* society' and so on. That is, with precisely the same problems, Language itself is seen as essentially unaffected by globalization (culture, society, and so on), and globalization is seen as just another context in which language is practised, a new one at best. This, of course, precludes the possibility that the modes of occurrence of language themselves change, and that the traditional concept of 'language' is dislodged and destabilized by globalization. In other words, it reduces the sociolinguistic issues of globalization to issues of *method*, while a serious consideration of them would require ontological, epistemological and methodological statements as well – it would see it as issues of *theory*.

This theory construction cannot be just another *linguistic* theory. It needs to be a theory of language in society or, more precisely, of changing language in a changing society. To some extent, this is already an ontic decision: the sociolinguistics we need is one that addresses not the traditional object of linguistics, but something far more dynamic, something fundamentally cultural, social, political and historical. That object cannot be understood as autonomous, but needs to be examined as part of the larger package: as the sociolinguistic side of a larger social system. This observation is not new; in some measure it even defines the sociolinguistic approach:

... it will not do to begin with language, or a standard linguistic description, and look outward to social context. A crucial characteristic of the sociolinguistic approach is that it looks in toward language, as it were, from its social matrix. To begin with language, or with an individual code, is to invite the limitations of a purely correlational approach, and to miss much of the organization of linguistic phenomena. (Hymes 1974: 75)

The sociolinguistic approach, Hymes continues, involves a shift 'from focus on structure to focus on function – from focus on linguistic form in isolation to linguistic form in human context' (Hymes 1974: 77). And it is this socio-linguistic approach that I shall try to use in the chapters of this book: an approach that looks at linguistic phenomena from within the social, cultural, political and historical context of which they are part; one that considers language as organized not just in a linguistic system but in a sociolinguistic system, the rules and dynamics of which cannot be automatically derived from considering their linguistic features; and one that so examines language in an attempt to understand society. (See Hanks 1996; Agha 2007; Blommaert 2005 for elaborate discussions.) An ethnographically formulated sociolinguistics, seen from that angle, is a critical social science of language.

There is a need for such a critical social science of language. Eric Hobsbawm recently reminded us of the fact that

the currently fashionable free-market globalization has brought about a dramatic growth in economic and social inequalities both within states and internationally. There is no sign that this polarisation is not continuing within countries, in spite of a general diminution of extreme poverty. (Hobsbawm 2007: 3)

In addition, 'the impact of this globalization is felt most by those who benefit from it least' (Hobsbawm 2007): there is a globalized '"reserve army of labour" of immigrants from the villages of the great zones of poverty', and 'while the actual scale of globalization remains modest … its political and cultural impact is disproportionately large' (Hobsbawm 2007: 4). Most people in the world still have no access to the new communication technologies that offer shortcuts to globalization, they live, so to speak, fundamentally un-globalized lives; but the elites in their countries have such access and use it in the pursuit of power and opportunities – a pursuit which does affect the lives of the 'un-globalized' citizens. Migration from the 'zones of poverty' into European societies, even if statistically restricted, is a major political factor in many European countries, has changed the face of some of its urban centres, has prompted or fuelled the rise of reactionary, racist or fascist right-wing groups and has generated a heightened awareness of politicized identities, of ethnolinguistic nationalism and of national chauvinism. It has also changed the face of multilingualism, as we shall see below, creating new and complex markets for linguistic and communicative resources. Such markets naturally include winners and losers, and many people nowadays find their linguistic resources to be of very low value in globalized environments. I have described this problem elsewhere as one of voice and mobility. That is, people manage or fail to make sense across contexts; their linguistic and communicative resources are mobile or lack such semiotic mobility, and this is a problem not just of difference, but of inequality. It is a problem exacerbated by the intensified processes of globalization

(Blommaert 2005: chapter 4, 2008). Globalization, thus, is like every development of the system in which we live, something that produces opportunities as well as constraints, new possibilities as well as new problems, progress as well as regression. A critical approach must at least provide an accurate diagnostic of these issues.

Before we can move on, we need first to find some bearings for this exercise. Sociolinguistics is changing, and so is its object. I start by sketching the general lines of this change; then I engage in its effects on what we understand by sociolinguistic diversity. In so doing, I first provide introductions to some of the key concepts of this book.

1.2   Two paradigms

Modern sociolinguistics drew an artefactualized image of language into time and space, but it did not necessarily destroy the old Saussurean synchrony. The artefactual image is the image developed in modern linguistics, of language as a bounded, nameable and countable unit, often reduced to grammatical structures and vocabulary and called by names such as 'English', 'French' and so on (Blommaert 2006; also Silverstein 1998; Bauman and Briggs 2003; Makoni and Pennycook 2007). Sociolinguistic studies of language variation focused strongly on diffusion – the spread of linguistic variables over a restricted horizontal space, as in the work of Trudgill, Labov and others (see Britain and Cheshire 2003). The conceptual development of space and time in such studies is superficial, and this is where we see that the Saussurean synchrony survived in modern sociolinguistics. There is attention for generational transmission (time) and distribution of variables in one locality or across localities such as cities, regions or countries (space). Labov's famous studies of New York City (1966) and of Martha's Vineyard (Labov 1972) are classics in this trend. Contact linguistics, in the meantime, focused on the sociolinguistic and linguistic patterns resulting from migration (Clyne 2003), and patterns of multilingualism resulting from migrations also drew the attention of scholars (Extra and Verhoeven 1998). One widespread problem with such studies is that the people whose language repertoires are studied, even if they are migrants, are 'fixed', so to speak, in space and time. The Saussurean synchrony was of course also a syntopy. The phenomenology of migration and diaspora became an object of theoretical elaboration in cultural studies, sociology and anthropology. Certainly in the context of recent globalization processes, notions such as transcultural flows, transidiomaticity and deterritorialization made their way into mainstream social science (Appadurai 1996; see also Jacquemet 2005). We now see that the mobility of people also involves the mobility of linguistic and sociolinguistic resources, that 'sedentary' or 'territorialized' patterns of language use are complemented by 'translocal' or 'deterritorialized' forms of language use, and that the combination of both often accounts for unexpected sociolinguistic effects. The possibility of frequent electronic contact with the country of origin, for instance, can generate new forms of language innovation (and thus contribute to language maintenance) in diasporic communities; small and marginal languages can, in the context of tourism, acquire new and unexpected forms of prestige (Heller 2003); popular culture such as hip-hop or Reggae can be a vehicle for the worldwide dissemination of particular language forms (Pennycook 2007; Richardson 2007), including new forms of literacy and message design (Kress and van Leeuwen 1996). All of these dimensions of mobility still collapse in concrete spaces where actual people live and interact with one another; the structure of people's repertoires and the patterns of multilingual language use, however, become less predictable and significantly more complex, as we shall see below.

The upshot of these developments is that we see two paradigms develop, one established and one emerging. The established paradigm is the *sociolinguistics of distribution* as sketched above, in which movement of language resources is seen as movement in a horizontal and stable space and in chronological time; within such spaces, vertical stratification can occur along lines of class, gender, age, social status etc. The object of study, however, remains a 'snapshot', in which things are in place, so to speak. The second paradigm can be called a *sociolinguistics of mobility*, and it focuses not on language-in-place but on language-in-motion, with various spatiotemporal frames interacting with one another. Such spatiotemporal frames can be described as 'scales', and the assumption is that in an age of globalization, language patterns must be understood as patterns that are organized on different, layered (i.e. vertical rather than horizontal) scale-levels. And while a sociolinguistics of distribution is by and large concerned with 'language' – linguistically defined objects – a sociolinguistics of mobility is concerned with concrete *resources*. Put more concisely, it is a sociolinguistics of 'speech', of actual language resources deployed in real sociocultural, historical and political contexts (Hymes 1996, chapter 3). I discuss this topic more fully in the next chapter. Access to and control over scales is unevenly distributed, it is a matter of power and inequality, as becomes clear when we consider typical resources for access to higher (i.e. non-local and non-situationally specific) scales such as a sophisticated standard language variety or advanced multimodal and multilingual literacy skills.

This second paradigm, of course, faces the challenge of incorporating a more profound theoretical understanding of space. Space, here, is metaphorically seen as *vertical* space, as layered and stratified space. Every horizontal space (e.g. a neighbourhood, a region, or a country) is also a vertical space, in which all sorts of socially, culturally and politically salient distinctions occur. Such distinctions are *indexical* distinctions, which project minute linguistic differences onto stratified patterns of social, cultural and political value-attribution.

They convert linguistic and semiotic differences into social inequalities and thus represent the 'normative' dimensions of situated language use (Silverstein 2006a; Agha 2007; Blommaert 2005). The stratified and ordered nature of such indexical processes I have called, by analogy with Foucault's 'order of discourse', *orders of indexicality* (Blommaert 2005: 69), and every (horizontal) space is filled with such orders of indexicality – with stratified normative complexes that organize distinctions between, on the one hand, 'good', 'normal', 'appropriate', and 'acceptable' language use and, on the other, 'deviant', 'abnormal' etc. language use. Orders of indexicality define the dominant lines for senses of belonging, for identities and roles in society, and thus underlie what Goffman called the 'interaction order' – which is an *indexical* order (Silverstein 2003a; Agha 2007). I return to this in the next chapter.

Movement of people across space is therefore never a move across empty spaces. The spaces are always someone's space, and they are filled with norms, expectations, conceptions of what counts as proper and normal (indexical) language use and what does not count as such. Mobility, sociolinguistically speaking, is therefore a trajectory through different stratified, controlled and monitored spaces in which language 'gives you away'. Big and small differences in language use locate the speaker in particular indexical and ascriptive categories (related to identity and role). As we learned from John Gumperz's work (e.g. 1982), this is rarely inconsequential. Below, I introduce such patterns of mobility and their effects on what we understand by sociolinguistic diversity.

1.3   Globalization, super-diversity and multilingualism

Super-diversity

The 'villages' traditionally addressed by sociolinguists have changed. As mentioned above, the current globalization processes are best seen as part of longer, wider and deeper globalization processes, in which they represent a particular stage of development. That development is real, however, and changes in economic and technological infrastructure have especially affected what we currently understand by mobility. Migration was long seen as people *emigrating* and *immigrating* – that is, a change in the spatial organization of one's life in an enduring way. People left their country and settled in another. In that new country, they lived separated from their country of origin, perhaps (but not necessarily) in ethnic communities. They took their languages and other cultural belongings with them, but the separation from the land of origin and the permanent nature of migration was likely to bring pressure to accommodate to the host society. A tradition of study emerged in Western host societies on such relatively isolated, stable and residential immigrant groups, often also consisting of large communities from the same country or even region of origin: Turks in Germany, Algerians and West-Africans in France, Caribbeans and East- or South-Asians in Britain.

The 1990s brought a change in the nature and profile of migration to Western host societies, and Steven Vertovec (2006: 1) summarizes that process with respect to Great Britain as follows:

Over the past ten years, the nature of immigration to Britain has brought with it a transformative 'diversification of diversity' not just in terms of ethnicities and countries of origin, but also with respect to a variety of significant variables that affect where, how, and with whom people live.

These variables, Vertovec explains,

include a differentiation in immigration statuses and their concomitant entitlements and restrictions of rights, labour market experiences, gender and age profiles, spatial factors, and local area responses by service providers and residents ... The interplay of these factors is what is meant here, in summary fashion, by the notion of 'super-diversity'.

The new migrants typically settle in older immigrant neighbourhoods, which thus develop into a layered immigrant space, where resident ('old') immigrants often rent spaces to newer, more temporary or transient groups, and where new segments of the labour market are developed. Many of the new immigrants live in economically and legally precarious conditions, and many of them are strongly dependent upon informal employment and solidarity networks such as churches (Blommaert et al. 2005; Blommaert, Collins and Slembrouck 2005a, 2005b). The extreme linguistic diversity in such neighbourhoods generates complex multilingual repertoires in which often several (fragments of) 'migrant' languages and lingua francas are combined. And such neighbourhoods often display a density of mediating institutions such as welfare and employment offices, as well as night shops, money transfer bureaus such as Western Union and – significantly – telephone and Internet shops where international phone calls and Internet access are offered at bargain prices.

Super-diversity poses descriptive as well as theoretical challenges. Descriptively, these globalized neighbourhoods appear chaotic, and common assumptions about the national, regional, ethnic, cultural or linguistic status of the inhabitants often prove to be useless. The presuppositions of common integration policies – that we know who the immigrants are, and that they have a shared language and culture – can no longer be upheld. In addition, the dense presence of telephone and Internet shops shows that even if new migrants reside in one particular place, they are capable of maintaining intensive contacts with networks elsewhere, including often their countries of origin. A burgeoning network of satellite and Internet providers also allows them to follow (and be involved in) events in their country of origin and to consume its media and cultural products. Their spatial organization, consequently, is local as well as translocal, real as well as virtual – and all of this has effects on the structure and development of language repertoires and patterns of language use. Theoretically, this stretches the limits of existing frameworks for analysing and understanding multilingualism and the dynamics of language change. We can illustrate the complexity of these phenomena and theoretical issues by looking at my own globalized neighbourhood in Berchem, an inner-city part of Antwerp, Belgium.

Multilingual repertoires and super-diversity

The repertoires of new migrants often appear to be 'truncated' (Blommaert, Collins and Slembrouck 2005a; see also section 4.1 below): highly specific 'bits' of language and literacy varieties combine in a repertoire that reflects the fragmented and highly diverse life-trajectories and environments of such people. Thus, recent West-African (e.g. Nigerian) immigrants in Berchem may combine one or more African languages with a West-African indigenized English, which will be used with some interlocutors in the neighbourhood, and will also be the medium of communication during weekly worship sessions in a new Evangelical church in the neighbourhood. English, however, is not part of the repertoire of most other immigrants in the neighbourhood. Most of the shops, for instance, are owned by Turkish or Moroccan people, who often use vernacular forms of German or French as 'emergency' lingua francas. Thus, when a Nigerian woman goes to buy bread in a Turkish-owned bakery, the code for conducting the transaction will, for both, be a clearly non-native and very limited variety of local vernacular Dutch, mixed with some English, or German, words. In the phone shops, vernacular English will have slightly more currency, because the phone shops are typically run by people from India or Pakistan. Note, however, that the particular varieties of English spoken in such transactions will be very different: none will be 'standard', each variety will reflect informal patterns of acquisition and an uneasiness in use.

The Dutch used in the bakery is a minimal, informally acquired small 'bit' of language, a specialized language skill, limited to specific domains of interactions, and showing significant limitations compared to fluent speakers. It is insufficient for successful communication in institutional encounters: bureaucratic procedures are in standard and literate varieties of Dutch, typically varieties that are associated with formal acquisition efforts. Thus, when a Nigerian woman goes to her daughter's school for consultation on her child's progress, she will have to revert to her non-native English. This will then be met by a Belgian–Flemish variety of English from the teachers, and the interaction will typically be less than smooth. The medium of communication between mother and child will be a mixed code, often blending unevenly distributed chunks of Dutch and English. Naturally the child, as a result of her immersion in a formal language learning environment, has access to more elaborate varieties of standard and local vernacular Dutch and will often have to assist the mother and the teacher in communication attempts. This, importantly, points towards another peculiarity of language in such neighbourhoods: the fact that language tasks often involve *collaborative work*. People may call on others, or others may volunteer to translate and assist in communication. This is not only the case for tasks that involve literacy; it can also be noticed in face-to-face encounters. People very often pool their competences and skills in particular languages when they have to accomplish demanding communication tasks.

At home, the Nigerian family will have access to television, and the choice will go to English-medium channels such as BBC World or MTV, with an occasional foray, often initiated by the children, into Dutch-medium children's programmes. There will be a very low level of consumption of local printed mass-media, and access to printed sources from Nigeria will be restricted. At the same time, telephone contacts in the native languages will be maintained with people back home and fellow migrants from the same region of origin, now living in Brussels, London or Paris. Occasionally, there will be mutual visits during which the African regional language might be the medium of communication among adults, while the children revert to vernacular forms of English to interact with each other. Their exposure to education environments in which different languages are the medium of instruction – Dutch and French, for instance – constrains the use of any other language.

Thus we see very fragmented and 'incomplete' – 'truncated' – language repertoires, most of which consist of spoken, vernacular and non-native varieties of different languages, with an overlay of differentially developed literacy skills in one or some languages (depending on the level of literacy at the time of migration). We also see how many communication tasks are accomplished collaboratively, by combining the resources and skills of several people. The particular patterns of such repertoires are difficult to establish in detail – here is the descriptive challenge. Repertoires such as these require close inspection; chapter 4 addresses this issue more fully. The sociolinguistic world of these people is strictly local (the neighbourhood) as well as widely translocal (involving the network of fellow migrants elsewhere, communication with people back home, and the media). And internally, we see variation in language repertoires, in which adults have different repertoires from children; fellow migrants from the same region now living elsewhere have different repertoires again.

The local environment of these migrants is abundantly multilingual. Since Nigerians are a very small minority, their languages are invisible in the public space. The older resident communities – Turks and Moroccans – do publicly display the formal, literate aspects of their multilingualism. We see Arabic and Turkish displayed in shops and on posters announcing cultural or political events. Such public language displays can index the size and the degree of solidification of particular immigrant communities. Thus, Albanian posters

Figure 1.1 Advertisement of the rates in a phone shop

Figure 1.2 Money transfer advertisement

have recently begun to appear, indicating the existence of a well-organized and resident Albanian migrant community in Belgium. Groups that have not yet achieved that level of stability and visibility revert to highly unstable forms of written language, mixing English and Dutch and betraying non-native pronunciation of words, as the display of rates in phone shops illustrates (figure 1.1). They are also addressed by fully globalized signs in (near-)Standard English, advertising services such as money transfer (figure 1.2) that cater to specific needs of recent and economically vulnerable immigrants.

Figure 1.3 'Liar Channel'

The uneven distribution of language resources, that is, degrees of public legitimacy of languages and of patterns of access to language resources, becomes clear when we examine figure 1.3, where we see how someone has changed the name of a large transnational advertisement bureau called 'Clear Channel' to 'Liar Channel' on a billboard. This is a playful language act, a case of 'ludic' English (Pennycook 2007: 30ff), revealing advanced competence in English and in literacy as well as a particular critical political stance. When we compare figure 1.3 with figure 1.1, we see how strongly the levels of literacy and command of language varieties differ within one topographically delineated community. The reason is historical and has to do with the particular social and cultural mix of the neighbourhood, which has of late also seen an influx of educated, middle-class native Belgians, attracted by affordable housing prices. These latter people have typically had access to prestige varieties of language and prestige forms of multilingualism – Standard Dutch and Standard literate English. Thus, highly advanced multilingual repertoires can be displayed alongside very incomplete ones, and the general picture is one of extreme mixedness. It is, consequently, hard to identify the 'dominant' language in the neighbourhood. Vernacular forms of Dutch would probably have the widest local currency; at the same time, various languages point inwards as well as outwards, to local communities and small networks in the neighbourhood as well as to translocal and transnational networks that have their 'hub' in the neighbourhood. Languages and language varieties operate and have validity at particular scale-levels, from the strictly local to the strictly global, with all sorts of intermediate scale-levels in between. In our example, the weekly worship session in the Evangelical church gathers several hundreds of people and so creates a translocal, but locally anchored, scale-level. And the occasional visits from and to fellow immigrants also creates a local–translocal scale-level. Each time, elements of the repertoires will have to be mobilized, because the different criss-crossing scales answer to different norms and expectations. A language variety that is good enough to perform adequately during the worship session is not necessarily good enough for buying bread in the bakery, or for talking to the schoolteacher.

Stratified distribution

If we now try to summarize some of the elements discussed so far, we see that a sociolinguistic analysis of such globalization phenomena cannot proceed on the basis of common notions of distribution. First, *what* is distributed is not easily defined, for we are never just talking about languages, but always about highly specific language resources (the 'little bits' of language I referred to earlier). Second, *how* these resources are distributed also requires a lexicon and imagery of considerable complexity, for there is no 'flat' distribution, no juxtaposition of particular resources. We see a range of densely layered, *stratified distribution patterns*, in which particular specific language resources are deployed (and deployable) on particular scale-levels and not on others; what is valid in one situation is not valid in another. I return to the issue of scales in greater detail in the next chapter. The point here is: some resources allow mobility across situations and scale-levels. Prestige varieties of language, such as Standard Dutch, for instance, would have currency across a wide range of situations; the same goes for prestige and literate varieties of English. These are high-mobility resources. Others – think of the African languages spoken by our Nigerian subjects – have very little in the way of mobility potential. Their range is largely confined to the adults in the family and the wider network, and to some restricted use with the children. Outside these situations, these languages have no potential for use. Institutionally they are often not even recognized as languages.

The key to understanding this complex pattern is *what counts as language* in particular contexts: what is ratified and recognized as a valid code for making oneself understood. The key is, in other words, *the indexical value that particular linguistic resources have* in certain spaces and situations. In highly complex neighbourhoods such as the one I discussed here, complex and truncated repertoires can have such validity, at least to the extent that particular ingredients of the repertoires are mapped onto particular micro-environments, networks or situations. Consequently, migrants are often confronted with situations in which the sociolinguistic and communicative requirements stretch their repertoires and complex patterns of shifting and mixing occur. As we shall see in the following chapters, conventional treatments of such patterns of shifting and mixing (for instance, 'code-switching', where 'codes' are understood as artefactualized languages) fail to do justice to their complexity.

The main parameters for the exercise have now been sketched and I am almost ready to address the challenge I described earlier. Since, as noted above, I am joining an emerging tradition of work on language and globalization, it is at this point good to take stock of part of the relevant scholarship.

1.4   The start of a tradition

The term *globalization* is most commonly used as shorthand for the intensified flows of capital, goods, people, images and discourses around the globe, driven by technological innovations mainly in the field of media and information and communication technology, and resulting in new patterns of global activity, community organization and culture (Castells 1996; Appadurai 1996). Being shorthand for highly complex forms of mobility, the term thus obscures important distinctions. However, failing to note them may result in confusion over what exactly our object is.

In the opening chapter of his *Age of Empire*, Hobsbawm asks how the world of the 1880s could be compared with that of the 1790s; his answer is: '[i]n the first place, it was now genuinely global' (Hobsbawm 1987: 13). In effect, the nineteenth century was the era of globalization, and Hobsbawm actually uses the term *globalization* for the process of capitalist expansion and deepening described in his *Age of Capital* (1975: 14n). This period coincides with what Wallerstein covers in his analysis of the development of the modern world-system, characterized by a 'geoculture' drawing on Enlightenment and capitalist values and mass politics (Wallerstein 2004, especially chapter 4). According to Wallerstein, this modern world-system has been in crisis since the late 1960s, and the phenomena we currently call 'globalization' (with economic delocalization, the destabilization of old social structures, new migrations, growing gaps between rich and poor, and 'terrorism') are features of that crisis. The point is that globalization cannot effectively be understood when it is de-historicized, or in Wallerstein's own terms:

If we look at globalization and terrorism as phenomena that are defined in limited time and scope, we tend to arrive at conclusions that are as ephemeral as the newspapers. By and large, we are not then able to understand the meaning of these phenomena, their origins, their trajectory, and most importantly where they fit in the larger scheme of things. (Wallerstein 2004: ix)

This slow and deep process of globalization can be called *geopolitical* globalization. It affects the deep social, political and economic fabric of societies, and it is an old process. There is, of course, another sense in which we currently use the term globalization. This latter sense can be called *geocultural* globalization. It refers to more recent developments *within* globalization, largely an effect of the emergence of new communication technologies, increasing and intensified global capitalist processes of accumulation and division of labour, and increased and intensified global inequalities resulting in new migration flows (in turn resulting in super-diversity in metropolitan areas). These geocultural globalization processes develop within a narrower timeframe, and as Hobsbawm's earlier observation tells us, their scope, speed and intensity do not correlate with those of geopolitical globalization. Such geocultural globalization processes have been impressively documented by Castells (1996) and Appadurai (1996), for example; but while they do affect the structure and fabric of social systems, there is very little *fundamentally* new to them. Developments in mass communication systems, for instance, have their precedents. People in earlier ages had similar feelings of revolutionary newness when the telegraph, telephone, radio or television became part of their world, and the invention of book printing may have been the biggest revolution of that kind. Each time, such developments affected the way people communicated, thought, organized themselves and acted. The current globalization phase is therefore another stage of development *within* globalization – even if this is perhaps the first stage that has received the name of 'globalization' (Arrighi 1997). This stage is interesting enough, particularly in the field of language, where we see how these new geocultural processes affect sociolinguistic patterns of language in society, the emergence of new multimodal forms of communication (Kress and Van Leeuwen 1996), and super-diverse patterns of urban multilingualism. But it is good to understand that such processes, and the timeframe in which they occur, can only be understood as part of larger, slower and more profound changes in society.

In the field of language, we are witnessing the modest beginnings of a tradition of scholarship that addresses globalization. I will briefly review three recent books that address, each in its own way, aspects of language in globalization. This review will, I hope, demonstrate some of the conceptual issues and difficulties involved in this exercise, as well as allow me to sketch my own agenda in this book. I will discuss Norman Fairclough's *Language and Globalization* (Fairclough 2006), followed by Louis-Jean Calvet's *Towards an Ecology of World Languages* (Calvet 2006) and Alastair Pennycook's *Global Englishes and Transcultural Flows* (Pennycook 2007). Each of these books explicitly addresses globalization as a topic and framework of analysis, but each of them addresses it from a different angle and perspective.

Fairclough's *Language and Globalization* is an ambitious attempt to bring critical discourse analysis to bear on globalization. The problem, however, is that it addresses geopolitical globalization within the timeframe of geocultural globalization. The globalization Fairclough examines started, apparently, in 1991 when the Cold War ended. Even if in his conclusion he warns his readers that 'globalization is not … a phenomenon which developed in the last decades of the twentieth century', adding that we are now witnessing just 'a distinctive contemporary surge in globalization associated especially with innovations in communications and information technology' (Fairclough 2006: 163), this wider horizon is never addressed in the book. What is addressed, and given focus, is *'globalism'*, the neo-liberal version of post-Cold War globalization propagated by Reagan, Thatcher and their followers. It is a highly specific, and very restricted, development within globalization. This neo-liberal global-ism takes the shape of widely disseminated discourses such as those of ('Western') management techniques, re-scaling processes, an intensified effect of mass-mediated communication and a global 'war on terror'. Fairclough analyses these distinctly recent phenomena mainly in relation to the current situation in Romania, a country awaiting membership of the European Union (EU) and therefore caught in a process of transition to neo-liberal globalism.

The line he follows is familiar to those acquainted with Fairclough's oeuvre. Fairclough accurately locates the processes to be considered at the level of discourse, not language. There are new texts and genres; these texts and genres point towards new discourses and relations between discourses, and these in turn point towards social change. Thus, 'new' managerial genres suggest historical breaks and discontinuities, and the texts he analyses suggest a histor-ical discontinuity which he calls globalization. There is a serious theoretical flaw in this line of argument because it leads to a 'snapshot' approach to history: all of this looks or sounds 'new', so it must *be* new. And the discursive novelty is then projected onto social systems, *as if a fundamental discursive change necessarily presupposes a fundamental social change*. Observable intertextual-ity becomes a substitute for history here: a crucial methodological flaw in much critical discourse analysis. This flaw becomes clear when Fairclough examines 're-scaling' processes in Romania (chapter 4). In Fairclough's interpretation, 'scale' is essentially spatial scope, and the 're-scaling' of Romania means, roughly, that Romania now becomes part of a larger complex, the EU. The argument here is: social systems within Romania now undergo influences from the EU. This can be seen in the appearance of new 'managerial' discourses and in the implementation of the Bologna Declaration in European higher educa-tion. For Fairclough, this is a new process; he prefaces his analysis with the statement that '[c]ontemporary globalization is also associated with the con-struction of other scales than the global scale', such as the 'macro-regional' scale of the EU (Fairclough 2006: 64). 'Contemporary' here stands for the post-1991 world order, and Romania is re-scaled from a nation state scale-level to a 'macro-regional' one.

Romania, of course, has been re-scaled before, in the sense of being made part of larger spatial units. The Cold War had its own global structures, in which the Warsaw Pact was as much a 'macro-regional' scale-level as the European Union, and the Comintern was as globalized an institution as the Organisation for Economic Co-operation and Development (OECD). Thus, the re-scaling transformations in Romanian higher education cannot possibly be new or unique; the higher scale-level has always existed, because (as Hobsbawm and Wallerstein never fail to remind us) in the modern world-system no nation state has been completely isolated. Thus, the current re-scaling process is not about *the introduction* of a new scale-level, but *a change in the operational structure* of that same scale-level. The appearance of the term 'international context' in a manual from the University of Bucharest is not, therefore, the 'texturing of *new* scalar relations' (Fairclough 2006:77); it is nothing more than a change in what 'international context' means, a reorientation of that scale-level away from the previous Communist international context to the EU. In other words, there is very little real fundamental re-scaling going on; there is a transformation of the face of the scales and of the practices and discourses they involve. Profound discursive transformation does *not* flag profound social-structural transformation here. It flags relatively superficial cultural, political and ideological transformations, part of the geocultural globalization processes mentioned earlier. The consequence of this confusion is that Fairclough claims to say something about geopolitical globalization, while in actual fact he is talking about geocultural globalization. He does this by committing a very common error: merging the 'real processes of economic globalization' with the ways in which they are represented discursively (Fairclough 2006: 5). The real processes, to be sure, are longitudinal, while the patterns of representation (including the use of the very term *globalization*) are recent innovations, and there is a confusion of long and short histories here.

The 'snapshot' approach has two very negative effects, apart from descriptive and interpretive distortions such as those about re-scaling Romania. One is the stereotyping of contemporary globalization processes as fundamentally and shockingly new things – as if the world we now live in is a totally new one. It is not. The second effect is related to this: the de-historization of the contemporary ('globalized') world is part of globalism as an ideology, as famously proclaimed in Fukuyama's (1992) *The End of History*. Fukuyama's argument was that the end of the Cold War marked the end of modern history, characterized by ideological and economic competition between systems. The end of the Cold War marked the beginning of a new world order, in which (neo-liberal) capitalism and (American-style) democracy were *universal* (also in the sense of 'natural'). The message was: forget about history prior to 1991, do not look for histories of systemic development, they are pointless. Thus, whenever we let the history of globalization begin with the advent of the Internet or with Reagan and Thatcher, we buy into this end-of-history claim, thus into globalism. Consequently, 'we tend to arrive at conclusions that are as ephemeral as the newspapers', as Wallerstein predicted.

A lesson to be learned from this is that, when discussing globalization, one has to be precise with respect to the historical framing of the phenomena one examines. As noted earlier, globalization is not one process but a complex of processes, evolving and developing at different scale-levels, with differences in scope, speed and intensity. Fairclough focuses strongly on relatively recent and superficial processes, which he then confuses with the larger and deeper processes. Not so with Louis-Jean Calvet, whose *Ecology of World Languages* takes us to the other extreme – to a timeless and macroscopic world, a galaxy of globalized languages.

Unlike Fairclough, Calvet does not attempt to analyse concrete instances of globalized language use. Instead he focuses on the way languages operate in today's world, a pattern which he describes as an 'ecosystem', or even a world-wide 'gravitational system' with different languages being 'constellations', defined by their relations with other languages and by their functions in the 'milieu'. Thus certain languages may be more central, others more peripheral in the galaxy, the gravitational force of which is instantiated by the existence of bilingual speakers. Each language possesses a 'valency', a capacity to populate a larger or smaller number of milieus and to transport itself into other milieus. Thus we get 'peripheral languages', 'central languages' (within one constellation), 'super-central languages' and 'hyper-central languages' (between constellations and galaxies). Ecosystems produce the materials they need to retain a balance – the principle of homeostasis. Linguistic ecosystems are in constant flux, as creoles and dialect continua exemplify, and changes in the ecosystem will trigger changes in languages and in their relative position vis-à-vis one another. These dynamics are the point where language practices and representations of languages come into the picture: the different ecological and gravitational forces also operate at the level of language-in-practice, and there is a politics of use and representation that informs the process.

Calvet, to be sure, contributes a whole set of new metaphors to the field of language and globalization. His book is replete with an appealing imagery of languages in orbit around one another, adapting to changing circumstances, gradually changing position and so on. The basic metaphors – those of ecosystems and of galaxies – have been employed elsewhere with varying success (we can think of Mühlhäusler 1996 and de Swaan 2001), and while they help us imagine large, macroscopic complexes of objects, their definition of the objects itself is usually shallow. Calvet's attempt rarely transcends the level of 'language' – of nameable and countable things like 'French', 'Hindi' or 'English'. The point we took from Fairclough, that globalization processes are *discursive* and consequently operate at sub-language levels such as register, genre or style, is absent from Calvet's discussion. Also absent is any consideration of real histories, of real social formations in time and space – there is, to stretch Calvet's own metaphors, no theory of the Big Bang in his description of sociolinguistic galaxies. Languages appear here as completely isolated items, as objects circling around one another in a galactic void, not in real social, cultural, political and economic spaces. The notion of homeostasis does not offer much analytic purchase either. Like so many ecological metaphors, it restricts itself to claiming that there is perpetual and inevitable change. The engines and agents of such change, and changes in such engines and agents, are not discussed. There are cases, for instance, where the '(super-)central language' changed, without much effect on the smaller languages: think of the change from German to English as language of colonization in Tanzania after World War I, or of the more recent change from French to English in Mauritius (Mufwene 2005, 2008). Calvet's book thus instantiates a particular genre of writing on globalization: one that tries to generalize ahistorically about the forces that govern this globalized world and produces eloquent and appealing imageries to that effect. I distinguished between geopolitical and geocultural globalization processes above; Calvet, let us say, discusses globalization in *geological* terms. The imagery is not a description, however, but a generalizing metaphor, and thus necessarily something that excludes detail, contradiction and complexity. One can borrow the metaphors to achieve particular aesthetic and rhetorical aims, but the analysis still remains to be done.

So one could say that Calvet offers us a theory of the infinitely big and timeless aspects of language in globalization. Although one could equally say that it does not tell us much about globalization, for languages are abstracted and extracted from their real 'ecological' habitat, from the real sociocultural, political and economic globalized world of which they are part and in which they operate. It does, however, emphasize the need to keep an eye on the bigger picture in which sociolinguistic globalization evolves – a point I take on board – and he also stresses the need to see such processes as inherently political, as a global politics of language – a point I also take on board.

Alastair's Pennycook's *Global Englishes and Transcultural Flows* does a far better job. While we saw confusion about what exactly was understood by globalization in Fairclough's work and a vacuum surrounding language in Calvet's, Pennycook articulates quite sharply what he understands by sociolinguistic globalization, and he adequately fills the space in which his 'hyper-central' language (English) moves. Pennycook opens by accurately observing that an analysis of contemporary sociolinguistic globalization processes requires a different set of theoretical and methodological tools, and he opts for a series of 'trans'- approaches ('transcultural', 'transidiomatic', 'translocal', 'transdisciplinary', 'translingual', 'transtextual') rather than for 'post'-, 'inter'- or 'multi'- approaches, in an attempt to do away with the legacies of modernist thought on language (and thus constructing a post-modern, or should we say 'trans-modern', theoretical framework). Established notions such as 'language', 'culture' or 'place' are not useful in an analysis of objects that are necessarily mixed, hybrid, local as well as delocalized (or delocalizable), dynamic and unstable. These objects are, moreover, not just 'linguistic'. The bits of language that are globalized are equally bits of culture and society. That means that they always become part of the local, while they are part of the global, and at the end of global processes of semiotic rearrangement we have local usage and abuse of sociolinguistic resources.

This is where we see how in Pennycook's attempt, the space of globalization is filled, not empty like in Calvet's treatment: in order to understand language globalization, we need to look at larger semiotic and cultural packages, and a purely synchronic analysis will not do. The packages need to be looked at historically, in their histories of becoming particular signs, and dynamically in their use, uptake and re-use sequences. Like Fairclough and to a lesser extent Calvet, Pennycook emphasizes the political and critical nature of such work throughout. Considering globalization phenomena involves an engagement with power, misrecognition and recognition, social justice and empowerment.

Hip-hop (Pennycook's main target of analysis) is a case in point. It is a multimodal (or better: transmodal) semiotics of music, lyrics, movements and dress that articulates political and sub-cultural anti-hegemonic rebellion as well as aesthetics, a philosophy of life and a particular range of identities. Its origins are in the US inner cities among African-American youths but it has spread all over the world and appears everywhere in a recognizable form, in spite of very significant local differences. Hip-hop artists all over the world use similar patterns of semiotic conduct (including the use of English stock terms and expressions), but wherever it occurs, hip-hop offers new potential for local identity formation (see also Richardson 2007). What happens with hip-hop is therefore 'the global spread of authenticity' (Pennycook 2007: 96ff), not just a flat distribution of cultural forms but a layered distribution in which local forces are as important as global ones. There is always 'a compulsion not only to make hip-hop locally relevant but also to define locally what authenticity means' (Pennycook 2007: 98), and while many 'global' (including English) features of hip-hop are adopted in this search for authenticity, many others are rejected as well, and alongside the globalized African-American English hip-hop register we often see the emergence of similar registers in the local languages as well, sometimes (like in Tanzania) leading to a new, localized, fully-fledged vernacular hip-hop tradition.

This is of course a strong critique of popular theses about English linguistic imperialism (Phillipson 1992; Skutnabb-Kangas 2000), and I return to this topic in the next chapter and elsewhere in the book. Rather than discussing the subject in terms of totalizing dominance, replacement and uprooting, Pennycook argues that global culture needs to be seen in terms of 'circles of flow' (2007: 122), large networks in which highly diverse forms circulate and are exchanged, and which can overlap and blend together. There is, thus, not one 'centre' for hip-hop, even if its urban African-American origins strongly suggest one, but multiple overlapping circles in which joint forms and modes of conduct can flow and be meaningful. This point needs to be taken on board and I develop it further in the next chapter, in the form of polycentricity (see also Blommaert, Collins and Slembrouck 2005b). It is of significance, because it helps to pull us away from the unified and unifying visions of globalization noticeable in Fairclough's book as well as in Calvet's, and to focus instead on sociolinguistic globalization as a chequered, layered complex of processes evolving simulta-neously at a variety of scales and in reference to a variety of centres. At the same time (and this is where Pennycook remains silent) the interplay of scales and centres requires a historical perspective. The origins of hip-hop are influences of a different order than those coming from the local environments in which it is produced: the former are more enduring and static than the latter – elements of stability, exchangeability and recognizability in a wildly diverse set of forms. References in the lyrics to race or gender are also of a different order than references to local politicians or radio stations. These orders, I argue, are historical orders that produce scale-levels in semiotic conduct.

The three books reviewed here all have their merits. Fairclough usefully draws our attention to the fact that we should not look at language but at discourse when we consider sociolinguistic globalization processes. We will have to focus on genres, registers, styles rather than on languages. This to some extent will deny us the comfort of the clarity of names such as *English* or *French*, but so be it. Calvet emphasizes the global politics of language, the fact that languages operate in relation to one another and occupy different (political) positions. Pennycook stresses the inadequacy of established conceptual tools in addressing the complexities of sociolinguistic globalization. He also stresses (like Fairclough) the critical importance of careful attention to these phenom-ena, and he demolishes the image of globalization as a unified and unifying process. All of these insights inform my discussion here. At the same time, we also saw recurrent conceptual problems in all three, notably in relation to the historical dimension of globalization processes. This has led to confusion over 'globalization' itself in Fairclough's work, to a less than useful abstraction of language in Calvet's work and to silence on the historicity of the processes of globalization in Pennycook's work.

1.5   The challenge again

This book proposes *a* sociolinguistics of globalization, not *the* sociolinguistics of globalization. It is a modest attempt at bringing together materials and building blocks for a paradigmatically different approach to language in society in the present age, and it builds on the shoulders of others, some of whose work I have just given attention. I cannot promise that I will offer solutions to all the problems I encountered in the work of others, but I will give it my best shot. Some of the main lines of my attempt have been sketched already. I categorically opt for a sociolinguistics of resources, not of languages, and mobility is a central theoretical concern in this sociolinguistics of resources.

Mobility is the great challenge: it is the dislocation of language and language events from the fixed position in time and space attributed to them by a more traditional linguistics and sociolinguistics (the Saussurean synchrony) that will cause the paradigm shift we are currently witnessing to achieve success. It is the insertion of language in a spectrum of human action which is not defined purely in relation to temporal and spatial location, but in terms of temporal and spatial trajectories that is the main objective here. In order to get there, the notion of 'mobility' itself must be examined, and an improved notion of 'locality' needs to be developed as well. This approach will, of course, raise questions about the nature of *resources* in this kind of sociolinguistics – the stuff that is mobile and travels across different localities – and it will also raise the question of 'history'. And a critical historical questioning of issues of resources and competence will compel us to consider the actual forms of *inequality* that characterize language in the era of globalization. The patterns of mobility will show various problematic aspects that are due to the particular structure of the localities between which resources travel. All of this will, furthermore, have to be demonstrated not as an effort of theory but as one of analysis, that is, as a practical research problem for which particular types of research design and data can be used. I try to be very generous with examples and analyses, and many if not most of the theoretical points are based on extended case studies. However, given the vast panorama of issues and phenomena that go under the umbrella of globalization, I cannot possibly aspire to offer a comprehensive analytical *tour de table*. My treatment will necessarily be selective and eclectic. I hope the reader will show tolerance for manifest gaps in my approach – I see this book as an invitation offered to others to participate in this exercise, and I hope others will fill the gaps.

While I sketched the phenomenology of language in the era of globalization in the most general terms here, introducing the notion of super-diversity to describe the conditions under which language occurs in contemporary urban centres in the West (and elsewhere), I try to delve deeper into this question in chapter 2. Starting from a number of observations from Japan, I show that mobility affects the nature and function of the conventional conception of 'language' in linguistics, calling for a different vocabulary to describe the way in which it is lived and practised presently. I offer three theoretical concepts for consideration: 'sociolinguistic scales', 'orders of indexicality' and 'polycentricity'. Together they provide a descriptive frame: language (here seen as the mobile resources mentioned earlier) needs to be seen as a phenomenon that occurs (or has the potential to occur) at different scale-levels. Mobility across these different scales involves important shifts in function, structure and meaning; and since globalization introduces the global as a relevant level of context, we can expect such shifts to occur generally. The shifts are shifts that involve the reordering of normativity: linguistic resources move through different orders of indexicality, and every move involves a different set of indexical potentials for the resources. What works well in one context may not work at all in another. The reason is that such orders of indexicality need to be seen as organized in polycentric systems, in which different centres – Bakhtinian 'super-addressees' from which real or perceived norms emanate – co-occur in complex (and often opaque) simultaneous relationships.

This is a different frame for understanding language and globalization from the more common ones such as that of 'linguistic imperialism'. The localism that is central to much discourse on linguistic rights and linguistic imperialism will be examined and opposed to a sociolinguistics of mobile resources. The frame I offer is based on mobility and on actual 'bits' of language, and I will illustrate some of its purchase by means of a small study of Internet language courses in American accent. Such courses make use of the defining technology of globalization (the Internet), and they construct surprisingly strict and punitive orders of indexicality that co-occur alongside those of (state-sponsored) education systems. People in India learn English at school, and that English is perfectly adequate for most of their business. But if they want to jump from the local/national scale to the transnational one, for instance by applying for work in the international call centres that are a booming industry in India, they need to 'go private' and learn an American accent from an Internet company. The rules for learning English at school and those of learning American accent are different, and both now co-occur in a polycentric environment for 'English'.

Selling American accent means selling an image of America, the world and one's own position therein, and chapter 3 elaborates this issue, focusing on issues of locality and taking the perspective of the periphery. The world is different when seen from the periphery rather than from the centre, and two pieces of analysis attempt to demonstrate this. I first examine the way in which in a 'globalized' Tanzanian novel, characters and elements of the plot are developed on the basis of a local topography of places and associative qualifications. The characters of the region move through Tanzanian physical and social space, and the author skilfully exploits the indexical nature of place names and geographical locations in his novel. The author himself produces a strongly local novel, written in Swahili, although his writing is fully globalized. He himself is a professor at an American university, and his novel instantiates much of what globalization is about: the mobility of signs across time and space, combined with a strong sense of the local. Mobility is the rule, but that does not preclude locality from being a powerful frame for the organization of meanings. Locality and mobility co-exist, and whenever we observe patterns of mobility we have to examine the local environments in which they occur.

We see this clearly in the second analysis I offer in chapter 3. On the basis of material gathered in a secondary school in a peripheral township in South Africa, I argue that the teaching of English there needs to be understood as proceeding within a strongly local economy of language and literacy, not in terms of universal standards of English. Teachers and learners all commit grave and frequent errors in their writings, if these are assessed from a strictly normative and absolutist viewpoint of North America or the United Kingdom. The co-occurrence of the same deviations, however, shows that they are systemic and belong to a system of 'peripheral normativity' which has its historical roots in the deep class and ethnic divisions that dominated South Africa until recently, and these are played out now against the backdrop of profound forms of social inequality in contemporary society. This analysis shows the power of locality. The world has not become a village but a network of villages, and the villages are organized very much like individual villages, with their own, relatively autonomous and self-regenerating rules and codes. I see this observation as cautionary for over-enthusiastic people for whom global-ization means first and foremost 'glocalization', the making of global localities with connotations of uniformization (so-called McDonaldization). There is an influence from the global and, to be sure, places do change, but the local is quite resilient as well and local criteria and norms define the processes of change. Global influences become part of the context-generative aspect of the produc-tion of locality: they become part of the ways in which local communities construct a social, cultural, political and economic environment for themselves (Appadurai 1996: 187).

The actual materials with which such context-generative dimensions of locality operate change, however, and chapter 4 delves into questions of resources and competence. Referring back to the discussion of English literacy resources in the township, we can see that much of the communication in English there had an 'unfinished' character, to the complexity of which traditional approaches to multilingualism (which assume the possibility of co-ordinated co-existence of 'languages') cannot do justice. I therefore propose a view of 'truncated' multilingualism: repertoires composed of specialized but partially and unevenly developed resources. We never know 'all' of a language, we always know specific bits and pieces of it. This counts for our 'mother tongue' as well as for the languages we pick up in the course of a lifetime, and this is perfectly normal. I contend that such 'truncated' repertoires are a better diagnostic of what real multilingual competence means in an age of global-ization, as they explain the unfinished character of communication, as well as the numerous problems that can occur in processes of mobility. The truncated repertoires are grounded in people's biographies and in the wider histories of the places where they were composed. They are 'placed' resources, some of which will allow mobility while others will not, and repertoire analysis can explain what goes on when people, carrying their language luggage, so to speak, move around, or when their messages move around.

I illustrate such processes with an extended analysis of a globalized genre with which many of us are familiar: email messages informing us that we are about to receive very large sums of money. Such messages are sent from the periphery of the world-system, from places such as Nigeria, to addressees in the centre of the world-system, people such as me. Their actual construction and composition raise a number of fundamental questions with regard to competence in the age of globalization, and it is clear that statements about how 'well' one 'knows a language' are uninformative in this respect. The people producing such messages display various forms of competence, and these competences are unevenly developed – they are truncated. The authors display a profound and amazingly sophisticated understanding of the computer hardware and the techniques for surfing the Internet, hunting for free and anonymous email providers and email addresses of addressees. An analysis of the genre features shows that they also display a degree of what we could call cultural competence: they have a clear, if incomplete, awareness of the genre features that are expected by their addressees in messages such as these. The messages display a canonical genre structure which mirrors that of business letters, personal narratives and so forth – genres that have a recognizable place in the repertoires of their addressees. But the actual implementation of such genres in fluent English text is quite problematic. While we see a very highly developed technological competence, and a moderately developed cultural competence, we see a weakly developed linguistic competence articulated in many of these messages. These differences between specific forms of competence seem to reveal different degrees of accessibility of communicative resources, technical resources being more democratically accessible than cultural ones and certainly more accessible than linguistic ones. The differences in the messages may therefore reveal inequalities, and I return to this later on.

Prior to that, however, the issue of history needs to be more fully developed. Mobility is something that has spatial as well as temporal features, and mobile text is text that has the capacity to travel through time and space. In chapter 5, I emphasize and illustrate some of the points made at several places throughout the previous chapters. When I discussed the issue of locality and argued that we need to see the world as a system of relatively autonomous local systems, we should also realize that such systems have their own historicity. This idea is crucial for understanding contemporary globalization because of the superficial uniformity that is sometimes discerned (and emphasized) in cultural globalization phenomena – the so-called 'McDonaldization' of the world. Even if similar features occur all over the globe, the local histories which they enter can be fundamentally different and so create very different effects, meanings and functions. This is an instance of what Hymes (1966; also Blommaert 2005: 70) called 'second linguistic relativity': even when linguistic structures are identical, their functions can differ, depending on the place of the linguistic resources in the repertoires. I give an example of two similar images of golf, discussing the way we should understand both images in terms of local historical conditions and environments. This leads to some reflections on differences between long and short histories – Braudel's (1949, 1969) distinction between slow, intermediate and fast time is not too far away – and on synchronization. I argue there that sociolinguistic reality is never synchronic but always *made* synchronic. In actual fact, what we see in a 'synchronic' sociolinguistic observation is a patchwork of composite parts that have very different origins and followed very different trajectories into people's repertoires. Understanding sociolinguistic reality as such a chequered pattern helps us provide better descriptions of change, and the chapter concludes with an example of how mass tourism affects the sociolinguistic environment in a small town in northern Finland.

With the issue of history, most of the theoretical points in the book have been addressed. What is missing is a perspective, something that gives direction to sociolinguistic work and determines why we should do a particular kind of sociolinguistics. Inequality is the theme of chapter 6, and much of what has been said in the first five chapters needs to be reread through the lens of inequality. We already saw how Hobsbawm warned us against the ways in which globalization has deepened inequality both within and across different societies, and we also know that Wallerstein defined the contemporary world-system as driven by inequality. There is, as we know, a widespread popular discourse that sees globalization as the spread of prosperity around the globe; the price to pay for this prosperity is allegedly cultural uniformization. While chapters 3 and 5 provide conditions for the aspect of cultural uniformization, arguing that processes of change need to be understood primarily from the viewpoint of locality, this chapter now responds to the claims about the prosperity- and opportunity-generating features of globalization. It also responds to another widespread image of globalization: that it undercuts the power of the nation state. In the two analyses I offer in this chapter, we will see that globalization is a problem and a threat for many people, and that these problems are very often generated or exacerbated by the workings of modern states.

The two analyses both fall within the domain of immigration. I open with an analysis of an asylum application case in the UK by a man from Rwanda. The man's application was turned down because his sociolinguistic profile did not match the one the UK Home Office deemed 'normal' for a Rwandan. My analysis shows that the applicant's sociolinguistic profile was fully realistic, at least if one abandons pristine images of a national order and accepts the chaos of civil war, displacement and destroyed lives in regions such as Rwanda. The analysis shows how the applicant – by definition a transnational, deterritorialized subject – was cast in a very modernist imagery of the nation state by the

Home Office. He was supposed to speak the 'national' languages of Rwanda (i.e. Kinyarwanda and French), and to know the things a 'normal' citizen of any country is supposed to know about his/her country: the flag, the landmarks and so on. Thus we see how this refugee was supposed to answer as a *national* subject, from within a supposedly stable and untroubled national order. The state – the Home Office in this case – formulated a very 'modern' response to the very 'post-modern' phenomenon of super-diversity.

The persistent use of frames derived from the modern nation state to address transnational, displaced migrants is a feature of inequality and defines many of the common responses to migration in central states of the world-system. Assumptions of uniformity, categorizability, transparency, fixedness and so on (the machinery of modernist bureaucracy, in short) underlie measures to accept or reject and to 'integrate' migrants in their host societies (Blommaert and Verschueren 1998). We see this in the second analytical vignette in this chapter, where data from a Dutch immersion class in Belgium are discussed. Migrant children enter such classes with truncated multilingual repertoires which often reveal important traces of previous learning processes: they speak (often standard) varieties of several languages and are often literate. These resources, however, are disqualified on the basis of a very modernist ideal of the monolingual state: if they do not know Dutch, they do not know *any* language, because no language other than Dutch will allow them to 'integrate' in their host society. We already saw above that the super-diverse neighbourhoods in which such children as a rule reside offer purchase for a whole range of languages, but the modernist imagination of monolingualism and social uniformity dominates the education system. Consequently, the learning process is slowed down because language learning is seen as a condition for any other learning, and the actual ways in which children use language(s) to communicate their (migrant) experiences are not used in the learning process.

Both analyses show that globalization is a process which, apart from people who benefit massively from it, also counts losers and victims, people for whom globalization is one more obstacle in life. They also show how the state is a critical factor in creating such problems. The state imagines itself in very modernist terms, and increasingly uses the modernist image of language as a tool to divide and discriminate migrants (cf. Bauman and Briggs 2003).

The storyline of the book has so far taken us from mobility and locality to resources and competence, and thence to history and inequality. We can see how mobility starts to reformulate classical sociolinguistic topics: locality, resources, competence, inequality all belong to the stock themes of sociolinguistics. When we see these themes from the perspective of mobility, however, they are transformed into theoretical territory for which we have as yet no sound and detailed map. I try to provide a sketch of such a map in chapter 7, taking stock of the preceding discussions and summarizing what could be useful for a sociolinguistics of globalization and pointing towards some effects and implications for scholarship. The purchase of my own proposals will be tested by applying them to the defining topic of globalization: English in the world. Taking the way in which this issue is currently framed in sociolinguistic work within the linguistic rights paradigm (in which indigenous languages are 'threatened' when English enters their space), I discuss the case of English in Tanzania, again a country in the periphery of the world-system. I first highlight the complex position of the Tanzanian state as one scale-level caught between others, and then I examine some of the different forms in which English occurs in Dar es Salaam. We will see that rather than an oppressive force, English enables people to construct meanings and functions that are new and creative. And at the same time, their English is local, and it operates within a local scale-level, as part of the production of locality. This final example should illustrate the potential of a new sociolinguistics to offer new, perhaps better, answers to issues that hitherto were addressed under the banners of oppression and imperialism, such as the relative position of 'small' languages vis-à-vis 'big' ones, language loss and language revitalization. It is essential, especially in light of what is covered in chapter 6, that sociolinguistics gives plausible and precise answers to language issues that can endanger individuals. I submit that only a particular kind of sociolinguistics can do that: the sociolinguistics of resources.

I have now described how I will take on the challenge I have set for myself, and I am ready to go. I will have to start by defining the sociolinguistic world in which we live, and this world – alas! – is messy, complex and rather unpredictable.

2 A messy new marketplace

Sociolinguistics is the study of language as a complex of resources, of their value, distribution, rights of ownership and effects. It is not the study of an abstract language, but the study of concrete language resources in which people make different investments and to which they attribute different values and degrees of usefulness. In the context of globalization, where language forms are perhaps more mobile than before, such patterns of value and use become less predictable and presupposable. Economic metaphors such as those developed by Bourdieu (1991) are particularly useful for a sociolinguistics of globalization. Recall that Bourdieu saw language as a market of symbolic capital and power, with people juggling for profit and with some people structurally having less capital than others. Bourdieu and his contemporaries Bernstein (1971) and Hymes (1980, 1996) all drew our attention to the same phenomenon: that the world of language is not just one of difference but one of inequality; that some of that inequality is temporal and contingent on situations while another part of it is structural and enduring; and that such patterns of inequality affect, and articulate around, actual, concrete, language forms such as accents, dialects, registers and particular stylistic (e.g. narrative) skills.

The symbolic marketplace described by Bourdieu and others was a local and relatively closed one. Its patterns of value attribution and the logic of the economic game were clear to most of the people involved in the transactions – the speaker from *la province* knew quite well that their speech was 'inferior' to that of the Parisian, and this awareness accounted for their tendency towards hypercorrection. When we address globalization, however, we address trans-local, mobile markets whose boundaries are flexible and changeable. And this is the theoretical challenge now: to imagine ways of capturing *mobile* resources, *mobile* speakers and *mobile* markets. A sociolinguistics of globalization is perforce a sociolinguistics of mobility, and the new marketplace we must seek to understand is, consequently, a less clear and transparent and a messier one. So let us engage with this issue now and see where it brings us theoretically.

Figure 2.1 Nina's derrière

2.1 Nina's derrière

A few years ago I was visiting an up-market department store in Central Tokyo, and in the very exclusive and expensive food section of that store I noticed a chocolate shop which bore the name *Nina's Derrière*. The stylized lettering and the choice of French betray an aspiration to considerable _chic_, and the prices of the chocolate on sale materialized that aspiration. But the name of the shop was, let us say, a rather unhappy choice, and I hoped that not too many Japanese customers would know enough French to understand the meaning of the name. I confess that I myself found the thought of offering someone a chocolate obtained from Nina's bum intensely entertaining. It was also useful in bringing an important point home to me. *This was not French*. At least: while the origins of 'derrière' are clearly French, and while its use in the shop's name drew on indexicals of French *chic*, the word did not function as a linguistic sign. Linguistically it was only French in a minimal sense, as a word whose origins lie in the stock vocabulary of the language we conventionally call French. Its Frenchness was *semiotic* rather than linguistic: important was not its linguistic function as a denotational sign, but the _emblematic_ function it had in signalling a complex of associative meanings, the things I captured under the term French *chic*. This is why the chocolate shop was still in business in spite of its dramatically inappropriate name: the sign did not function linguistically in the context of a Tokyo department store – linguistic knowledge of French being a very rare commodity in Tokyo – but it functioned, and functioned well, emblematically. The sign suddenly becomes a *linguistic* sign only when someone like me, who has

Figure 2.2 Keikyu phone card

linguistic competence in French, sees it *and reads it as an instance of (linguistic) French*. Prior to that the sign is not 'French' but 'Frenchness'. At least, as long as the sign remains in its particular environment. When it is 'exported', so to speak, to the environment that someone like me brings along, it changes.

The world is full of examples of signs that shift functions depending on who uses them, where and for what purpose. We see the same phenomenon in figure 2.2, a phone card from Tokyo, that advertises the Keikyu fast rail connection between Haneda Airport and Central Tokyo.

This simple and mundane object (a typical instance of the multitude of 'unimportant' language objects that litter our world) is amazingly complex both linguistically and semiotically. We see three writing systems – Kanji characters, Katakana script and Roman alphabet – and three 'languages' – Japanese, English and French. The French *LeTrain* is accompanied by a Katakana transliteration that instructs Japanese customers to read it as *rutoren* ([ɾətorɛn]). Interestingly, the French here is meant to be spoken, and spoken correctly. The English is confined to one word *with*. It connects two Kanji words and if we translate the whole phrase, it reads 'Haneda *with* Keikyu'. The English here is strange. There are perfectly adequate Japanese equivalents for such a function word as *with*, and even icons such as arrows could have worked. The choice, however, was for English, and there it stands: *with*. The problem, however, is that unless you know the two Kanji words on either side of it, *with* has no meaning or function. It is not English linguistically, because English competence does not allow you to understand what *with* stands for there. You need to know Japanese in order to make sense of *with* in this phrase, and so, somewhat provocatively, one could say that *with* is linguistically not English but Japanese. It is English emblematically, like *Nina's derrière* was French emblematically and (one would certainly hope!) not linguistically.

Figure 2.3 'Lced Coffce'

In both examples we see how language material shifts meanings and functions when it is mobile. The French and English elements considered here were mobile *semiotic*, rather than *linguistic*, resources. In moving from a space where people have sufficient linguistic competence to project linguistic functions onto the signs (e.g. France in the case of French) to a space where such competences cannot be presupposed (e.g. Japan), the sign changes from a linguistic sign to an emblematic one. It ceases to be something that produces linguistic meanings, because the ones consuming it cannot extract such meanings from the sign. When someone like me then, in Japan, comes across such signs, they re-become linguistic signs.

Or the sign can travel. Globalization involves delocalized production in major industries, including printing, and figure 2.3 shows us an instance of delocalized printing work. The picture was taken in London Chinatown. We see a bilingual poster, advertising, in Chinese and English, a range of cold drinks.

Whereas the Chinese is correctly written, the English contains quite spectacular typos: *Lced* 'iced', *dlrink* 'drink', *coffce* 'coffee', and so forth. Since written signs are always traces of human activity, one can speculate about the processes that generated this poster. Imagine a print shop in China, where a handwritten text is handed down to a typesetter. The typesetter does not know English, and so while the handwritten Chinese characters do not present any difficulties, the English handwritten text is *not language but a meaningless design*, a set of forms to be copied in print. Poor handwriting, such as not closing the first *e* in *coffee*, can result in it being read as *c* instead of *e*, and thus emerges the printed form *coffce*. *The text only becomes English when it is transferred to London*, and posted there against the window of a grocery store in Chinatown. It is in London that people can detect the deviations in spelling, question them or find them amusing. Such value judgments were impossible in the printing shop in China. At the same time of course, for many customers in Chinatown the Chinese in the poster is just a meaningless design. In its transfer to London it ceased to be a linguistic representation and it became a set of forms signalling Chineseness and thus fitting in Chinatown.

I am deliberately overstating my case here, because I wish to emphasize a point: that semiotic mobility has all sorts of effects on the signs that are involved in such mobility. Such processes need to be understood because they are at the heart of globalization as a sociolinguistic phenomenon. In the context of globalization, linguistic resources change value, function, ownership and so on, because they can be inserted in patterns of mobility. For this, I would suggest, we need a particular set of conceptual tools, and in the remainder of this chapter I will introduce three central concepts: scales, orders of indexicality and polycentricity.

2.2   Sociolinguistic scales

We have seen in our discussion of Fairclough (2006) how the notion of 'scale' was used essentially to denote spatial scope. We have also seen how this raised several problems, the most important of which was that a purely spatial use of the term de-historicizes the processes it is supposed to capture. So let us see what better use we can find for a notion such as 'scale'. We said above that when people or messages move, they move through a space which is filled with codes, norms and expectations. Scale is a metaphor we can use to imagine such moves.

The metaphor of scale is borrowed from fields such as history and social geography (Swyngedouw 1996; Uitermark 2002). Scales and scaling processes are an important part of the theoretical toolkit of World-Systems Analysis (Wallerstein 1983, 2000). According to World-Systems Analysis, social events and processes move and develop on a continuum of layered scales, with the strictly local (micro) and the global (macro) as its extremes and several intermediary scales (e.g. the level of the state) in between (Lefebvre 2003; also Geertz 2004). Events and processes in globalization occur at different scale-levels, and we see interactions between the different scales as a core feature of understanding such events and processes. Appadurai's (1996) notion of 'vernacular globalization' is a case in point: forms of globalization that contribute to new forms of locality. This locality, however, is destabilized – the immigrant neighbourhood no longer looks like the 'traditional' neighbourhood – because of influences from higher-level scales: migration and diaspora, neighbourhood multilingualism, the presence of the homeland in economies of consumption and in public identity display (Mankekar 2002).

The point of departure: horizontal and vertical metaphors

The point of departure for what follows is the non-unified nature of socio-linguistic phenomena. The point has often been noted: acts of communication are all uniquely contextualized, one-time phenomena; yet we understand them because of their manifest lack of autonomy: their consistence with previous traditions of making sense, their connection to shared, enduring (i.e. historical) patterns of understanding such as frames. This dual nature of language practices, both as an individual, one-time and unique phenomenon and, simultaneously, as a collective and relatively stable phenomenon, has often been captured under labels such as 'micro' and 'macro'. The connection between such levels has often been described as complex, difficult, unfathomable. Yet, several very useful theoretical tools have been developed, explicitly identifying the instanta-neous transition from one level to another in communication: Gumperz's (1982) notion of 'contextualization', Goffman's (1974) 'frames', the Bakhtinian con-cept of 'intertextuality' (as further developed, e.g., by Fairclough 1992) and Bourdieu's (1990) 'habitus' – to name just the most widely recognized ones.

In all cases, the concepts identify *the jump from one scale to another*: from the individual to the collective, the temporally situated to the trans-temporal, the unique to the common, the token to the type, the specific to the general. And *the connection between such scales is indexical*: it resides in the ways in which unique instances of communication can be captured indexically as 'framed', understandable communication, as pointing towards socially and culturally ordered norms, genres, traditions, expectations – phenomena of a higher scale-level. The capacity to achieve understanding in communication is the capacity to lift momentary instances of interaction to the level of common meanings, and the two directions of indexicality (presupposing – the retrieval of available meanings – and entailing – the production of new meanings; Silverstein 2006a: 14) are at the heart of such processes.

Reviewing current theorizing about such scalar phenomena, we see that a lot of thinking has gone into the connections and movements – sophisticated concepts such as 'intertextuality' and 'entextualization' are results of that. What exactly it is that is connected and moved between, however, has by and large been neglected as an area of theorizing. One effect has been that notions of 'contextualization' (the process of conversion) have been better developed than notions of 'context', the spaces in and between which contextualization hap-pens. (See Hanks 2006 for a recent survey.) I have been using the term *scale* here as an attempt to at least provide a metaphor that suggests that we have to imagine things that are of *a different order*, that are hierarchically ranked and stratified. The metaphor suggests spatial images; however, these images are *vertical metaphors of space* rather than *horizontal* ones, which are implicit in terms such as *distribution*, *spread*, and even *community* and *culture*, among others. Scales offer us a vertical image of space, of *space as stratified* and therefore power-invested; but they also suggest deep connections between spatial and temporal features. In that sense, scale may be a concept that allows us to see sociolinguistic phenomena as non-unified *in relation to a stratified, non-unified image of social structure.* Note that the introduction of 'scale' does not reject horizontal images of space; it complements them with a vertical dimension of hierarchical ordering and power differentiation. Let us look at these aspects of scales in some detail.

Scales as semiotized space and time

To be sure, a notion such as 'scale' is the construction of an analytic image – something which Wallerstein warns us is an invention of social-scientific, traditional thought (Wallerstein 1997, 2001: chapter 10). In particular, our current attempt at 'spatializing' sociolinguistic theory risks being flawed by that institutional problem inscribed in the division of labour between the social sciences: the separation of time and space as different aspects of social life and social phenomena. Against this separation, Wallerstein pits the notion of TimeSpace – a 'single dimension' which locks together time and space (Wallerstein 1997: 1; also Fals Borda 2000). Every social event develops simultaneously in space and in time, often in multiply imagined spaces and timeframes. So here is one critical qualification: a notion such as scale refers to phenomena that develop in TimeSpace. Scale is not just a spatial metaphor.

Talk about 'time' and 'space', however, is slippery, and we must add a second necessary qualification. The phenomena that develop in TimeSpace are *social* phenomena, and the TimeSpace in which they develop is consequently an 'objective' (physical) context *made social.* It is an often repeated assertion: people make physical space and time into controlled, regimented objects and instruments, and they do so through semiotic practices; semiotized TimeSpace is social, cultural, political, historical, ideological TimeSpace (Lefebvre 2003; also Haviland 2003; Goodwin 2002). A third necessary qualification to be added follows from the previous one. The semiotization of TimeSpace as social contexts always involves more than just images of space and time. As we shall see, a move from one scale-level to another invokes or indexes *images of society,* through socially and culturally constructed (semiotized) metaphors and images of time and space. The general direction of such moves can be formulated as follows:

	Lower scale	Higher scale
Time	Momentary	Timeless
Space	Local, situated	Translocal, widespread

In social interaction, such TimeSpace moves – 'scale-jumping', as they are called by Uitermark (2002: 750) – are converted into interactional patterns that index norms, expectations and degrees of generalness of positions. They are converted, in other words, into *statements that index social order*, and the TimeSpace imagery provides rich indexicals (sometimes iconically) for aspects of a real or imagined social order. Consider, by way of illustration, the following bit of (imagined) interaction between a tutor (T) and a PhD student (S):

s: I'll start my dissertation with a chapter reporting on my fieldwork
t: We start our dissertations with a literature review chapter here.

The tutor performs a scale-jump here, in which he moves from the local and situated to the translocal and 'general', invoking practices that have validity beyond the here-and-now – *normative validity*. This 'upscaling' is articulated through a change from personal and situated to impersonal and general – compare S's use of *I* and *my*, as well as his use of the future tense, with T's *we* and *our*, T's use of the timeless present and his invocation of *here*: a community larger than just the student and the tutor. The student's utterance was centred on his own work and plans; the tutor's response re-centres it on a higher scale-level: that of the larger academic community and institutional environment of which both are part. The individual plan of the student is countered by an invocation of general rules and norms, valid 'here' (i.e. valid for the particular student as well). The tutor's move is a vertical move performed in a stratified, hierarchically layered system, in which higher scale-levels (institutional and community norms and rules) prevail over lower scale-levels (the individual concerns of the student). It is, of course, a power move in which a higher level of relevance, truth, validity or value is called in to cancel the suggestion made by the student, in which individuals have been replaced by institutionally circumscribed roles, and in which the *specific* case is measured against *categories* of cases: from token to type, from contextualized to decontextualized. The scale-jump thus made is a complex one, in which various kinds of semiotic transformations occur:

Lower scale	Higher scale
Momentary	Timeless
Local, situated	Translocal, widespread
Personal, individual	Impersonal, collective
Contextualized	Decontextualized
Subjective	Objective
Specific	General, categorial
Token	Type
Individual	Role
Diversity, variation	Uniformity, homogeneity

And all of this is produced through simple grammatical, stylistic and generic operations in the utterance: small formal cues that release dense indexical meanings.

The fact that these operations are performed here by the tutor and not by the student is, of course, not accidental. As Uitermark (2002) notes, some people or groups can jump scales while others cannot, and 'outscaling' is a frequent power tactic: lifting a particular issue to a scale-level which is inaccessible to the other, as when a lawyer shifts into legalese or a doctor into medical jargon. Jumping scales depends on access to discursive resources that index and iconicize particular scale-levels, and such access is an object of inequality. As Conley and O'Barr's (1990) work on small-claims courts demonstrated some time ago, discursive resources that are empowering at one scale-level (e.g. issue-centred emotive discourses) can be disempowering at higher scale-levels (where a law-centred rational discourse dominates). Power and inequality are features of scaling, of the asymmetrical capacity to invoke particular scale-levels in the interpretation of an act; scales provide contexts with possible regulations of access.

The simple lexical and grammatical operations performed by the tutor, thus, trigger a whole range of indexical shifts, redefining the situation, the participants, the topic, the scope of 'acceptable' statements on the topic, and so forth; they also firmly set the event in a normative, general norm-oriented frame. This complex indexical shift can now be described not as a series of individual operations, but as *one vertical move within a stratified social meaning system*, enabling and mobilizing the various forms of indexical re-ordering of the statement. Introducing a notion such as 'scale' for describing current phenomena in communicative action has the advantage of introducing a layered, stratified model of society as a frame for the interpretation of such phenomena. Power and inequality thus become incorporated into our ways of imagining such phenomena, and rather than seeing them as an exceptional aberration in social life (as in many analyses focused on power), they can be seen as an integral feature of every social event. It is the new image of society introduced by the tutor's statement that organizes the new indexical order: he introduces a rigid, norm-oriented, trans-personal social space – a different power regime for the interaction which reorganizes the 'footing' (Goffman 1981) on which the participants can interact with one another.

In sum, scales need to be understood as 'levels' or 'dimensions' (Lefebvre 2003: 136–150) at which particular forms of normativity, patterns of language use and expectations thereof are organized. Scalar processes are processes of shifts between such scales, and we should recall that such shifts involve complex re-semiotizations of TimeSpace: new images of time and space, new patterns of acting upon them. In this more complex understanding, the notion of 'scale' may allow us to understand the dynamics between local and translocal forces discussed in chapter 1 as well as in the examples given earlier in this chapter. Different scales can interact, collaborate and overlap or be in conflict with one another, because each time there are issues of normativity at play. To these issues we now need to turn.

2.3   Orders of indexicality

Different scales organize different patterns of normativity, of what counts as language. This may quickly be turned into an image of chaos and of fragmentation (and quite a lot of post-modernist literature would make this interpretation), but for reasons that are discussed later in this book, such interpretations are not helpful. The processes we see are *not* chaotic but ordered, although they are of considerable complexity. Normativity is, by its very essence, a form of organization and order. So we need to look for conceptual tools that help us imagine this complex form of organization and order, and I will turn to the notion of 'orders of indexicality' for that (cf. Blommaert 2005: 69ff).

The point of departure is quite simple: indexicality, even though largely operating at the implicit level of linguistic/semiotic structuring, is not unstructured but *ordered*. It is ordered in two ways, and these forms of indexical order account for 'normativity' in semiosis. The first kind of order is what Silverstein (2003a) called 'indexical order': the fact that indexical meanings occur in patterns offering perceptions of similarity and stability that can be perceived as 'types' of semiotic practise with predictable (presupposable/entailing) directions (see also Agha 2003, 2005). 'Register' is a case in point: clustered and patterned language forms that index specific social personae and roles can be invoked to organize interactional practices (e.g. turns at talk, narrative), and have a prima facie stability that can sometimes be used for typifying or stereotyping (e.g. 'posh' accents – see Rampton 2003). Speaking or writing through such registers involves insertion in recognizable (normative) repertoires of 'voices': one then speaks *as* a man, a lawyer, a middle-aged European, an asylum seeker and so forth, and if done appropriately, one will be perceived as speaking *as such* (Agha 2005). Thus, indexical order is the metapragmatic organizing principle behind what is widely understood as the 'pragmatics' of language.

Such forms of indexical order sometimes have long and complex histories of becoming (Silverstein 2003a and Agha 2003 offer excellent illustrations). These histories are often connected to the histories of becoming of nation states and to their cultural and sociolinguistic paraphernalia – the notion of a 'standard language' and its derivative, a particular 'national' ethnolinguistic identity (Silverstein 1996, 1998; Errington 2001). Yet, they also display a significant degree of variability and change, they can erupt and fade under pressure of macro-developments such as capitalist consumer fashions, as is evident from Silverstein's (2003a, 2006b) *oenologia* – the register of contemporary wine connoisseurs (see also Agha 2005, 2007). Indexical order of this sort is a positive force, it produces social categories, recognizable semiotic emblems for groups and individuals, a more or less coherent semiotic habitat.

It does so, however, within the confines of a stratified general repertoire in which particular indexical orders relate to others in relations of mutual valuation – higher/lower, better/worse. This is where we meet another kind of order to indexicalities, one that operates on a higher plane of social structuring: an order in the general systems of meaningful semiosis valid in groups at any given time. This kind of ordering results in what I call orders of indexicality – a term obviously inspired by Foucault's 'order of discourse'. Recall that Foucault was interested in the general rules for the production of discourses: their positive emergence as well as their erasure and exclusion. He started from the hypothesis

that in every society the production of discourse is at once controlled, selected, organized and redistributed by a certain number of procedures whose role is to ward off its powers and dangers, to gain mastery over its chance events, to evade its ponderous, formidable materiality. (Foucault 1984 [1971]: 109; see also his notion of 'archive', Foucault 2002 [1969]: chapter 5)

If we now paraphrase Foucault's hypothesis we see that ordered indexicalities operate within large stratified complexes in which some forms of semiosis are systemically perceived as valuable, others as less valuable and some are not taken into account at all, while all are subject to rules of access and regulations as to circulation. That means that such systemic patterns of indexicality are also systemic patterns of authority, of control and evaluation, and hence of inclusion and exclusion *by real or perceived others*. This also means that every register is susceptible to a politics of access. And it also means that there is an economy of exchange, in which the values attached by some to one form of semiosis may not be granted by others: the English spoken by a middle-class person in Nairobi may not be (and is unlikely to be) perceived as a middle-class attribute in London or New York.

'Order of indexicality' is a sensitizing concept that should index ('point a finger to') important aspects of power and inequality in the field of semiosis. If forms of semiosis are socially and culturally valued, these valuation processes should display traces of power and authority, of struggles in which there were winners as well as losers, and in which, in general, the group of winners is smaller than the group of losers. The concept invites different questions – sociolinguistic questions on indexicality – and should open empirical analyses of indexicality to higher-level considerations about relations within sociolinguistic repertoires, the (non-)exchangeability of particular linguistic or semiotic resources across places, situations and groups, and so forth. It invites, in sum, different questions of authority, access and power in this field.

2.4   Polycentricity

One such question is: how do we imagine these patterns of authority and power? One way of answering that question is to suggest that authority emanates from real or perceived 'centres', to which people orient when they produce an indexical trajectory in semiosis. That is, whenever we communicate, in addition to our real and immediate addressees we orient towards what Bakhtin (1986) called a 'super-addressee': complexes of norms and perceived appropriateness criteria, in effect the larger social and cultural body of authority into which we insert our immediate practices vis-à-vis our immediate addressees. And very often, such authorities have names, faces, a reality of their own; they can be individuals (teachers, parents, role models, the coolest guy in class), collectives (peer groups, sub-cultural groups, group images such as 'punk', 'gothic' etc.), abstract entities or ideals (church, the nation state, the middle class, consumer culture and its many fashions, freedom, democracy), and so on: the macro- and micro-structures of our everyday world. The point is: we often project the presence of an evaluating authority through our interactions with immediate addressees, we behave *with reference to* such an evaluative authority, and I submit we call such an evaluating authority a 'centre'.

The authority of centres is evaluative, and it often occurs as an authority over clusters of semiotic features, including *thematic domains, places, people* (roles, identities, relationships) and *semiotic styles* (including linguistic varieties, modes of performance etc.). Thus, broaching a particular topic will trigger a particular semiotic style and suggest particular roles and relationships between participants, and certain types of communicative events require appropriate places and occasions – *Not here! Not now! Not while the children are listening!* (Scollon and Scollon 2003, Blommaert, Collins and Slembrouck 2005a). One speaks differently and as a different person about cars or music than about the economy or about sex. In one instance, one can speak as an expert using a particular register indexing membership of expert groups, in other instances one can speak as a novice; one can shift from a very masculine voice on a particular topic (e.g. sex or cars) to a gender-neutral voice (e.g. when discussing the war in Iraq), each time also shifting registers, often even accents, pace, tone and rhythm (a declarative tone on one topic, a hesitant one on another). And topics, styles and identities belong to specific places and are excluded from other places (a thing that becomes apparent during after-hours escapades at scientific conferences). Each time one orients towards other centres of authority offering ideal-types of norms or appropriateness criteria, as it is called in pragmatics: the places where 'good' discourse about these topics is made.

It is the packaging of topic, place, style and people that makes up the index-ical direction of communication: the fact that certain topics require specific semiotic modes and environments, and so organize identities and roles (Agha 2005). Goffman (1981), as we already saw, called such patterns 'shifts in footing': delicate changes in speaker position that are accompanied by shifts in linguistic and semiotic modes and redefine the participant roles in the interaction. We are now in a position to empirically 'dissect' footing and bring it in line with larger organizational features of life in society.

It is obvious that even though places impose rules and restrictions on what can happen in communication there, every environment in which humans convene and communicate is almost by definition polycentric, in the sense that more than one possible centre can be distinguished. One can follow norms or violate them at any step of the process, and sometimes this is wilfully done while on other occasions it comes about by accident or because of the impossibility of behaving in a particular way. Again, Goffman's descriptions of the multiple layers that characterize mundane interaction scenes are informa-tive. For instance, Goffman distinguishes between 'focal' and 'non-focal' activities occurring in the same event – as when a pupil in class produces an offensive reaction to a teacher's question, giving off negative impressions (focal, for the teacher) as well as positive ones (non-focal, towards his peer group who studiously try to avoid being classified as 'nerds'). In our own research on asylum seekers' narratives, we often found that 'truthful' accounts by the applicant were interpreted as 'implausible' (i.e. untruthful) by the interviewers, because describing the chaotic and often paradoxical realities truthfully often iconically resulted in a chaotic and paradoxical story. Interviewees oriented towards 'the truth' as defined by situated, densely con-textualized realities in countries like Africa, for example, while interviewers oriented towards a particular textual (bureaucratic) ideal of decontextualizable coherence, linearity and factuality (Blommaert 2001a; chapter 6 below). Both centres were always present in such a polycentric interview situation, although the interviewers' centre was often 'non-focal', kept in the background during the interview itself. Thus, in telling 'the truth', the applicants were often 'wrong-footed' by the interviewers; in the real world, the dominant order of indexicality is that of the interviewer and their bureaucratic apparatus.

Polycentricity is a key feature of interactional regimes in human environ-ments: even though many interaction events look 'stable' and monocentric (e.g. exams, wedding ceremonies), there are as a rule multiple – though never unlimited – batteries of norms to which one can orient and according to which one can behave (as when the bride winks at the groom when she says 'I do'). This multiplicity has been previously captured under terms such as 'polyphony' or 'multivocality'. A term such as 'polycentricity' moves the issue from the descriptive to the interpretive level. Again, my attempt here is aimed at sensitizing others to the fact that behind terms such as 'polyphony', social structures of power and inequality are at work. Such structures – orders of indexicality – account for the fact that certain forms of polyphony never occur while other forms of polyphony miraculously seem to assume similar shapes and directions. The bride can wink at her groom, but baring her breasts would be highly unusual. Certain voices, like the bureaucratic one in the asylum system, *systemically* prevail over others, because the impact of certain centres of authority is bigger than that of others. The multiplicity of available batteries of norms does not mean that these batteries are equivalent, equally accessible or equally open to negotiation. Orders of indexicality are stratified and impose differences in value onto the different modes of semiosis, systematically give preference to some over others, and exclude or disqualify particular modes.

Both concepts, 'order of indexicality' and 'polycentricity', thus suggest a less innocent world of linguistic, social and cultural variation and diversity, one in which difference is quickly turned into inequality, and in which complex patterns of potential-versus-actual behaviour occur. They also enable us to move beyond the usual sociolinguistic units – homogeneous speech communities – and to consider situations in which various 'big' sociolinguistic systems enter the picture, as when people migrate in the context of globalization, or when in the same context messages start moving across large spaces. In both cases, people do not just move across space; given what has been said above, we also realize that they move across different orders of indexicality. Consequently, what happens to them in communication becomes less predictable than what would happen in 'their own' environment. Sociolinguistics in the age of globalization needs to look way beyond the speech community, to sociolinguistic systems and how they connect and relate to one another. Big things matter if we want to understand the small things of discourse.

2.5 A sociolinguistics of mobile resources

Power and mobility

Scales, orders of indexicality, polycentricity: we now have the basis for a little vocabulary that will enable us to talk about language in globalization in a different way. The three concepts I introduced had several things in common. One such thing was their emphasis on power: all of the concepts suggest layering and stratification in hierarchical systems of value for semiotic resources. In any and every social interaction, *specific* semiotic forms will be expected and be valued as the 'best possible' resources. In pragmatics, such phenomena of selection for preference have been described for decades in terms ranging from 'felicity conditions' to 'appropriateness criteria' (see e.g. Levinson 1983), and let us not forget 'politeness' research as a culmination point in such studies (cf. Eelen 2000). Likewise, the Hymesian notion of 'communicative competence' has often been described as the capacity for 'adequate' linguistic performance in a given social situation. Understanding what such forms of adequacy and appropriateness may be in a context which we are now compelled to imagine as complex and mobile, requires a new vocabulary. The three terms I propose here can be assessed with regard to usefulness.

A second feature shared by the three concepts is their spatiotemporal sensitivity. They need to be read in sequence to be clearly understood like that. In other words, sociolinguistic phenomena in a globalization context need to be understood as developing at several different scale-levels, where different orders of indexicality dominate, resulting in a polycentric 'context' where communicative behaviour is simultaneously pushed and pulled in various directions. The French on the Keikyu phone card was both strictly local (a Tokyo sign) as well as translocal (a French sign); the translocal scale-level, however, was not equally accessible to every consumer of the sign. For local people operating within a local order of indexicality, the French made good sense as an emblem of 'Frenchness', with its connotations of *chic*. For people such as me, who brought along a practical linguistic competence in French, it made sense in a very different way: it became a 'typically Japanese' way of using French, that is, a form that is detached from its conventional 'French' (i.e. translocal and linguistic) functions and is relocated in a local, Tokyo semiotic economy. It became, in short, an *exotic* French form, and note that the qualification of 'exotic' is an assessment made at one particular scale-level and within one particular order of indexicality – that of the translocal scale. Resetting this Keikyu phone card from its local, Tokyo, context to its translocal, 'French', context involved an operation in which the sign was resemiotized, subject to very different procedures of meaning attribution. The sign was made to travel, it was *mobilized* by a feature of globalization: a tourist (me) picking it up in its place of origin (Tokyo) and subjecting it to my own (Francophone) procedures of 'reading' and 'decoding'. By doing so, I lifted the sign out of its TimeSpace frame and brought it into quite a different TimeSpace frame, one for which it was not intended, and one in which it could, consequently, acquire 'exotic' meanings.

It should be clear that we are relatively far removed from a traditional sociolinguistic discourse of language mixing and shifting here. Conventional approaches to code-switching would not be able to tell us much about signs such as the 'Haneda *with* Keikyu' or the 'LeTrain' examples given here. For one thing, there is far more than 'language' (in the sense of 'Japanese', 'English' and 'French') at play here. As I noted in the beginning, the Keikyu phone card contains three such 'languages' (even if in minimal, one-word forms) as well as three scripts and a compound image of a plane and a train. It is, of course, a multimodal sign, and shifts occur here in a vastly more complex field than that of 'language' alone. What we observe is clearly not just a *linguistic* problem, it is a *semiotic* one. Consequently, we need to look at resources, actual situated resources as deployed by real people in real contexts, and recontextualized by other real people such as myself. We are witnessing repertoires here, constructed out of bits and pieces of conventionally defined 'languages' and concretely assuming the shape of registers and genres, of *specific* patterns of language in communicative forms such as a phone card, a poster or a shop sign. The target of our analysis is resources, and even if such resources can be conventionally tagged as 'belonging' to language X or Y, it is good to remember that the whole point is about the dislodging of such resources from their conventional origins. The French on the Keikyu phone card becomes a problem not because of its linguistic features – not because it is 'French' – but because of the particular ways in which it has penetrated the semiotic repertoire of people in Tokyo and has acquired meanings and functions there. This, I would say, is a sociolinguistics of mobile resources, no longer a sociolinguistics of immobile languages.

Locked in space: on linguistic rights

Naturally, this theoretical stance comes at a price. Such forms of inter-language penetration have often been captured in a totalizing but comfortable discourse of language(s), with which we now have to disagree. There is by now a well-entrenched and very respectable branch of sociolinguistics which is concerned with describing the world of globalization from the perspective of linguistic imperialism and 'linguicide' (Phillipson 1992; Skutnabb-Kangas 2000), often based on particular ecological metaphors. These approaches start from a socio-linguistics of distribution and oddly assume that wherever a 'big' and 'power-ful' language such as English 'appears' in a foreign territory, small indigenous languages will 'die'. There is, in this image of sociolinguistic space, place for just one language at a time. In general, there seems to be a serious problem with the ways in which space is imagined in such work. In addition, the actual sociolinguistic details of such processes are rarely spelled out – languages can be used in vernacular or in lingua franca varieties and so create different sociolinguistic conditions for mutual influencing; English sometimes 'threatens' other former colonial languages such as French, Spanish or Portuguese, rather than the indigenous languages (a phenomenon noted primarily in former exploitation colonies, and less prominent in former settlement colonies; see Mufwene 2005, 2008); or sometimes the 'threat' to indigenous languages can come from dominant local ('indigenous') languages rather than English, as we shall see further in this book. So there are several major problems with the literature on linguistic rights.

One major problem is the way in which authors appear to assume the spatial 'fixedness' of people, languages and places. The discourse of minority rights is in general a discourse of strict locality, and the first lines of the UN Declaration on the Rights of Persons Belonging to National or Ethnic, Religious and Linguistic Minorities read: 'States shall protect the existence and the national or ethnic, cultural, religious and linguistic minorities *within their respective territories*, and shall encourage conditions for the promotion of that identity' (quoted in Skutnabb-Kangas and Phillipson 1999). This Declaration is an agreement between states, which are here presented as territorially bounded entities in the space of which a particular regime can and should be developed with respect to 'minorities', defined in the same move as minorities within that particular ('state') territory. The rights granted by this Declaration are territorially bounded and organized rights, and distinctions between groups evolve along the classic Herderian triad of territory–culture–language (Blommaert and Verschueren 1998).

This discourse of locality is usually couched in environmental–ecological metaphors: a particular place is characterized by specific features ranging from climate through biodiversity to people, cultures and languages. The relationship between these different components is seen as a form of synergy: it is through human variability that diversity in the environment is sustained, for the languages and cultures of local people provide unique views on this environment and help sustain it. See, for example, the point of view articulated by one of the most vocal advocates of linguistic rights, *Terralingua* (1999, from their website http://cougar.ucdavis.edu/nas/terralin/learn.html):

We know that a diversity of species lends stability and resilience to the world's ecosystems. Terralingua thinks that a diversity of languages does the same for the world's cultures – and that these manifestations of the diversity of life are interrelated.

This diversity is invariably seen as something that needs to be preserved, consequently. It literally needs to be 'kept in place'. To go by the words of Skutnabb-Kangas and Phillipson (1995: 84): '[t]he perpetuation of linguistic diversity can ... be seen as a recognition that all individuals and groups have basic human rights, and as a necessity for the survival of the planet, in a similar way to biodiversity' (see also Skutnabb-Kangas and Phillipson 1999; Nettle and Romaine 2000; see May 2001, Blommaert 2001b and Mufwene 2002 for a critique).

There is a linguistic–ideological dimension to this, in which it is assumed that language functions in a community because it provides *local* meanings: meanings that provide frames for understanding the local environment, to categorize and analyse the (strictly) local world. References to the unique worldviews enshrined in these languages often revolve around local functionality as well: the worldviews are expressed in terms and grammatical relations that address or articulate a local decoding of the world. Let us return to Skutnabb-Kangas and Phillipson 1995: 89):

Linguistic diversity at local levels is a necessary counterweight to the hegemony of a few 'international' languages. The 'World Languages' should, just as roads and bridges, be seen as tools for communication of ideas and matter, but the creation of authentic ideas and products (instead of mass-products) is in most cases necessarily best done locally.

The worldviews are invariably local (or territorialized) worldviews, linked to particular regional surroundings. A people's language localizes these people, it sets them within a particular, spatially demarcated ecology.

It is this view of local functionality that underpins the strong claims, cited above, that the survival of minority languages is crucial for the survival of the planet, for with every language that disappears a uniquely functional local set of meanings about the environment is lost. Languages are seen as local repositories of knowledge, and such local forms of knowledge are essential for understanding the (local) world. Consequently, when people are moved into a different environment, the language may lose (part of) its functions. Conversely, when another language is introduced in a particular environment, it may as well be dysfunctional for it does not articulate the particular local meanings required for the sustenance of this environment. This idea in turn underpins the idea of linguistic imperialism, invariably conceived as a non-local language (usually the ex-colonial language, and usually English) penetrating or invading local spaces and disturbing the ecological balance that existed between people, their language and culture, and their environment (Skutnabb-Kangas 2000; Skutnabb-Kangas and Phillipson 1995, 1999 and Heugh 1999 provide examples).

In sum, what we see here is how language functions are territorialized, tied to particular local environments apparently constructed as static. Language apparently works excellently in its own, original place, and it loses functions as soon as the stable, original, 'autochthonous' (or 'native', 'aboriginal') link between language and place is broken. Consequently, a programme aimed at stimulating or promoting these local languages (invariably mother tongues of apparently inherently monolingual and monocultural people) ties the speakers of these languages to a place and reinforces the presumed fixed connection between people and their environment – a clear reflex of the Saussurean synchrony.

All of this sounds more or less acceptable, at least when some aspects of reality are conveniently overlooked. A rather disturbing aspect of contemporary reality, as we know, is *mobility*. In contemporary social structures, people tend to move around, both in real geographical space and in symbolic, social space. And all of these processes of mobility appear to display complex connections with language (Rampton 1995, 1999), including language attitudes and language planning.

Language as a social thing, i.e. something in which people have made investments and to which they have attributed values, seems to have awkward relations to space, the main axes of which are those of territorialization and deterritorialization. Territorialization stands for the perception and attribution of values to language as a local phenomenon, something which ties people to local communities and spaces. Customarily, people's mother tongue (L1) is perceived as 'territorialized language', alongside orality and the use of dialects. All of these forms of language emanate locality. Conversely, deterritorialization stands for the perception and attribution of values to language as something which does not belong to one locality but which organizes translocal trajectories and wider spaces ('scale-jumps' in the terminology developed earlier in this chapter). Second or other languages (L2) as well as lingua francas and diaspora varieties, standardized varieties and literacy are seen as 'deterritorialized language', language that does not exclusively belong to one place (Jacquemet 2000, 2005; Maryns and Blommaert 2001).

Language variation allows, defines and organizes spatial trajectories. Literacy allows a text to be moved, both physically across spaces in the world, as well as symbolically, across social spheres and scales. A standard variety of a language allows moving to adjacent places where people speak similar dialects, as well as across social spaces, into the elite. International languages such as French or English allow insertion in large transnational spaces and networks as well as access to the elites. The different 'types' of languages, in short, allow access to different scales. All of these scalar patterns of mobility are real, they revolve often around life-chances and opportunities, and consequently people often articulate relations between language or code choices and spaces. The choice for English or French rather than indigenous languages in education is at the grassroots level often motivated by means of discourses of 'getting out of here' and towards particular centres – metropolitan areas – where upward social mobility at least looks possible.

Moving through the various levels of education often involves moving through layered, scaled regimes of language, each time seen as enabling deterritorialization and hence social as well as geographical mobility. Senses of belonging to a particular community conversely often go hand in hand with the creation (or re-creation) of particular varieties that tie people to that community while at the same time indexing displacement and deterritorialization. 'Gangsta' English, for instance, is widespread in African urban centres as a language of the townships and the slums, where particular, often imaginarily violent youth cultures develop (see chapter 7 below for a more extensive discussion). Such linguistic ideologies connecting language varieties to dynamics of locality and mobility, active both at the folk and at institutional levels, often foster resistance to the promotion of indigenous, minority languages – a point often reported by fieldworkers, but rarely written down in publications.

Although one might deplore this, the reasons are usually sound enough. Symbolic marginalization is often just one correlate of real, material marginalization (Fraser 1995, Stroud 2001); L1 promotion is a form of symbolic upgrading of marginalized resources, and resistance is often based on an acute awareness of the persistence of real marginalization. If performed within a monoglot strategy (i.e. a strategy aimed at constructing 'full monolingualism' and rejecting bilingualism as a road to language attrition or language death), L1 promotion, is thus seen as an instrument *preventing* a way out of real marginalization and amounting to keeping people in their marginalized places and locked into one scale-level: the local. Imagine a family in the very marginalized and poor north-eastern parts of South Africa, speaking Venda. Education in Venda is likely to be perceived as keeping people in the marginalized region, as long as good, white-collar jobs and higher education are in effect concentrated in places like Johannesburg – and require access to English and/or Afrikaans. If the family wants to offer its children upward social mobility, then, it needs to offer them geographical mobility and consequently linguistic mobility as well. Language shift, under such conditions, is a strategy for survival. In the eyes of the speakers, the upgrading of marginalized symbolic goods may still be seen as less empowering than the creation of access to the real prestige goods. Mufwene (2002: 377) captures the core of this 'wicked problem' well: '[i]t sometimes boils down to a choice between saving speakers from their economic predicament and saving a language'.

The crux of the matter is that we need to think of issues such as linguistic inequality as being organized around concrete resources, not around languages in general but specific registers, varieties, genres. And such concrete resources follow the predicament of their users: when the latter are socially mobile, their resources will follow this trajectory; when they are socially marginal, their resources will also be disqualified. In both cases, the challenge is to think of language as a mobile complex of concrete resources. If we fail to do that, we risk drawing a caricature of social realities and becoming very upset about that caricature rather than about an accurate replica of social processes. This, needless to say, is a pointless exercise. The matter is of fundamental importance and is easily misunderstood, and this is why I am emphatic about it. In what follows I will try to provide a clear illustration of what we are talking about: the mobility of concrete semiotic resources (not 'languages') in a globalized context. There is always a tension between an ideologically perceived 'language' and sociolinguistically perceived 'resources', as we shall see presently; globalized economic forces exacerbate and exploit such tensions.

2.6   Selling accent

Language policy revolves around the production and enforcement of norms for language use, and its success is measured by the degree to which policy-preferred norms are accepted and spread. Traditionally, the state is the major player in the field of language policy. It regulates which language(s) and forms of literacy are 'official' and 'national', and it imposes rules and constraints on the use of languages and scripts in its realm. Usually, the state was and is concerned with standardized 'languages', that is, with one layer of linguistic variation. The state, however, has always had to share the space of norm definition and normative conduct with other actors – the family is one very important such actor, while civil society actors such as churches are others. Media, by and large, traditionally supported the 'official' norms imposed by the state. Intralanguage variation – dialects, accents – was and is within the purview of the individual citizens or of groups using them to flag particular identities. At the national level, they are very often seen as the fabric of national identity and local (sub-state) authenticity and often cherished as such (see e.g. Elmes 2005).

I have to cut quite a few corners here, but the point I wish to make is that (1) the state is traditionally a very powerful actor in the field of language norms and traditionally has the monopoly of formal policy making; but (2) the state has never been the only player in the field of language norms. It has always been a major player, but never a completely hegemonic player; there is always a form of polycentricity, a division of labour between the state and other actors in this field, and formal language policies compete with the language politics of other actors in complex webs of language policing activities. (3) The language policies of the state are traditionally aimed at 'languages' only; the state is usually tolerant when it comes to the co-existence of a multitude of dialects and accents in the national language(s) on its territory. In Belgium, for instance, the state makes no effort to combat regional variation in the national languages French, Dutch and German, even if the education system forcefully promotes standard varieties of these languages, and even if a modest complaints culture exists about the use of regionalisms and dialects in the media.

I will use these general introductory remarks as the backdrop for an argument that runs as follows. The traditional tolerance of state policies towards intra-language variation such as dialects and accents is not matched by the politics of language of globalized, private enterprise actors. While the state focuses on language, new actors of language commodification focus on accent and discourse, thus creating a market in which sharp distinctions between speaking right and speaking wrong are articulated. Such distinctions draw on globalized orders of indexicality, normative complexes in which imageries of global success and failure are used, and English – the language that defines global-ization – is of course the core of such orders. The outcome of this is a competitive market not just of English but of English accents which defies the traditional tolerance of the state policies, as well as popular (and academic) perceptions of accent as producing authenticity. It creates a new commodified dialectology and raises quite complex issues on normativity and identity, as well as on the shifting balance between formal language policies and equally for-malized language politics in an age of globalization. It is an instance of Foucaultian 'policing' – the rational production of order – and it works through an infinitely detailed attention to conduct (what Foucault (2005, 2007) called 'the care of the self', the perpetual micro-practices of subjectivity). Accent courses produce a regimented subject that is subjected to rules of 'normal' speech – speech that is invisible because it is uniform and homogeneous. Let us now examine the procedures by means of which this subjectification is effected.

The Internet and the commodification of accent

Replacing to some extent the older industry of correspondence courses, the Internet offers a wide and virtually uncontrolled space for language learning packages. They come in all shapes and sizes, and I will focus on websites offering courses in American accent. I do this because they manifestly bank on two different things: (1) the worldwide 'stampede towards English' (de Swaan 2001) inspired by the global perception of English as the language that defines upwardly mobile trajectories; (2) a particular imagery of the USA and American cultural symbols as being in the forefront of globalization and of upward global mobility. In other words, we get the so-called 'McDonaldization' of the world caught metonymically in packages for acquiring an American-sounding variety of English. What is spread is, of course, not just the product but also the adjectives used to qualify it, not just the language as linguistic structure but the language as a densely loaded ideological format, something that is far more than a language but also an acquirable imagery of the self as being 'in the world'.

Let me note from the outset that, although American accent websites may offer us the most outspoken examples of such dense ideological packaging, websites offering packages in other languages and varieties do the same, be it slightly less explicitly. They all offer language and the social trajectories it is supposed to provide or open. American accent websites are not unique but illustrative of a broader pattern of ideological packaging of commodified languages and varieties. We should also observe right from the start that these websites never offer 'a' language in its totality. What they offer is a *register* – a specific bit of language tailored to the immediate needs or desires of the customers. What is offered is something that gives the impression of language, a *pragmatic* and *metapragmatic* component to language competence that indexically emanates the right ideological package. The point is not to *learn* American English, but to *sound* like an American. The language policing here operates on sub-language objects.

Note also that the real US society is of course very much a 'multi-accent' society. Apart from the well-known regional varieties (e.g. Texan, Appalachian) a visit to any big hotel in the USA teaches us that Latino, Eastern European and Asian accents are very much accepted as working varieties of American English. The 'American accent' sold by the Internet companies we consider here is often

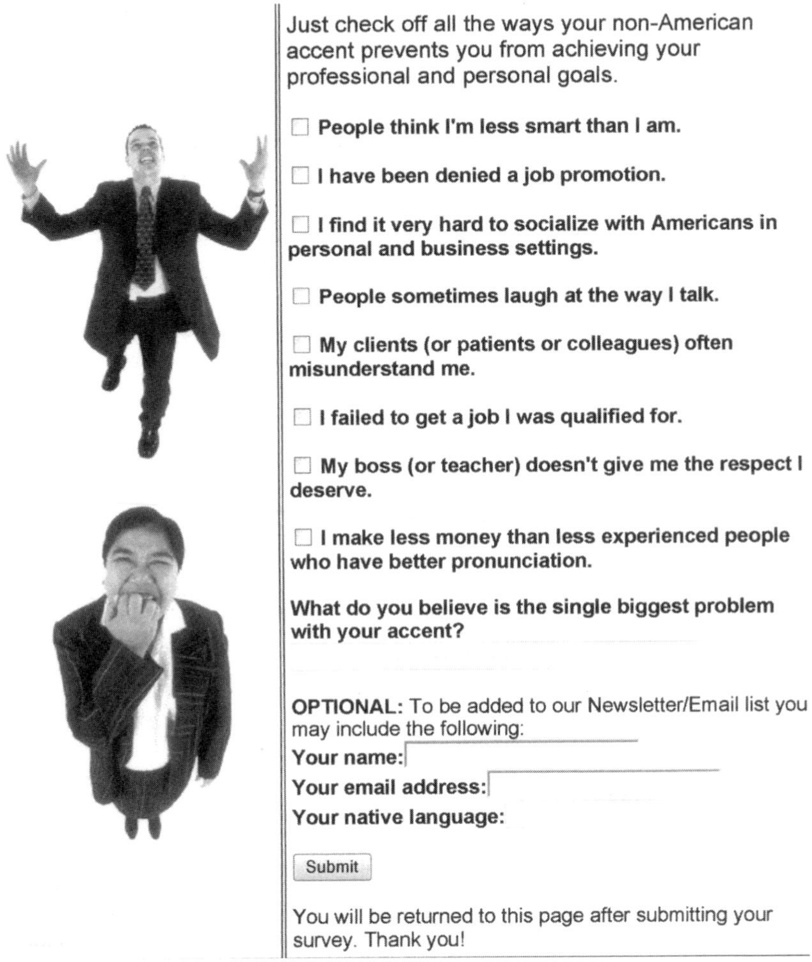

Just check off all the ways your non-American accent prevents you from achieving your professional and personal goals.

☐ **People think I'm less smart than I am.**

☐ **I have been denied a job promotion.**

☐ **I find it very hard to socialize with Americans in personal and business settings.**

☐ **People sometimes laugh at the way I talk.**

☐ **My clients (or patients or colleagues) often misunderstand me.**

☐ **I failed to get a job I was qualified for.**

☐ **My boss (or teacher) doesn't give me the respect I deserve.**

☐ **I make less money than less experienced people who have better pronunciation.**

What do you believe is the single biggest problem with your accent?

OPTIONAL: To be added to our Newsletter/Email list you may include the following:
Your name:
Your email address:
Your native language:

Submit

You will be returned to this page after submitting your survey. Thank you!

Figure 2.4 'American Accent Now'

based on the East-Midwest (Michigan, Illinois) accent, presented here as the neutral, 'accent-less' American accent. That in itself deserves more discussion space than I can spend on it here. The point is: Internet providers sell a 'standard (ized) accent', a regional accent ('American') that carries all the ideological features of a standard(ized) language. With these two caveats in mind, let us now turn to the websites themselves.

Consider figure 2.4, taken from a website called 'American Accent Now' (www.American-accent-now.com).[1]

We see several things here. First, of course, we see two figures: a manifestly happy young white man, and a manifestly frustrated Asian woman. We can assume that the man has acquired an American accent (or had one right from the start) and that the Asian woman has not. The reason why she is frustrated can be read from the boxes one can check to demonstrate the ways in which a 'non-American accent prevents you from achieving your professional and personal goals'. Respondents – prospective customers – are requested to identify the 'single biggest problem with your accent'. The two categories can be divided as follows:

Professional:
- I have been denied a job promotion
- My clients (or patients or colleagues) often misunderstand me
- I failed to get a job I was qualified for
- My boss (or teacher) doesn't give me the respect I deserve
- I make less money than less experienced people who have a better pronunciation

Personal:
- People think I'm less smart than I am
- I find it very hard to socialize with Americans in personal and business settings
- People sometimes laugh at the way I talk

We now begin to discover the strange world we have entered. It is a world in which indexical values and social effects of language – usually tacit ideological features of language use – are made very explicit both in text and in images. The key to getting the jobs one deserves and to earning the money one is entitled to is pronunciation. An image of personality is invoked that makes this reduction possible: the prospective customer is already smart, entitled to better jobs and a superior income, and entitled to respect from their superiors. So acquiring the accent will, so to speak, release all of these qualities to be seen for everyone. Acquiring an American accent will, in the eyes of the interlocutors, turn you into the person you really are.

Not everyone is a prospective customer of course. As we can see in the images used by American Accent Now, the frustrated subject was Asian and the happy one was what is known in the USA as a 'Caucasian'. Websites make general targeted statements about 'strong foreign accents':

A strong foreign accent can prevent you from achieving your professional or personal goals and reaching your full potential. People shouldn't have to ask you to repeat what you said. In today's competitive corporate environment, clear pronunciation and correct grammar are a must. (Accurate English, www.accurateenglish.com)

What is meant by 'strong foreign' accent is often documented in the FAQ or Testimonials pages of such websites, and almost invariably this is done by reference to 'national' accents. Some European accents such as French, German and even British accents are seen as particularly prone to misunderstanding, Asian accents such as Indian, Chinese and Japanese accents naturally move in the danger zone of globalized comprehensibility, and Middle Eastern accents are problematic throughout. They are problematic in contacts with 'native speakers':

Our accent reduction and American pronunciation courses will teach you to create the sounds of Standard American English and give you greater confidence in your communication skills with native speakers of English. (Accurate English)

[Testimonial from an 'Iranian dental student'] Hi, my name is Sanaz. About a year ago when I came to the US, I was very confused. I was in culture shock. Thanks to God, it happened to me to meet very lovely people. They gave me courage to deal with all new things, as well as they helped me to improve my English, and gave me confidence to speak English. Among them two people were so special for me – Sheri and Mark [the Accent Workshop trainers]. Not only they were fabulous teachers, they were very helpful friends. You can always trust their opinion. I'll never forget the great influence that Sheri and Mark have on my English. I'm really happy to meet them. (The American Accent Workshop, www.accentworkshop.com)

Sanaz experienced 'confusion' and 'culture shock' upon his arrival in the USA, and the American accent course gave him 'courage' and 'confidence' to speak American English, and this capacity clearly helped him overcome his initial feelings. Note the frequent references to 'feel-good' factors such as 'confidence'.[2] Speaking in an American accent makes people more confident in contacts with their American native-speaker counterparts:

[Testimonial from a Spanish male Laboratory manager] The Accurate English accent reduction courses should be a 'must' for all professionals whose foreign accent gets in the way of clear communication. Taking the courses has greatly improved my pronunciation of American English sounds and made a big difference in my speech. My presentations at work are much better. I speak with more confidence and authority. (Accurate English)

[Testimonial from an Israeli male computer consultant] Before I started taking the classes, I couldn't pronounce certain vowel sounds correctly. Lisa [the trainer] identified the issues and taught me to listen and to express myself in a native way. Her customized method allowed me to quantify my weekly improvements. After a relatively short time, I noticed major progress in the way I speak. This lead [sic] to an unexpected increase in my confidence when communicating. I highly recommend the American Pronunciation course. (Accurate English)

The benefits of accent modification can be yours!
• Clear, understandable speech
• Efficient, effective communication
• Career opportunities
• Improved job performance
• Successful public speaking
• More confidence
  (Advance American Accent Training, www.advanceamericanaccent.com)

The 'confidence' promised or reported in these examples is a mixture of personal and professional features. People are more confident in general, they feel better after having taken the courses, and they also perform better in their jobs. The Spanish Laboratory Manager reported significant improvements in his presentations at work, and Advance American Accent Training promises not just 'more confidence' but also 'career opportunities' as well as 'improved job performance'. The implicit image is that of a 'professional', someone whose job is a central part of their life, and for whom professional unhappiness is equal to personal unhappiness. Most websites, thus, would suggest mixtures of professional and personal results for their accent courses, and we see a sort of continuum here, with some websites suggesting more professional benefits than personal ones. Consider the next example, from the Accent Reduction Institute (www.lessaccent.com), a website that shouts 'Lose your accent in 28 days!':

The Accent Reduction Institute (ARI) is the industry leader in American Accent Training, providing non-native English speakers with proven techniques to quickly master English pronunciation. ARI provides the tools to help people maintain their unique cultural identity while:

> Eliminating language barriers and miscommunications
> Increasing sales and profitability
> Communicating expertise to customers
> Building strong teams
> Increasing efficiencies
> Raising self-confidence

'Self-confidence' has been pushed into a small corner here, and the main advertisement claims are about professional aims. Note, however, that customers can 'maintain their unique cultural identity'. I shall come back to that below. Communicaid (www.communicaid.com), in the meantime, is clear about its business-oriented efficiency:

Why American Accent Training? With the proliferation of offshore operations in locations as diverse as India, the Philippines, South Africa and China, organizations need to ensure that their offshore employees are able to communicate effectively with customers and colleagues alike. A vital ingredient of successful communication for your overseas staff is their accent when speaking English.

The impact of First Language Influence (FLI) on an offshore employee's accent can not be underestimated. American Accent training from Communicaid will help your overseas staff to minimise the influence of their first language while maximising their communication with your customers through a neutral accent. Whether through online American Accent Training courses, virtual American Accent training or face-to-face accent instruction, Communicaid offers scaleable American accent training solutions for your organization's offshore operations.

A Communicaid American Accent Training course will provide your offshore person-
nel with the ability to:

- Communicate more efficiently and effectively with customers and colleagues by reducing their first language influenced accent
- Build rapport and empathy and strengthen relationships with customers and colleagues through more successful communication
- Enhance your customer experience and satisfaction

The target groups are here, clearly, the ever-increasing workforce of international call centres, and most of the American accent websites make explicit or
implicit reference to call centres as a target or a success story. Thus, the
Testimonials page of the Pronunciation Workshop (www.pronunciationwork-
shop.com) reports:

This is by far, the MOST EFFECTIVE English Pronunciation programme I have ever
seen. I am an American Accent Trainer in India and have trained 22,000 agents. After
taking this programme, I wish there was a way to go back and start all over again.
(Oorvakx Boyce, American Accent Trainer, India)

I am the Head of the Training Department of the World's Second Largest Call Center
Company in India. We have footprints in over 40 countries around the world
including many centers in United States as well. I have been working in the Call
Center Industry in India for the past 8 years. Because we cater to America, for years
we have been searching for a cost effective training method to learn the American
style of English Pronunciation, however, have had no luck…that is, until we found
the PronunciationWorkshop programme. While searching through Google one day, I
came across the PronunciationWorkshop website and watched the free demo ……We
found that demo to be SIMPLY AMAZING STUFF !!!!!!! Instead of showing
diagrams, visuals combined with phonetics, there was Paul.. A LIVE
TRAINER…… SHOWING HIS MOUTH FORMATION and the TECHNIQUES
to get a clearer sound. I quickly showed it to my CEO and he was amazed as well.
What's unique about Paul's course is how simple it is…as well as fun to watch. My
staff always looks forward to working on this programme…We seem to learn something new every time we watch another video, and it has made remarkable changes in
our speech and English skills. We have implemented this training approximately six
months ago to improve our customer satisfaction scores. Not only have we seen
significant improvements with our scores, but our Average Call Handle Time per
customer has reduced approximately by 29% in the last 4 months as the agents do not
need to repeat themselves. Looking into the success of the programme at our centre
we have also asked Paul to develop a certification programme. I myself, as well as
members of my staff have gone through telephonic training with Paul, one-on-one.
Paul makes learning so much FUN and has changed the way we speak English!!!.
Today I am proud to say that the entire training department has become Certified by
Pronunciation Workshop. I cannot praise this course enough (…) It is truly quite an
achievement and I know you will be extremely pleased as well. (Joy Deb Mukherjee,
Director of Training, India)

The truly remarkable thing about Paul's [the trainer] programme is how simple and effective it is…and his engaging persona really pulls you in. Here in India, using this programme we are able to take an individual who is UNEMPLOYABLE for the offshore booming call centre industry, and make him EMPLOYABLE, with a good job which pays well, in less than two and half months… That's the Power of Paul's programme!!! He is changing lives on the opposite side of the world! (Sanjay Mehta, Managing Director, Teleperformance India)

And American Accent (www.americanaccent.com) sees a direct link between its online teaching methodology and its prospective customers, the call centre workers:

It Works
Quick, Easy and Fully Automated
Given the powerful combination of high aptitude and a proven methodology, designated trainees *easily* and *quickly* pick up on the accent.

    People used to think that classroom training is the best method, but for the ideal call centre candidate, you *want* someone who is completely comfortable in the virtual environment – from initial training through to long-term job satisfaction.

Global indexicals of success

American accent, personal happiness and self-confidence, smooth and efficient communication with Americans, job satisfaction, business opportunities and money: this is the package sold by these dot-com businesses. The package consists of 'language' itself (or register-bits thereof) as well as representations of it and of what it has to offer its speakers, and, at a very implicit level, representations of 'America', of what America is as a society and of the socio-cultural preferences and expectations of 'Americans'.[3] Following Silverstein (2006b: 485) we can call this 'semiotic consubstantiality': you are (or become) what you speak, and speaking it (mysteriously) transforms you into what is indexically suggested by the speech. The providers sell these consubstantialities to the people who are at the heart of globalization processes: expatriate (i.e. deterritorialized or peripatetic) professionals hungry for success, opportunity and money, and call centre operatives in 'delocalized' and inherently mobile areas of the business world. And they sell them by means of that defining technology of globalization: the Internet. The target audiences for these websites are *not* the masses of poor migrants from the margins of the world, not the Philippine domestic workers who have become one of their nation's main export industries, and not the housewives who join their expatriate husbands. The target audiences are the scale-jumpers who embody globalization as a success story – they are, in other words, a very small segment of the flows of people that characterize contemporary globalization. And one of the advantages of these materials is that they begin to show us a picture of what 'success' means within this imagery of globalization. For what the websites do is to abundantly flag what Silverstein (2006b: 486) calls (with respect to dictionary cautions such as 'slang' or 'obscene') 'register alerts'. Such alerts 'give normative indexical properties of a lexeme's appropriateness-to and effectiveness-in co(n)texts … of occurrence: where to use it, and what, socially speaking, will happen when you do'. If we replace 'lexeme' by 'accent' we have, I believe, an accurate description of what these websites try to achieve: to overtly specify the rich indexicals that come with the language in normative terms; to explicitly describe, in sum, an order of indexicality for the use of such an accent: you *must* use this accent if you want to become the person you intend to be. Naturally, there is a hierarchization involved in this: not every kind of speech is adequate and only this kind of speech will do.

We see this clearly from the way in which the websites define the exercise they expect from and offer to coach to their customers. First, it is not just about *acquiring* a new accent, but even more about *getting rid of* another accent ('Lose your accent in 28 days!'). Hence the often-used label of 'accent reduction' as a descriptor of the courses offered. The existing accents are wrong:

We focus on correcting your biggest speaking errors first. After the first lesson, you will already feel more confident about your speech. (Accurate English)

Nobody had ever been able to tell me what exactly was wrong with my speech until I took the Accurate English accent reduction course. There was a noticeable difference in my speech after only a few lessons. I see this course as an investment in my future. I learned how to strengthen my 'Chinese tongue' to create the sounds of good American English. (Testimonial page, Accurate English)

They are also, as we saw in several of the examples above, an obstacle to personal and business success, a source of frustration (recall the image of the Asian woman!), something that can hamper individuals and corporations in their ambition. So what is at stake is, one could say, linguistic purification as the first step to linguistic readiness for the globalized world. And at the core of this process of purification we see an image of the regimented subject, someone who can face the challenges of post-modern, globalized existence provided they submit to the process of purification and, consequently, sacrifice their individual agency in a quest for uniformity and homogeneity.

At this point, the locality and authenticity we encounter in popular, political and academic discourses on dialects and accents are far away. There is little value to the linguistic signs of belonging and authenticity that usually go under the label of 'accent'. Or at least: there is clearly a *differential* value to different accents. While foreign accents are remarkable, audible and problematic, and hence need to be reduced or eliminated, American accent itself is unmarked, unremarkable, unnoticed. Once you acquire American accent, your speech becomes 'normal', invisible, unremarkable, and can so become a vehicle for 'efficient', 'smooth', 'clear', 'confident' and 'convincing' communication (see Accurate English's website banner: 'Helping foreign professionals to communicate with *confidence, clarity* and *accuracy*'). American accent is not really an 'accent' like a German-English or Indian-English accent, for example – it is a neutral tool, a purely linguistic-communicative instrument. Thus, in the examples above, we saw how Communicaid projected trained employees as 'maximising their communication with your customers through a *neutral* accent' while they minimize 'the influence of their first language' (italics added). And in their FAQ section, American Accent reassures its customers as follows:[4]

Is this slang?
   No, of course not. Standard American English pronunciation is different from spelling, but it is not slang.

American accent, thus, is the 'exnominated' accent, to use a term coined by Barthes (1957) to denote the bourgeoisie. The bourgeoisie, Barthes said, was so hegemonic that they ceased to be perceived and named as bourgeoisie; they were just 'the people'. American accent, then, is the accent that is no longer an accent but just a vehicle for doing stuff. It is just a 'normal', expected, customary and efficient *language*. (This is where we see how American accent is ideologically represented as a standard(ized) language.) If you use it well, it helps you achieve the goals you have set in life: prosperity, success, happiness. And while, as the Accent Reduction Institute claims, customers can 'maintain their unique cultural identity', if they wish to be the globalized actors they aspire to be, they need to change and become sociolinguistically invisible. Their 'unique cultural identity' should not transpire from their speech. As for American cultural identities, they can also be studied in courses provided by the websites:

The American Psyche
Typical culture pieces seek to inform a trainee of facts about America. This information, however, is readily available via the media and the Internet, and can be easily acquired once the student has a standard accent. The AAT culture piece, on the other hand, deals with the American psyche. Trainees learn how Americans think, what is important to them, and how best to get them to respond in the desired way. (American Accent)

Thus, one remains 'Indian' while one can sound 'American'. And to the extent that accents betray the life-histories of their users, and in particular the histories of institutionalized and mundane language usage and learning, sounding American means that all of this has to be backgrounded. An Indian accent in English is the result of language learning processes in India, and the accent displays all the sociolinguistic diacritics we know: age, gender, class, educational background and so on. An American accent course removes all of this identificatory uniqueness and replaces it by an exnominated and translocal, presumed neutral and uniform accent.

The effort that trainees should invest in this process of removal and replacement is considerable. Apart from a significant financial divestment in registering for the courses, they are expected to buy books, CDs and DVDs, have telephone tutorials with their trainers, record their own speeches and listen to them, seek informal communication opportunities with 'native speakers', and even attentively watch TV:

> When you are watching TV look at the mouth movements of the speakers. Repeat what they are saying, imitating the intonation and rhythm of their speech (Accurate English)

But as we saw in an earlier example, the effort pays: 'our Average Call Handle Time per customer has reduced approximately by 29% in the last 4 months as the agents do not need to repeat themselves'. We also saw in several examples given earlier that individuals referred to their experience with such courses as events that made them gain self-confidence, the respect of their peers or superiors, and upward social mobility. Here is an ideologically rich and well-matured sign: the idea that hard work to change oneself will result in material as well as symbolic rewards. The American dream is here projected onto the symbolic currency marketed by these businesses: American accent.

Summarizing, we see the following picture. Customers who subscribe to these courses buy a package consisting of language as well as of representations of language, society and selves. They are expected to change themselves by 'reducing' their non-native accents in English, and by adopting, with great investments of effort, an accent that makes them sociolinguistically inconspicuous and changes their speech from something that contains side-tracking 'noise' (their 'foreign accent') to a normal, uniform, unpeculiar and thus no longer distracting tool of communication. This effort is rewarding, because it will remove the frustration resulting from (repeated) misunderstandings due to the 'noise' in their speech, it will allow Americans, thus, to see them for what they truly are, and this then will offer socially upward mobility. This, I would venture, is the cultural semantics of these courses, the ordered complex of indexicals suggested by American accent courses as a way to global success.

Discussion

This cultural semantics is a bit disconcerting, of course. We live in a world in which language learning environments, especially for English, become highly diversified and now include purely formal environments (state-controlled official curricula and school programmes) as well as purely informal ones (the global media and popular culture empires), with several hybrid forms in between such as the websites examined here. In this highly polycentric learning

why? who not a simple ideology?

environment, some actors are subject to formal and sometimes rather rigid state policies – as the formal learning environments typically are – while others escape such forms of imposed normativity. The websites discussed here, I suggest, contain a very clear and rather transparent language policing which, while being informal (in the sense of 'not controlled by external authorities'), is stable, predictable and hegemonic. It taps into widespread and very powerful images of globalization as centred on the USA and revolving around English, corporate culture and individual spatial and social mobility. These images show traces of one of Appadurai's (1996) 'idioscapes' – globally distributed socio-cultural and ideological scenarios – notably of what Fairclough (2006) called 'globalism'. This is an effect undoubtedly of the particular composition of their projected audiences: prospective customers, as said earlier, do not belong to the 'losers' of globalization but rather to its 'winners': globally mobile professionals who have the wherewithal to make the best of the opportunities offered by globalization processes. But its remarkable uniformity betrays the self-evidence of a strong hegemony for such views among the community of users of these websites.

This, of course, should warn us against making quick generalizations about language in globalization. We are not facing the emergence of a wholesale new global order of discourse here, but rather a highly niched phenomenon that affects the lives of relatively restricted groups of people, and that is an *effect* of larger and slower globalization processes – the deregulation of international business activity and labour, the development of virtual spaces for communication, commodification and learning such as the Internet, and the power of more general ideologies and discourses such as globalism. Sociolinguistic globalization is not the engine behind globalization, but an epiphenomenon of larger processes that are of a far more fundamental nature and have a far greater historical depth. Most people in the world do *not* want to spend money to learn American accents. In effect, most people could not care less.

Having said that, phenomena such as the ones examined here still do teach us a thing or two about language in globalization. One thing we see here is that the object of globalized commodification is *accent* and not *language.* This is a commodified dialectology, not just language learning. Investigations such as the ones reported here provide us with a more fine-grained view of sociolinguistic globalization processes. They are definitely not uniform, nor are they exclusively uniformizing: they are layered processes developing at several, very different scale-levels. The global purchase of English – what de Swaan (2001) called the 'stampede towards English' – is a phenomenon at one scale-level, a very general one and consequently one that, in actual sociolinguistic practise, would appear as a relatively widespread but superficial phenomenon. The marketing of American accents, on the contrary, revolves around specific socio-linguistic registers targeted at specific (rather small) groups. These groups, we can assume, already 'know English', but they require a more specific set of linguistic, pragmatic and metapragmatic skills – to sound like an American. The scale of such processes is far smaller than that of 'global Englishes', but the process appears a lot more developed and to have a more profound impact. Given the homogenizing 'semiotic consubstantiality' we witnessed in these dot-com Englishes, we could say that this (rather than the 'imperialist' spread of English *tout court*) is real 'McDonaldization': customers are expected not just to buy the language but also the whole indexical (that is: ideological) package it contains, and to do so from within a narrowly defined 'globalist' worldview. These are different processes, to be sure – perhaps complementary but *of a different order*. And I would suggest that a sound sociolinguistics of globalization should not just look at the world and its languages, but also to the world and its registers, genres, repertoires and styles, if it wants to have any empirical grounding. It is in small-scale, niched phenomena such as those considered here that we see real language: language that is invested by real-world interests and language that matters to real people. This, naturally, is no longer the 'linguistic' language, neither is it the language used in official language policies, but it is the sociolinguistic language and the language of the everyday politics of language, produced and articulated in a polycentric environment by a multitude of (often ephemeral) actors.

This leads us to a second point about globalization. Given the intense poly-centricity of learning environments and the fact that globalization processes develop at several different scale-levels, the issue of *normativity* becomes quite complex. What is the status of language norms, who produces them and who enforces them? These are questions that now require a detailed examination of actors, instruments, goals and resources. American accent websites cater for a market that is not serviced by the national formal learning systems. Indians who have acquired English at school and seek employment in global call centres need to be retrained in American accent, because their school English bears too many traces of what in our examples was called 'strong foreign accent'. The state offers 'English' (with an accent), the Internet companies offer another (a *better*) accent. Thus we see how actors collaborate in the production of language norms in an interdependent complex of actors: the school system produces 'English', using its own pedagogies and orders of indexicality; but in order to acquire the specific kind of English that offers jobs in the globalized economy, people need to turn to private providers, who impose yet another set of norms and rules of proper speech. These private providers are not tied to the national order of things, their activities are 'border busting' in nature, and interestingly their cultural semantics revolves around uniformity, homogeneity and submission – a very modernist response to globalized, post-modern pressures.

An important feature of globalization processes is the fact that they blend the local and the translocal in complex networks (Castells 1996). Local sociolinguistic systems, consequently, are shot through by traces and fragments of translocal ones, without, however, becoming less local (as we shall see in chapter 3). And the language that is 'good' in the local sociolinguistic system may not be good enough in the translocal ones – which is why Indian call centre workers need to learn *American* English and should not use their local accents. We thus see various orders of indexicality operating in the same polycentric environment, often without manifest overlap or confusion but 'niched' and confined to particular sets of communicative tasks. Highly skilled individuals such as the globalized professionals targeted by the American accent marketeers acquire, and must acquire, the resources that allow them to operate within and across these different orders of indexicality. Predictably, language thus becomes something that requires continuously more investment from its users, and language learning (more specifically, the learning of specific registers tailored to particular communicative tasks) will increasingly become a balancing act between formal and informal learning processes. It becomes, in effect, a permanent 'care of the self' in Foucault's (2005) sense, a permanent quest for order by attending to the small details of linguistic conduct. Highly specialized providers such as the ones described here, capable of offering these microscopic definitional registers of subjectification as operational (linguistic) and ideological (indexical) packages may thrive in this brave new world of language.

2.7   Conclusion

So how messy is this new globalized marketplace now? In this chapter, we have covered quite a bit of space, starting from some strange phenomena in which we saw how 'language' surrenders (or at least, dramatically changes) its customary functions due to patterns of mobility. Mobility does some things to language, to be sure. In an attempt towards structuring our understanding of such patterns of mobility, I then offered a small vocabulary, consisting of the concepts of scale, orders of indexicality and polycentricity. I suggested that we should understand communication phenomena as developing at different scales, on which different orders of indexicality operate, resulting in a polycentric context for such communication phenomena – that is, a context in which multiple normative complexes are simultaneously at work, but are of a different order. We saw such forms of polycentricity in the various examples given in this chapter, notably in the ways in which Internet language-learning providers sell American accent: they create an order of indexicality that operates alongside, but not necessarily in conflict with, state-organized normative complexes valid in formal education systems. The local and the translocal appear together, as different forces operating on the same object – language.

The result was complexity, but it was not chaos. It is too easy to see the late-modern globalized world as one in which order is lost and replaced by disorder, fragmentation and chaos, as a place where no single instrument of power can fully dominate and impose its rules on the field. Instruments of power now do co-occur in complex patterns of power-sharing (as we saw in the case of the Internet American accent providers), and the simplicity of modernist under-standings of the world can no longer be maintained. But there is still order – a more complex kind of order, but a real one. The fact that the state now competes with numerous other actors in the field of language normativity does not abolish the state as a relevant level of power; it couches the state in a wider field of power relations, in which its orders of indexicality now co-exist alongside numerous others in a layered, scaled, polycentric environment. We shall return to the power of the state in chapter 6. The analytical task now is to describe and interpret polycentricity, not simple dominance. We have to come to terms with notions such as micro-hegemonies: restricted, 'niched' hegemonies that co-exist with others in polycentric environments. Such a view can profitably replace older views of hegemony, articulated, for example, in linguistic rights discourses where a single hegemony (that of English) and a single actor (the state) are seen as defining the patterns of sociolinguistic life. There is not much purchase in these views in an age of globalization, I am afraid.

3   Locality, the periphery and images of the world

The world has become a complex place – that was the main line of argument in the previous chapter. In order to understand that place, we need to inquire into the way in which that place is imagined, represented and enacted by its inhabitants. This chapter will explore the conceptual complex that is central in globalization studies and hinges on notions such as centre and periphery, locality, flows, scales, networks, global economy and so forth. All of these notions refer to space and movements in/through space, and in particular the notion of 'flow' has already been productively adopted in sociolinguistics, as we saw earlier (Pennycook 2007). Theoretically, as we have seen, the main challenge for disciplines such as anthropology, sociology or sociolinguistics consists in loosening the connection between culture and a particular territory. Whereas more traditional approaches appeared to tacitly assume that societies and their features 'belonged' to one particular geographical area (think of our discussion of the linguistic rights paradigm in the previous chapter), and thus attributed an *absolute* spatiality to culture, the emphasis on situatedness emphasizes flows, trajectories, movements and thus the *relative* spatiality of culture. Hannerz (1991: 116–117) summarizes this as follows:

> The connection between cultural process and territory, we should remind ourselves, is only contingent. As socially organized meaning, culture is primarily a phenomenon of interaction, and only if interactions are tied to particular spaces is culture likewise so.

Thus, whereas, according to Hannerz, traditional anthropology was concerned with culture as 'a matter of flow of meaning in face-to-face relationships between people who do not move around much' (1991: 117), it is one of the main assumptions of globalization studies that multiple cultures can exist in one space and that, conversely, one culture can be produced in different spaces. The thematization of space and place (the latter denoting a space made social, hence becoming a space in which humans make social, cultural, political and historical investments) is thus a crucial ingredient of the process of coming to terms with globalization (Crang 1999), of producing globalized locality, of 'vernacularizing' globalization (Appadurai 1996: 10).

This is an elementary cultural activity which we see articulated – in very Whorfian ways – in language structure and discourse. I will argue that doing so in a particular language reveals 'vitality' in that language, in the sense that the language resources are proved to be up to the task of globalized meaning production. This will open up a range of issues related to 'big' and 'small' languages, language choice and other matters, that deserve our attention because, as we saw in the previous chapters, they are often caught in totalizing discourses of 'imperialism' and 'linguicide'. I will make my argument with respect to Swahili. This is somewhat off-mark in the literature on globalization, which is strongly focused on 'big' globalized languages such as English, French and (increasingly) Chinese, and on communicative channels such as electronic mass media and popular culture. We should not forget that many (indeed, very many) 'smaller' languages are effectively globalized, and Swahili is one of them, as we shall see presently.

3.1   Writing locality: a globalized Tanzanian novel

I will consider one particular cultural form: written literature from the 'periphery'. In particular, I will try to show how a novel, *Miradi Bubu ya Wazalendo* ('The invisible enterprises of the patriots') by Gabriel Ruhumbika, carries various kinds of spatial semiotizations that point towards locally salient centre-versus-periphery models and towards flows and translocal transactions. These models remind us of Wallerstein's (1983) World-Systems analysis, which hinges on a view of the world as divided into such centres, semi-peripheries and peripheries, between which an intricate division of labour exists (which is, in Wallerstein's analysis, global capitalism). At the micro-level of the novel itself, space is used as a powerful literary–stylistic device. It attributes identities to the characters; it casts their actions and their biographies in a recognizable local social semiotic; and spatio-semiotic features organize the meta-story of Tanzanian postcolonial politics. It is a form of cultural vernacularization, of the production of locality. At a macro-level (the level of the cultural act of writing itself), the novel illustrates the deterritorialized, network and translocal nature of contemporary cultural and political processes as well as the capacity of contemporary literacy to 'repatriate' meanings (Appadurai 1990: 307). This latter dimension challenges established views of African literature – here, Swahili literature – as necessarily produced in Africa and tied to a particular place. Though by now it may sound rather evident that African literature can be diasporic, the theoretical implications of this may be far reaching. Precisely this globalized dimension of the novel makes its strongly local flavour peculiar, and demonstrates the dynamics of Swahili as a globalized, vital language.

I will start by providing some background information on the novel. Next, we will move into an analysis of spatial semiotics in the novel itself, showing how a particular social and political geography of the country dominates the framing of characters and events along a centre/periphery axis. After this, I will return to the deterritorialized nature of the act of writing itself and the effect this has on the way in which we view 'local' literatures and literary actors.

The invisible enterprises of the patriots

Miradi Bubu ya Wazalendo was written in 1992 and published by Tanzania Publishing House in Dar es Salaam, Tanzania. It is written in the national language of Tanzania, Swahili, and it adds to the impressive modern written literature in that language. Especially in the postcolonial era (and notably under *Ujamaa* socialism), writing in Swahili was a densely symbolic act: it carried meta-meanings that indexed patriotism, loyalty to the nation and its political doctrine, and a democratic (socialist) attitude (Blommaert 1999b, chapter 4). Writing a literary piece in the national language was a political statement in its own right, and those doing it performed a cultural politics as much as producing a cultural product. This intense politics of literary codes and forms undoubtedly contributed to the vitality of the language after independence: it mobilized intellectuals and artists into conscious linguistic 'development', and it gave them a voice of their own as a *national* intelligentsia, a committed vanguard of people who shaped the minds of their people by shaping their language. The author, Gabriel Ruhumbika, was very much a member of this vanguard. He was born in 1938 on Ukerewe Island in Lake Victoria, in the British Mandate of Tanganyika. Ruhumbika was a professor of literature at the University of Dar es Salaam between 1970 and 1985, and he was one of the country's leading radical intellectuals (see e.g. Mbuguni and Ruhumbika 1974). After 1985, he moved to the USA and became a professor of English at Hampton University, Virginia, and afterwards a professor of comparative literature at the University of Georgia. *Miradi Bubu ya Wazalendo* was written in the USA but published in Dar es Salaam.

The book is a political novel, and its title already announces this. The term *wazalendo* 'patriots' was one of the key terms in the lexicon of Tanzania's *Ujamaa* socialism, a particular brand of socialism developed and propagated as the state ideology by the first president of Tanzania, Julius Nyerere.[1] Ruhumbika's novel is hard to read without any knowledge of the *Ujamaa* socialist period in Tanzania, for it is intended as a retrospective commentary on the *Ujamaa* political system and what it did to the country. Tanzania emerged out of the union of Tanganyika and the former British Protectorate of Zanzibar in 1964. Tanganyika had won its independence after a period of peaceful transition in 1961 under the leadership of Julius Nyerere's TANU party (Tanganyika African National Union); Zanzibar became independent in 1963, but the Sultanate installed by the British was soon overthrown by a popular revolution, the leaders of which sought closer union with socialist Tanganyika. The union led to a socialist radicalization within the new Republic of Tanzania, and this radicalization was codified in 1967 in the so-called Arusha Declaration which proclaimed *Ujamaa na Kujitegemea*, 'socialism and self-reliance'. The main features of this state ideology were egalitarianism, the absence of exploitation, political and economic non-alignment, pan-Africanism, and self-reliant small-scale agricultural development (in '*Ujamaa* villages') as the backbone of the economy (see Pratt 1976).

Ujamaa was, certainly in the years following the Arusha Declaration, very popular with the younger intelligentsia, largely based at the University of Dar es Salaam, of which Ruhumbika was a member. The university was a centre of radical political activity, not only nationally but also internationally (Othman 1994), and many of the young intellectuals saw themselves as the leading vanguard in a socialist revolution (see Shivji 1996 for excellent examples). Consequently, many intellectuals vigorously supported TANU (which had become the single party of the country), though their emphasis on a radical socialist strategy was not always welcomed by the TANU leaders (Blommaert 1999b, chapter 2). The Tanzanian *Ujamaa* economy collapsed in the 1970s and the country was further impoverished by a war against Idi Amin's Uganda in the late 1970s. From that point onwards, disillusionment about TANU and socialism was great. Nyerere voluntarily stepped down from the presidency in 1985, and his successor, Mwinyi, almost immediately signed a re-structuring agreement with the International Monetary Fund. *Ujamaa* was abandoned as a new official state ideology of economic liberalism replaced *Kujitegemea*, 'self reliance', and a multiparty system was installed.

It is against this background of general disillusionment that *Miradi Bubu* has to be set. Written by an erstwhile radical supporter of *Ujamaa*, it reflects on power abuse, inequality, class determinism and injustice in socialist Tanzania. It does so by telling the story of two Tanzanians, Saidi and Nzoka. They are the main characters in the novel. Part of Saidi's story involves two other men, Mzee Jabiri and Munubi, whose lives are sub-plots in the novel.

The plot of the book consists of five parts, summarized as follows.

Part 1:

Mzee Jabiri   Mzee Jabiri lives in Masasi, in southern Tanganyika. He has two children late in life, but his daughter and wife die of an unknown disease. He leaves Masasi with his only surviving child, the boy Saidi. They travel to Tanga in the north and get a menial job in a sisal plantation owned by a white man. Mzee Jabiri gets badly injured during work in the fields. The supervisor, Munubi, forces the white plantation owner to drive Mzee Jabiri to a hospital. Jabiri dies before they reach the hospital. The plantation owner dumps Mzee Jabiri's body in a sewage pit.

Part 2:

Supervisor Munubi   Munubi leaves the plantation with Saidi and travels to a relative's house in Mombo. There, he arranges for Saidi to be brought to relatives of his in Dar es Salaam. Munubi himself finds a job on a sisal plantation in Morogoro, central Tanzania. The plantation is owned by a white South African, and Munubi, as a supervisor, is supposed to administer corporal punishment to the workers. When he does so, however, Mzee Jabiri's ghost appears in his sleep. Munubi flees to another place and he continues to move from one place to another until independence. After independence, he gets a job as a supervisor in Kilosa, on a farm owned by an Englishman. Munubi marries a woman there and builds himself a house outside the farm compound. The farm owner disagrees with this and fires Munubi. Mzee Jabiri's ghost incites Munubi to correct this injustice, and Munubi kills the farmer. Munubi is tried and hanged for this murder.

Part 3:

Ndugu Saidi   Saidi has found his way to Dar es Salaam, where he lives with a relative of Munubi's. He finds a job as a houseboy with an Indian family, and then he works as a shopkeeper in the Indian neighbourhood for nine years. In his spare time, he is a volunteer worker for TANU, the leading independence party. After some time, he gets hired by TANU as a messenger. His salary is lower than what he earned from the Indians, but he is committed to TANU's cause and accepts the bad labour circumstances. Saidi lives in a one-room flat in Kariakoo, the market area of Dar es Salaam. When Nyerere becomes president in 1962, Saidi joins his personal staff as a messenger. In the meantime, he has let his friend and colleague Nzoka move into his house. Saidi marries Chiku, and between 1962 and 1967 the couple have three children. In 1967, with the Arusha Declaration, TANU installs a number of official commissions and Nzoka becomes the leader of one such commission. He appoints Saidi as a messenger to the commission. Saidi decides to build a house of his own in Manzese and the family moves into the half-finished house without electricity or running water in 1970. By 1981, Saidi has nine children and is struggling to make ends meet. The country is economically devastated, and things get worse after the liberalization of 1985 and 1986. Saidi's two oldest daughters become prostitutes. His oldest daughter Idaya murders her child and is imprisoned. When Nyerere steps down in 1985, Saidi is made redundant. He receives a very small sum of money and some praise for his patriotism, but lives in abject poverty in Manzese.

Part 4:

Executive Director Nzoka   Nzoka was born in the Mwanza region of northern Tanzania. He fails to qualify in a state exam and is not eligible for studies abroad. Instead, he organizes a trade union and manages to impress Nyerere because of his organizational and propaganda skills. Nyerere hires him to canvass popular support. He joins the TANU headquarters in Dar es Salaam in 1956, moves into Saidi's apartment, and becomes Nyerere's personal assistant. He marries Beatrice and earns enough to move to the European quarter in Oyster Bay. Nyerere sends him to various international colleges to complete his training. He travels to Ghana and Israel, and then to Ruskin College, Oxford, to Lumumba University, Moscow, and to the University of Sussex. By 1967, Nzoka has five children. He becomes the executive director of the State Commission for Planning, Wealth, Savings and Progress. This ends his friendship with Saidi as well as his marriage with Beatrice. Nzoka had committed adultery. He remarries and divorces several times, including a woman called Rosemary, a German female professor, and an Indian woman (who converts him to Islam). He becomes Head of the Armed Forces. He falls in love with a prostitute but marries her daughter and converts to Catholicism. By 1985, Nzoka has 32 children, all of whom are finishing their studies or are being taken care of by nannies. He lives in luxury while the country has become one of the poorest in the world.

Part 5:
Epilogue   Saidi decides to make the injustices he has experienced public at a ceremony at which he is thanked for his years of service. He walks up to Nyerere, the farewell gifts in his hand, but the latter does not recognize him, despite the many years of contact. Nzoka, who is also present, senses Saidi's plan and announces to Nyerere that Saidi intends to offer him the gifts he has just received, out of gratitude for what he (Nyerere) has done for the country. Saidi is praised for his patriotism but is not given the opportunity to speak out.

The social semiotics of Tanzanian space

People attribute meanings to the spaces they know and use (see e.g. Feld and Basso 1996; Low 2001). Such spaces are filled with symbols and attributes, and using them creates indexical ties to them. The symbols and attributes not only refer to the objective place, but also to a particular atmosphere associated with it, including the people living in it, as well as their class and other cultural peculiarities.[2] Thus a Cockney accent does not only identify one as being from London, it also carries class, gender and other cultural indexicalities. Code-switching may index the particular flavour of a place and may thus 'make a person speak from that place' as it were (see Rampton 2001, Maryns and Blommaert 2001; Blommaert 2005, chapter 8). Inhabitants of a particular place distinguish between 'good' and 'bad' neighbourhoods or parts of a country, and upward social mobility is often associated with (and practically effected by) moving from a 'bad' to a 'good' place. Features of particular places, such as the Eiffel Tower in Paris or the Statue of Liberty in New York, 'can be used to defend local identity, sell development sites, comment ironically on local trans-formations, or simply situate a plot development in films' (Wong and McDonogh 2001: 98). They can, consequently also be used to situate a plot development in a novel. Obviously, some of the indexicalities carried by places are meaningful only to 'locals', but some are meaningful to outsiders too.

Ruhumbika uses places and spatial trajectories that are indexically highly salient to Tanzanians (see also Lewinson 2003). Investigating them may lead us to a local perception of centres and peripheries, a World-Systems model trans-posed to one particular area. Recall that Wallerstein's model operated at the global level; we see here a 'fractal' replication of this model at a lower – national – scale-level. This fractal phenomenon may direct us to cultural and social patterns in which social behaviour appears to be organized on the basis of perceptions of opportunities (generally located in 'centres') and of social mobility and ambition. Focusing on how, for instance, opportunities and social mobility are perceived, it may also direct us to empirically graspable forms of transnational flows: Appadurai's '-scapes' (1996). Let us now examine the way in which such patterns are used in *Miradi Bubu*; we will first articulate some of the widespread attributes and associations tied to particular places and regions in Tanzanian popular imagery.

Tanzania is an overwhelmingly rural country with one big urban centre: Dar es Salaam. The official state capital is Dodoma, a small city in the geographical centre of the country, but all major services are concentrated in Dar es Salaam: the harbour, the international airport, the Parliament, ministries, embassies, the University, the most prestigious schools, headquarters of businesses and inter-national organizations, big international hotels, and so forth. Dar es Salaam also hosts a small community of expatriates from the West, as well as an older population of Indian descent who have traditionally controlled retail business and parts of the local industry, international trade and banking. The city is the centre of Tanzanian cultural life and it is the home of most prominent music bands, authors and artists. Dar es Salaam is the prestige place in Tanzania: white-collar careers are invariably made there, money and opportunities for obtaining money are concentrated in Dar es Salaam. The city is associated with highlife (involving both its joys and vices), access to international contacts and power: an imagery that has deeply penetrated popular consciousness and has been articulated in songs and popular novels (Blommaert 1998, 1999b: chapter 4). It is, in short, a scale-level of its own.

There are no other cities that can compete with Dar es Salaam. Arusha in the north is an important city, and so is Mwanza on Lake Victoria, but none of them comes close to Dar es Salaam in the terms sketched above. In general, the northern part of the country around Lake Victoria and the Kilimanjaro region are 'better' regions with some degree of economic prosperity. The inhabitants of these regions, and notably the Chagga, the Haya and the Sukuma ethnic groups are often seen in popular imagery as being shrewd businesspeople and competent organizers, very often holding positions of considerable power. The southern and central parts of the country are 'bad' regions. People from those regions are economically very poor and politically they are less weighty than their northern countrymen. The Makonde, Makua, Hehe, Gogo and other inhabitants of the southern and central regions are often perceived as being among the poorest and most disenfranchised Tanzanians. Adopting World-Systems terminology, we arrive at this pattern: Dar es Salaam is the absolute centre of the country, the northern regions are semi-peripheral, while the central and southern parts are peripheral.

Dar es Salaam is, as noted above, the most prestigious place in Tanzania. But Dar es Salaam itself is divided into several areas, many of them carrying the same kind of associations as the ones attached to (semi-peripheral) regions. The city is located on a lagoon with a natural harbour, and the city centre itself borders this lagoon and is quite old. The city centre is affluent and dominated by multi-storey bank and hotel buildings. It is surrounded by old, densely popu-lated areas, and the boundary of central Dar es Salaam is formed by a largely dried-out river bed, Msimbazi Creek, running from north to south. The main axes of the city centre are two big roads: Ali Hassan Mwinyi Road coming from Bagamoyo in the north and ending at the waterfront, and Morogoro Road, connecting with Ali Hassan Mwinyi Road at the waterfront and moving west in the direction of Morogoro and Tabora. The northern and western axes are the main traffic arteries, but also the main social–geographic axes of the city.

The western axis is the popular, lower-class axis of the city. Moving west from the waterfront, close to the very centre of town, is Uhindini – the Indian quarter littered with oriental-style old stone buildings, mosques, small busi-nesses and shops. A bit further west, and separated from Uhindini by Mnazimoja Park, lies Uswahilini – the Swahili quarter, a huge collection of small houses with corrugated iron roofs populated by Africans from all over the country. The centre of this part of town is Kariakoo, the market area. It is a rather poor but very lively area, with lots of shops, bars and restaurants and with dense traffic caused by the daladala, small, privately operated buses. Kariakoo is the centre of highlife and popular music. Across Msimbazi Creek along Morogoro Road lie a number of overcrowded popular areas: Magomeni, Manzese and Ubungo. Manzese is the poorest of them, and Manzese is often associated with violence, crime and abject poverty among the inhabitants of Dar es Salaam.

The northern axis is the elite, upper-class axis of the city. The most presti-gious quarter is Oyster Bay, a beautiful area along the shore with a concentration of spacious detached, gated houses, embassies and fine hotels and restaurants. Oyster Bay is traditionally the home of expatriates and affluent or prominent Tanzanians. The area is somewhat sheltered and separated from downtown

Dar es Salaam by Msimbazi Creek. Equally prestigious are Msasani further north, and recently also Mbezi Beach, several miles further north along Ali Hassan Mwinyi Road. In between lies Mwenge, a popular neighbourhood located at an intersection of Ali Hassan Mwinyi Road and a couple of roads connecting it with Morogoro Road. This connection between the western and northern axes runs through Sinza, a middle-class neighbourhood with some prestige and marked by bars, restaurants and hotels. On the other side of this connection lies the campus of the University of Dar es Salaam, again a rather prestigious area and home to the intellectual elite.

We can now turn to the way in which these local social and sociocultural semiotics of space are applied in *Miradi Bubu*. We can sketch two profiles for the main characters in the novel on the basis of spatial associations and trajectories. En route we will also see how particular activities, jobs and attributes are attached to certain places.

Saidi and his father come from the Masasi region in the south of Tanzania, and they are Makonde people, thus from the periphery. Disease strikes their region, and they are forced to seek refuge elsewhere. Saidi travels to Tanga in the north (a wealthy area) as a migrant worker and finds a job on a sisal plantation, often seen as one of the 'lowest' jobs. The Tanga sisal plantation is the site of gross exploitation and abuse, and in order to save Saidi, the supervisor Munubi sends him to Dar es Salaam, where he lives with a Makonde family. Munubi himself travels on to Central Tanzania, and finds poorly paid and exploitative jobs in Morogoro and Kilosa. Saidi first finds jobs with Indian employers. There is no mention of education at all, he embarks on a career of low-paid, unqualified, menial jobs. When he gets hired by TANU it is as a messenger. He then moves to an apartment in Kariakoo, and later to Manzese. All of his life is spent there, he has not travelled, apart from the move from the local, Tanzanian periphery to the local centre. But in this centre (Dar es Salaam), he lives in the periphery – the Manzese slum where life is tough.

Nzoka comes from the Mwanza region in the north, and he is a Sukuma, from the semi-periphery. He has had some education, although he failed in a crucial state exam. He appears to be an excellent organizer, and this buys him a ticket to the centre, Dar es Salaam. He travels extensively and to prestigious places, either politically (Ghana, Lumumba University) or academically (Oxford, Sussex University). He travels, and he acquires educational qualifications as well as, inevitably, prestige. He first lives in Kariakoo with Saidi, but then moves to Oyster Bay. Nzoka's life is spent in the centre in two ways, first as opposed to his region of origin, then as opposed to the country as a whole when he travels abroad.

We see how Saidi and Nzoka move through these spaces filled with symbols and attributes. We also see how feature clusters emerge in ways that allow informed readers to make all kinds of meaningful inferences with respect to people, places, activities, and value attributions. In a very sketchy way, such inferences could be represented as follows:

Saidi:

> Southern Tanzania, Makonde > poverty, no education, lower class
>
> Sisal plantations > menial jobs
>
> Dar es Salaam, Indian quarter > servant, lower employee
>
> Kariakoo > lower middle class, messenger
>
> Manzese > poverty, prostitution, crime

Nzoka:

> Northern Tanzania, Sukuma > relatively prosperous, ambitious, educated
>
> Political activism > power, education, skills
>
> Kariakoo > lower middle class
>
> Travels abroad > elite, government official, intellectual
>
> Oyster Bay > upper class, government official
>
> Multiple marriages (including foreign spouses) > wealth, status, cosmopolitanism

The connections that are made are connections between space, activities and attributes, and status or value. We can identify two directions in this set of connections, roughly definable as 'margin-directed' versus 'centre-directed':

> Margin-directed: the south, lack of education, unskilled jobs in someone's service, low wages; in Dar es Salaam: Manzese; no international contacts. Locality.
>
> Centre-directed: the north, education, qualified white-collar jobs, international contacts; in Dar es Salaam: Oyster Bay; abroad: intellectual and political centres of excellence. Mobility.

Two particular features stand out as critical in determining one's position either in the margin or in the centre: education and international contacts or translocality. Both are closely connected. Nzoka's success appears to lie in his articulateness, and he derives considerable prestige from his education abroad. Nzoka is capable of 'moving around', both as a professional by travelling to prestigious international places, and in his private life by crossing ethnic, racial and religious boundaries in marriage and by living among expatriates in Oyster Bay. This, however, appears not to be merely an individual accomplishment: it is *determined* by his background. Nzoka comes from a part of the country which is already close to the socio-economic centre. As a northerner, he seems to have been dealt the right hand of cards right from the start. Saidi, in contrast, has no education and grows up in terrible circumstances. Consequently, he spends his life in 'fixed' places: among members of his ethnic group and in the socio-economic periphery, even in Dar es Salaam. He comes from the south, the poorest region of the country, and he appears to be destined to remain in the periphery.

The way in which, through all this, we see the emergence of centre–periphery perceptions at three scale levels is interesting. At each of them we see a number of attributions in action:

> The strictly local level, in Dar es Salaam: Manzese versus Oyster Bay. What Saidi is and what happens to his family – poverty, a perpetual struggle to survive, prostitution and murder – is something that is not unexpected, given his location in Manzese; conversely, Nzoka's wealth, power and cosmopolitanism are things that come with his location in Oyster Bay. Manzese is the periphery and Oyster Bay is the centre.

> The national level: various parts of the country and trajectories followed by people allow presupposable inferences as to status, social class and opportunities. The south is the periphery, the north is the semi-periphery, and Dar es Salaam is the centre. Education is not easily accessible in the south and more accessible in the north; these differences have an impact on the opportunities people get in Dar es Salaam.

> The transnational level: Tanzania versus the rest of the world. Prestige is derived from being able to leave Tanzania and visit prestigious places and institutions outside Africa; poverty and failure are indexed by a life spent inside the country without opportunities to travel.

From these perspectives, we notice how strongly such centre-versus-periphery perceptions organize the description of the characters and the structure of the plot. The life histories of Saidi and Nzoka are deeply anchored in a set of meaningful spatial associations that have to do with the opportunities people have and can have in the Tanzanian world. One can become a success story because he is able to 'move out', first to prestigious places in Dar es Salaam, then to European and American prestigious places, and in between, as he crosses ethnic, racial and religious boundaries. Much of his ability to move regionally and socially is (pre)determined by his regional background. The other character remains a poor man because his background prevents him from 'moving out'. Saidi follows a trajectory that brings him from one periphery to another, and the low status and disenfranchisement that he carries with him from Masasi sticks with him all the way through. In a way, he never 'moves out': he does not move out of poverty, misery, violence, his country, and his ethnic and social group. The characters evolve in one of Appadurai's 'ideoscapes': an ideology of mobility and adaptation to criteria established in the centres of the world-system – Europe and North America – as the key to success. Conversely, locality and localism stand here for poverty and failure. This is a widespread social and cultural script that probably accounts for a lot of social processes in contemporary Africa.

These social attributions of space and spatial trajectories obviously carry deep political meanings. In effect, the kind of trajectories sketched by Ruhumbika form an important part of his critique of *Ujamaa* Tanzania. The promise of *Ujamaa* was to build a classless society in which every African would have equal opportunities and in which *Uzungu* ('the ways of the West') would no longer be the model for success in society. His two protagonists inscribe themselves in the *Ujamaa* project, both become active in the struggle for independence and both become aides to Nyerere. In spite of their very different regional origins and social trajectories, both also speak this emblem of *Ujamaa*: Standard Swahili. But the deep cleavages that characterized the country before independence – regional differences in wealth and opportunities, and class differences – persist after independence. Those who previously had few opportunities for upward social mobility still remain the losers; those who were less underprivileged and followed the track of education and internationalization (i.e. opted for *Uzungu*) are still the ones who make it. Class, as inscribed in all these cleavages, persisted throughout *Ujamaa*, and patriotism was not enough to attain equality as a citizen. So whereas *Ujamaa* was launched as a localizing political strategy – an *African* socialism emphasizing African roots and values – only those who got inserted in translocal, globalized trajectories of education and mobility made it. The world-system won. Consequently, images of globalization and the way in which Tanzania is inserted in globalization processes are powerful organizing principles in *Miradi Bubu*, and we begin to see how a novel written in an African language is fully globalized. Discourses of globalization have become part of the stylistic apparatus that Ruhumbika can deploy in Swahili and while the semiotics of space in the novel draws heavily from local images of space, these local images appear to be saturated with globalized tropes of locality and mobility. The resources of the language have changed.

The repatriation of critique

It is not just the resources that have changed: the language can be used in different networks as well. We now move into the other aspect of our discussion: the way in which *Miradi Bubu* is itself a rather typical globalization phenomenon. We concluded our discussion in the previous section by stating that globalization was an important motif in the novel. Yet, it is hard to characterize the novel as anything other than 'local': written for Tanzanian readers in their national language, and drawing on contextual information much of which is only accessible to Tanzanians. We also noted earlier that Ruhumbika wrote the novel while he was a professor in the USA. So what we have on our hands is a novel produced in the centre of the world-system for consumption in the periphery, Tanzania, and the choice of language as well as the cultural semiotics of space articulated in Swahili provide evidence for this.

The novel, consequently, is a typical product of contemporary globalized cultural processes, and we should heed Hannerz's advice (1991: 126) to 'think about the flow between places as well as within them' when studying such products of culture. Hannerz adds that the communities within which cultural products are produced and circulated are more and more 'ecumenical', made up by networks that are translocal and often involve deep differences in outlook and framework. Thus,

through the operation of the varied frameworks for cultural process, and the interaction between them, some meanings and meaningful forms become much more localized, much more tied to space, than others. (Hannerz 1991: 126)

Clearly, the community within which *Miradi Bubu* is produced and circulated is ecumenical and diasporic: we have an expatriate author writing for a readership which is, perforce, largely made up of politically and artistically sensitive intellectuals, most of whom are in his homeland and in East Africa. So the ecumene is restricted. The novel is written in Swahili and it draws heavily on 'local' Tanzanian meaningful forms, strongly 'tied to space' in Hannerz's terms. Consequently, the community can sensibly be defined as Ruhumbika on the one hand (and perhaps some students of African studies programmes in the USA and Europe, myself included), and a small group of Tanzanian (or East-African) intellectuals on the other hand. In that sense, *Miradi Bubu* is a 'local' novel destined for circulation in a network which is confined to those who are privy to the intricate local semiotics he uses in his work, as well as to the code in which it is written. It is a Tanzanian novel.

But things are obviously not that simple, because locality and mobility co-occur. We have seen in the previous section that Ruhumbika draws on local meanings against the background of globalization imagery containing centre-versus-periphery models. His 'local' critique against *Ujamaa* is done by means of 'translocalization', i.e. by means of arguments and tropes that define – anachronistically – the failure of *Ujamaa* as a failure to recognize the dynamics of the modern world-system. It is a critique which is built on cosmopolitanism as a worldview, an awareness that localism in social organization is an error, and that centre–periphery patterns are a reality. So in order to construct a local critique of Tanzania, Tanzania has to be lifted out of its shell, delocalized, and placed into the world-system. Nzoka is the key in this: his mobility and its resulting prestige and success demonstrate how insertion into transnational channels of power and prestige shapes success in Tanzanian society. Thus, interestingly, we see how a novel that is hard to read if one does not have access to the local semiotics of places, people and activities at the same time trans-localizes this semiotics and places it in the context of Tanzania-in-the-world.

It is perhaps at this point that we can begin to understand what globalization and its reflexes on literature involve. They involve a dynamics of semiotic localization and delocalization in such a way that Hannerz's space, to which meanings are tied, can be seen as *elastic* space, a space that can be reduced and expanded almost line by line and episode by episode. Ruhumbika speaks from *within* Tanzania and from *outside* Tanzania at the same time. We get images of what it means to be from southern Tanzania both within Tanzania *as well as* in the world: the local periphery is also a global periphery, for peripheries and centres are relatively stable while they operate at various levels of awareness and activity. Consequently, being marginal in Tanzania *is also meaningful in the world*, and this stretching of local meanings into translocal ones may offer us a better understanding of poverty and disenfranchisement in the periphery.

The message is, however, primarily for Tanzanians to pick up. Ruhumbika's diasporic act of communication should be repatriated, in Appadurai's sense, and thus recontextualized and re-entextualized in Silverstein and Urban's (1996) sense. But repatriation does not necessarily mean localization. The strength of the motif of mobility, both within and outside Tanzania, and its connection to success and failure as well as to an assessment of *Ujamaa*, make it hard to read this book as other than a translocalization of the history of Tanzania. As is perhaps the case with all diasporic literature, this may precisely be the novel's Achilles' heel. In the process of repatriation, the localization of the messages in the book may be challenged by the translocal dimension it necessarily has: that of a critique from afar by an outsider who does not suffer from the conditions of life he criticizes in his book. And thus, whereas the book is by all standards fully Tanzanian, its status as 'Tanzanian' may perpetually be challenged by Tanzanian critics. The repatriation of meanings produced by expatriates is always a political issue, and even at that level Hannerz's ties between cultural products and space crop up.

The cultural codes of globalization

Ruhumbika's choice of Swahili (rather than English, his working language as a professor in the USA) encodes this complex semiotics. In itself, the choice to write a novel in Swahili is a highly meaningful act: it dramatically restricts the scope of the readership to the groups described above, and this prejudices sales figures, international acclaim and other rewards of successful authorship. To some extent, it 'hides' the novel in a corner in the world, it locks it in a narrow space of circulation and uptake. All of this is indisputable: even to many people strongly interested in African literature, my discussion here (written, of course, in English) will be their first encounter with Ruhumbika's novel. In that sense, the dynamics of localization and translocalization always come with a price: the choice to avoid the global lingua francas seems to immediately marginalize cultural products, and minimize the symbolic bonuses one could get from cultural production.

It is indisputable, however, to the extent that one views globalization as a process of uniformization, and to the extent that cultural globalization processes are seen as the production of a global monoculture. Things are different when we see globalization in the terms sketched earlier in this book: as a more 'niched' complex of processes, developing at several different scale-levels, some of them truly global, others regional, national or even sub-national. Appadurai's 'vernacular globalization', I would suggest, is globalization at one particular scale-level, lower than the fully global one: it is the connectedness of small pockets of people located (and 'local') in different parts of the world, sharing cultural products and being involved in processes of joint cultural production, the 'networks' described by Castells (1996). Ruhumbika's book is globalized within such a network, it is globalized at a sub-global scale-level within the communities sketched above. At that scale-level, a strong articulation of locality can be expected, and the choice of Swahili, as well as the strongly local social semiotics of space contribute to that. There is nothing paradoxical to that – the seemingly odd combination of outspoken locality and outspoken globalization – if one understands the nature and scope of the particular communication network for which this cultural product was designed. It was designed for a dispersed world-wide network in which this sense of locality is politically, culturally and artistically meaningful, for a network that shares the indexicals that render it meaningful.

Let me summarize what we have seen so far. We saw how an African language, Swahili, could become the vehicle for discourses of translocality and locality, in a complex balance which reflected the particular kind of globalization in which it was used: sub-global, niched globalization within a particular network of communicators. An African language such as Swahili could become the cultural code for globalized cultural production at a particular scale-level, and it was even *the best* cultural code for this particular network. This, I would say, is an aspect of vitality: these opportunities for using such languages in globalization are relatively new (they follow the increasing connectivity in diasporic networks), there are plenty such opportunities, and a quick look at the Internet shows that they are used by many people to articulate the new cultural forms of vernacular globalization. Ruhumbika uses an 'old' format, that of the postcolonial Swahili novel, to articulate a new (translocal) critique of the (local) past. The format, thus, becomes new, and the language encodes this innovation. I find this a very hopeful sign for African languages, and see this as a necessary qualification of the more widespread views of sociolinguistic globalization, in which English is seen as a linguicidal force. It no doubt is, but perhaps only at certain scale-levels, not at others, and seeing globalization as something that operates at a variety of levels can help us understand the real dynamics of vitality and endangerment of African languages.

This also counts for other languages that do not belong to the sociolinguistic top of the world. Cultural products such as music, art, cinema and (to a lesser

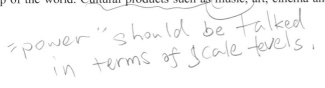

=power "should be talked
in terms of scale levels.

extent) literature appear to open new avenues to survival for languages whose fate would be otherwise pretty gloomy. We see how, for instance, hip-hop appears to offer new opportunities for 'small' languages to articulate globalized meanings in a new and invariably innovative cultural genre. Pietikäinen (2008) mentions the Sami rap artist Amoc, who makes widely sold and popular records in the Inari Sami language – a language that counts (in optimistic accounts) about 300 speakers and is solely spoken in one town in northern Finland. Inari Sami thus gets a new lease of life through the globalized vehicle of hip-hop. Similar phenomena can be observed in various places in Africa, and elsewhere, where we see local languages and language varieties being used in rap music and being disseminated via this medium to otherwise inaccessible audiences. The spread of globalized cultural formats and the emergence of globalized communities of consumers thus create new, and positive, opportunities for languages to circulate – even if the languages are changed in the process, and even if the locality they articulate only makes sense in the context of the translocal circulation of signs and meanings in which the language is involved.

3.2   Locality and the periphery

The images of the world that we saw in Ruhumbika's work were local images, they were images of and from the periphery of the world-system. Ruhumbika drew on a local social topography in which places and trajectories acquire meaning and structure events and subjects, the same kind of social topography that gives names such as 'Paris' or 'The White House' much more than just a geographical meaning. Such topographies belong to the local cultural codes, the complexes of local meanings that provide rich indexicals to place names. The spaces they index so begin to structure discourses of ascriptions, discourses in which events and people acquire characteristics that are sensed to be attached to these places.

This is a rich field for research on globalization processes, because whenever people communicate, they communicate from and on particular places. Their contextual situatedness as communicators also includes spatiotemporal situatedness. This is not the same as spatiotemporal fixedness, for the patterns of mobility we associate with globalization obviously trigger expected and unexpected phenomena at this level. A Tanzanian friend of mine who had studied in Lancaster, UK, sent home pictures of himself next to a radiator – a very mundane object for people in Lancaster, so mundane that very few people would find it worthy of photographic recording. The picture (in which he himself was tightly packed in layers of clothing), told a story, however: the story of how cold it was in Lancaster, so cold that people had heating systems in their houses, and even with such heating systems people from Tanzania would have to wear sweaters and scarves – it was *that* cold. My friend was

translocalization (Radiator)
vs.
glocalization (McDonald's)

communicating *about* Lancaster, but *from* Tanzania, from within a frame of meaningfulness that was Tanzanian. It was from within that Tanzanian frame that the radiator in his student room acquired the emblematic value that it had in the picture. He was, thus, translating one form of locality into another, in a process of mobility – the transport of local English practise into a local Tanzanian universe where it is assigned a localized Tanzanian interpretation. Communication, thus, always involves issues of transporting the signs or objects attached to one place into those of other places, where they can be re-interpreted otherwise. It always involves the mobilization of meanings.

This is 'translocalization' – a term I prefer (like Appadurai 1996) over the more common one 'glocalization', which is slightly misleading because it suggests the global-in-the-local. I see locality transported into locality, and while such a process is indeed definitional of semiotic globalization processes, the localities do not necessarily become more 'global' or 'deterritorialized' because of such patterns of translocalization. They remain as local as before, even when elements from a higher scale-level (the translocal) are being imported ('re-territorialized', we could say). Meanings are primarily imported into local systems of meaningfulness, where they are changed and interpreted on the basis of such systems – like when a Lancaster radiator becomes an emblematic sign in Tanzania of the climate in northern Britain. This point merits some emphasis, because while processes of global flow are by now quite well described, their uptake has been less well understood so far, and such forms of uptake need to be understood in terms of locality. We need to gain a clear sight of what locality means if we want to understand globalization. I am not happy with views of globalization in which the local is only seen as the stable and traditional, and I am equally unhappy with views in which locality is seen as the effect of deterritorialized 'place-making' (cf. McKay and Brady 2005; also Bubinas 2005; Mankekar 2002). Such views are too much tainted by existing emphases on globalization as primarily diasporic in nature, while more specific forms of semiotic mobility – like the photos of radiators moving from Lancaster to Tanzania – are overlooked or neglected.

This is particularly at issue when we consider globalization processes from the centre to the periphery. There, and rather persistently, we see how global images, discourses and patterns of conduct become relocalized into existing strong and perduring patterns. Even if such peripheral local communities are 'touched' by globalization, they remain firmly local in structure, self-presentation and image. Change is gradual, step-by-step and slow, and the 'old order' of things persists while elements of the new order creep in. This is what we saw in the Tanzanian novel: the local semiotics of space was used in a translocal, globalized act of communication, which then became relocalized among the Tanzanian readers of the novel. The language, Swahili, itself func-tioned as the carrier for this process of blending the old and the new, and so became a vehicle for cultural innovation. Languages and discourses move around, but they do so between spaces that are full of rules, norms, customs and conventions, and they get adapted to the rules, norms, customs and conventions of such places before moving further on their trajectories. This dynamic of localization, delocalization and relocalization is essential for our understanding of sociolinguistic globalization processes. This will also become clear when we engage with the next series of examples, in which we see the sociolinguistic emblem of globalization, English, make its way into a newly democratic education environment in the townships of South Africa.

3.3   The norms of the periphery

Societies marked by deep inequality characteristically produce different layers and niches in which very different ways of life are developed on the basis of rules, norms and opportunities not valid elsewhere. The dynamics within such spaces lead one to suspect that they have a degree of autonomy vis-à-vis the wider system; yet, they are often seen only *in relation to* the wider system: as 'peripheries', 'margins', 'backward areas', 'poor neighbourhoods' and so forth. There is a politics of semiotic stratification that assumes the existence of a uniform system, in which a ranking of 'good' and 'worse' places can be made. This mechanism is homogenizing, and it often appears as a discourse of standards, 'normalcy' and monocentricity, where the norms and customs of the 'centre' (i.e. usually the middle class) are taken to be the only valid ones and the only ones guaranteeing upward social mobility and success. Failing to meet such norms is then seen as failing to meet *the* norms – failing to comply with the only perceived possible trajectory for success in society. And those who fail to meet the norm are, in one move, rapidly qualified as problems, 'abnormals', 'marginals' etc. (Foucault 2003). Education, as a system designed for cultural and social reproduction, is of course a case in point.

Such homogenizing approaches to differences in an unequal society, I intend to demonstrate, obscure an accurate view and appraisal of the local dynamics in parts of the system. The 'margin', so to speak, is not necessarily a space in which people *fail to meet norms*, but it can as well be seen as a space in which *different but related norms are produced*, responding – 'ecologically', so to speak – to the local possibilities and limitations. Such norms, of course, do not matter much in the larger scheme of things. Lifted out of their local context, they bump into the homogenizing, singular images of normativity dominant in most societies and get disqualified without much ado (Blommaert, Creve and Willaert 2006; also Milroy and Milroy 1991; Silverstein 1996; Bonfiglio 2002). This, however, is a process that deserves substantial attention, because it is a process often only understood, not in its own terms, but in terms of the homogenizing normativity itself. Disqualifying 'deviant' norms almost automatically effaces these norms as existing, socially and culturally valuable and above all *productive* problem-solving instruments. This is a classic problem of hegemony in social science: emphasis on a limited number of categories and notions makes other categories and notions invisible, even if they might be crucial for an accurate understanding of the very social processes of exclusion and erasure that made them invisible (cf. Irvine and Gal 2000). Investigating deviation is therefore (in an echo of Foucault) an investigation of power.

I will focus here on literacy practices in Wesbank High, a township school in the Cape Town area, South Africa, suggesting that 'deviant' normativity in language – specifically, orthographic 'errors' – becomes a *productive* instrument that allows teachers to work with groups of learners displaying wildly different backgrounds, capacities and skills. I will suggest that there is an ad hoc consensus over local normativity, a normativity that relates to the sociological and cultural environment (a 'realistic' form of normativity, in other words) and thus creates opportunities for 'realistic' appraisals of learning trajectories. It has to be seen in terms of local – restricted – repertoires of literacy, an economy of literacy in the townships which exists alongside other economies, in which more diverse and extended repertoires are available. Such ad hoc norms, therefore, do not counter the dominant (curriculum) norms, nor do they disqualify them; they suggest a local level of organization in which different solutions are developed to local problems. In that sense, the production of local, deviant normativity is both a problem and a solution, as we shall see. It is a problem because it remains 'insufficient' in terms of the dominant norms; it is a solution because it allows for a productive teaching practise in school as well as for a degree of community development and identity construction.

A detailed decoding of the conflictual and ambivalent nature of such processes may be fundamental for an understanding of patterns of inequality in societies such as contemporary South Africa. Imagining literacy normativity not as one uniform object, but as an ecologically and economically localized one, is an important first step towards analysing it with more sensitivity to local context, use and function. For a sociolinguistics of globalization, it is important to see the way in which globalized language material – normative English literacy – enters and becomes adapted to a local sociolinguistic environment, and begins to function there as a local resource, only loosely connected to its globalized origins. This local resource belongs to a language, English, but it is more productive to see it as it is: as a set of specialized, localized semiotic resources that is related to a local economy of signs and meanings. The next chapter will elaborate further on this theme, but first we need to specify the particular processes we are considering here. In what follows, I shall first provide some general contextualizing remarks. Next, I shall engage with a number of issues emerging from fieldwork in Wesbank High, focusing first on the density of occurrences of 'deviant' literacy features and then on local views of the function and value of linguistic resources. I will then sketch a pattern of the production of locality in Wesbank High, and what are commonly regarded as 'errors' committed against a single norm will be converted into productive mechanisms for the construction of peripheral normativity: a normativity that relates to the sociology of the periphery. This, then, should illustrate the dynamic of localization, delocalization and relocalization in globalization processes and so show us the core of sociolinguistic globalization processes.

The field and the issues

The Wesbank settlement is by all standards a peripheral community, isolated from neighbouring areas and plagued by a variety of social and economic difficulties. Wesbank was one of the first post-apartheid housing projects. Prior to the start of the housing project, the area was an informal settlement (i.e. a slum) known as Camelot. In September 1995 the Provincial Administration of the Western Cape decided that Wesbank should become an area for the relocation of 'maximum subsidy' (i.e. minimum income) families. Former place of residence, colour or other social diacritics did not play a role. The building works started in 1997 and, given the critical nature of the housing problems in the Cape area, proceeded at a rapid pace and with a limited budget. The houses were built with brick walls and corrugated iron roofs, without thermal insulation. Every house has one toilet and one washing table. The houses are uniform and excessively simple in structure – people call them 'matchbox houses'. The bright colours in which they were painted quickly gave rise to another nickname: 'Smarties town', after the coloured chocolate Smarties (M&Ms).

People started moving into Wesbank in 1999, and at the time of the fieldwork in 2004, the community consisted of an estimated 25,000 people, living in 5,145 housing units. Due to the dominance of socio-economic criteria in the selection of inhabitants, the population in Wesbank was and is very diverse: Wesbank houses people who lived in other townships in the Cape Town area and in the numerous informal settlements mushrooming around the city, as well as recent immigrants from the Eastern Cape province and from further afield. Black, coloured and (some) white people live in the same community. Most of the inhabitants are coloured and speak Afrikaans, though 25 per cent are black and speak Xhosa. The Xhosa community lives together in one section of Wesbank (Dyers 2004a, 2004b). Wesbank is a community with very limited public infrastructure and a serious degree of spatial isolation, caught between highways and inadequately integrated in the local 'taxi' transport network (Jonckers and Newton 2004: 113–118). Apart from 'shebeens' (local, illegal bars) and other small-scale shops, there is one supermarket. There are one secondary and three primary schools catering to many thousands of learners, only one open-air bus-stop and no community centre or hospital. The unemployment rate in Wesbank is very high, perpetuating the poverty which characterized the eligible population. One has to start one's own small business or leave the community to find a job, and commuting out of Wesbank involves considerable travel expenses.

Wesbank High is the only secondary school in the area, and its new and well-constructed facilities rank among the best and most welcoming in the whole of Wesbank. It is situated on the edge of the settlement, at a certain distance from the main road, and is therefore shielded from busy traffic and passage. The building is surrounded by a high fence and a gate provides access to the school grounds. The building is organized around a large central patio. The school has an (embryonic) library annex and computer-room; there are some (modest) sports facilities at the back of the building; a vegetable garden is under construction. Apart from daytime teaching activities, there are also evening adult classes.

Wesbank High is a dual-medium school, which means that subjects are offered in two languages: English and Afrikaans. In 2004 the school counted nine grade 8 classes, nine grade 9s and five grade 10s. Every grade had two class groups having English as the medium of instruction, and it must be noted that only the rarest of learners in these groups had English as their mother tongue. The rest of the classes had Afrikaans as the medium of instruction, and mostly this was the learners' mother tongue. This distribution can immediately serve as an indicator of the balance between black and coloured learners in the school. The majority was coloured and took Afrikaans-medium classes. Very few black learners joined them there, as most black learners attended English-medium classes, where one found few coloured learners. Although this seems a simple language issue, it had social and sociolinguistic repercussions, as we shall see further on.[3]

The error as terror: deviation and normativity in Wesbank High

Teachers in Wesbank High face a number of challenges: large classes with a very heterogeneous population with respect to backgrounds, capacity and levels of achievement; a poor and marginalized community; an under-resourced school in which special educational needs cannot be adequately addressed. Let us now have a look at some classroom activities in Wesbank High. I will restrict myself to observations on literacy practices and the way in which we see complex relations towards norms there. This restriction is a matter of space, not of methodology, and it is useful to emphasize that the observations on literacy are mirrored in the spoken varieties of learners and teachers as well (for a detailed study, of relevance to our concern here, see Kapp 2001).

Getting it right   Regardless of their average scores all learners shared some problems, and one major problem was command of basic literacy skills. A close examination of the data gathered among learners reveals that almost all of them consistently (and with amazing frequency) produced particular types of writing features:

(i) the erratic use of capitals (not using them where needed, using them where not needed);
(ii) difficulties with singular and plural marking;
(iii) difficulties with verb inflections, esp. plural marking and tense marking;
(iv) problems with the use of definite and indefinite articles (not using them where needed);
(v) a wide range of spelling problems, mostly a result of phonetic spelling (writing according to pronunciation);
(vi) a tendency to aestheticize writing, even while struggling with basic writing skills – writing as drawing.

These features occurred regardless of the languages used by learners (we shall later see that they also occur in the teachers' writing). In addition, many learners had more specific problems with completing relatively undemanding syntactic and grammatical tasks in English. Let us look at a small random sample from the data gathered. First, observe these examples of erratic capital use:

1. Because they thought that is a Gun Sound and the boy wasn't back @ home.
2. If I loved him, He would marry me
3. ja, Ek dink daar is toekoms, … (yes, I think there is a future,…)
4. Watte taal hou jij Niks van nie? (Which language do you dislike)
5. BECAUSE You can Communicate with Everyone with it.
6. You can go to the far lands that they speek other language lets say maybe they speek french they may understand english.
7. English. because it's the oFFicial Language in South Africa

Example 6 already shows that apart from the erratic use of capitals, learners also struggled with spelling. Here is a sample of the spelling problems we encountered in our data, and as noted above, many of them have to do with phonetic writing. We see, for instance, errors that seem to have their origin in 'accent-in-writing': local ways of pronouncing words reflected in writing (cf. Blommaert 2008).

Xhosh/Xhoza (Xhosa), Fraans (Frans), spesel (special), dearist (dearest), sewand (selwand), emegency exit (emergency exit), amtelle/amtelik (amtelike), Englis (English), defferent (different), importend (important), neve (never), disent (decent), ather (other), whe (when), hotal (hotel), iconomy (economy), trave egent (travel agent), trasport (transport), eirs (ears), anather (another), pefect (perfect), merriage (marriage), the (there)

Related to the former category, some forms betray interlingual influences from Afrikaans on English and vice versa:

Africaans, Afrikans (Afrikaans), Franch (Frans), populare (popular), becouse (because), finde (find), importante (important), famile (family), countrie (country), somethinge (something), Engilhs (Engels)

We also see homophone spellings: spelling a word in a way that allows homophonous realization in local varieties of speech

now (know), noyse (nose), a price hate/apesiheth (appreciate), sutch (such), mybe (maybe), eath (earth), restaurand (restaurant), Afrikaan (Afrikaans), Soud-Africa (South Africa), language (language), meter (matter), there leder (their leader), leyzy (lazy), us (use), mothe language (mother language), no (know), learne (learner), sow (so), verry (very), everry (every), othe/ather/arther (other), som (some), busness (business), arwer/awer (our), rase (race), speek (speak), lurners (learners)

Some errors might be based on the complexity of the graphic form: inverted order of symbols, confusion about the graphic representation of sounds etc.

whit (with), South Africka/Soud-Afica (South Africa), people/peop/peaple (people), a noteher (another), mith (might), aers (ears), coputer aided design (computer aided design), pleke (plekke), meste (meeste), Nedelerlands (Nederlands), feel unappreciatel (feel unappreciated), beutyfull (beautiful), becuase (because), langage/langauge/languge (language), somethimes (sometimes), liek/lick (like), tuong/tounge/togue (tongue), the want (they want), speck (speak), moust (most), aproff (a proof), respectfull (respectful), leasten (listen), weather (wether)

Figure 3.1 is an example of a word order task in English; figure 3.2 is an example of an orthographic (spelling) correction task. Figures 3.3, 4 and 5 show how all these isolated difficulties combine in creative writing. Figure 3.6, finally, shows another widespread feature: the tendency to create an aesthetic textual product in spite of the difficulties in handling literacy codes.

These features of writing are not unexpected: they are features of 'grass-roots literacy', and very widespread in Africa and elsewhere. They can be encountered in many places in the world where people are inserted in sub-elite literacy economies and have restricted literacy repertoires, and often assume the shape of a skeleton writing competence in which acoustic images of words are noted in an unstable spelling system. Grassroots literacy, I insist, need not be seen as 'bad literacy' or 'restricted literacy' in Jack Goody's terms (Goody 1968). Such terms suggest a particular (inferior) position on one uniform continuum of 'quality' in literacy, whereas it is far more useful to see grassroots literacy as a particular, locally constructed and constrained literacy 'culture' with a degree of autonomy vis-à-vis related literacy cultures, including that of elite, normative literacy. It is a form of literacy which results in very restricted literacy repertoires and in which, consequently, the norms and codes of literacy are deployed differently, in a different system of visualization of meaning. It is not ortho-graphy, but *hetero-graphy*, the deployment of literacy techniques and instruments in ways that do not respond to

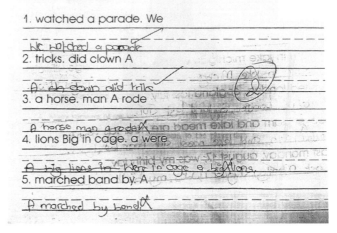

Make a sentence by putting each group of words in the correct order.

1. watched a parade. We

2. tricks. did clown A

3. a horse. man A rode

4. lions Big in cage. a were

5. marched band by. A

Figure 3.1 Syntax assignment

institutional ortho-graphic norms but that nevertheless are not completely chaotic, even if such chaos appears to be the most conspicuous feature (Blommaert 2008; see Prinsloo and Breier 1996 and Thesen and van Pletzen 2006 for studies of contemporary South Africa). There is order in the chaos, and this order invites (as yet unexplored) rich comparative study: we see recurrent 'errors', widespread as *types* in the examples given here as well as in those found elsewhere, and rather than seeing this as an *absence* of order and consistency, one can also see it as the *presence* of a different kind of order operating within a restricted repertoire. These forms of literacy respond to *local* issues of function and need; they are, in other words, ecologically embedded in the community in which they operate (cf. Barton 1994; Barton and Hamilton 1998; Street 1995; Jaffe 2000; Collins and Blot 2003).

This view, in which such forms of writing are seen as belonging to a particular local literacy culture, complicates matters that otherwise might seem overly clear. For one thing, it does not help to dismiss the learners' writing as littered with orthographic errors: there is a more productive hetero-graphic way of seeing it. It does not only exist in relation to one (institutional) norm of writing, but it exists in relation to a multitude of such norms. Also and consequently, superficial comparison with similar forms of writing produced, for example, in the UK or the USA is not helpful either, as this would again suggest one uniform literacy complex that functions as a yardstick for assessing degrees of quality in

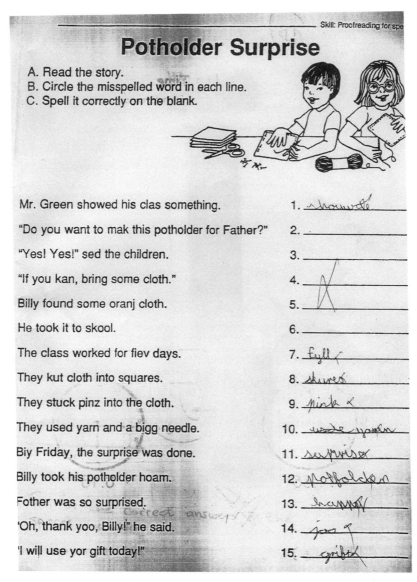

Figure 3.2 Spelling assignment

literacy. Even if we see similar graphic realizations in contemporary and historical examples of writing from the West, the particular histories of becoming of such forms as well as their contemporary embeddedness in socio-economic, cultural and ideological contexts call for deeper and more nuanced

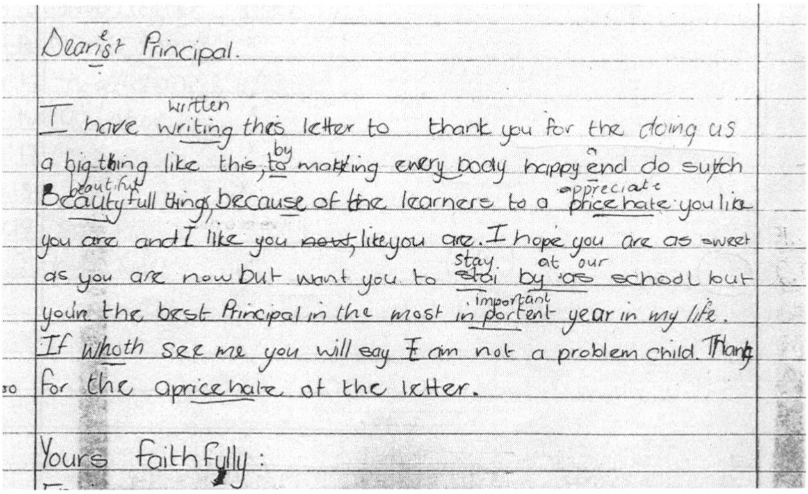

Dearest Principal.

I have writing this letter to thank you for the doing us a big thing like this, by making everybody happy end do such Beautyfull things, because of the learners to a appreciate you like you are and I like you not, likeyou are. I hope you are as sweet as you are now but want you to stay by as our school but your the best Principal in the most important year in my life. If whoth see me you will say I am not a problem child Thanks for the apricehate of the letter.

Yours faithfully:

Figure 3.3 Letter to the Principal

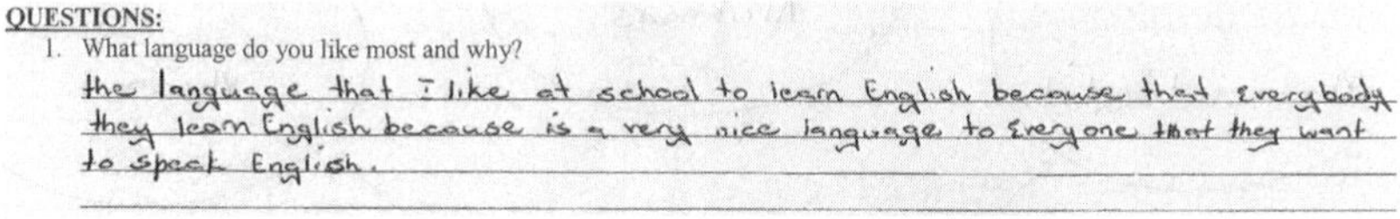

QUESTIONS:
1. What language do you like most and why?

the language that I like at school to learn English because that everybody they learn English because is a very nice language to everyone that they want to speak English.

Figure 3.4 'The language I like most'

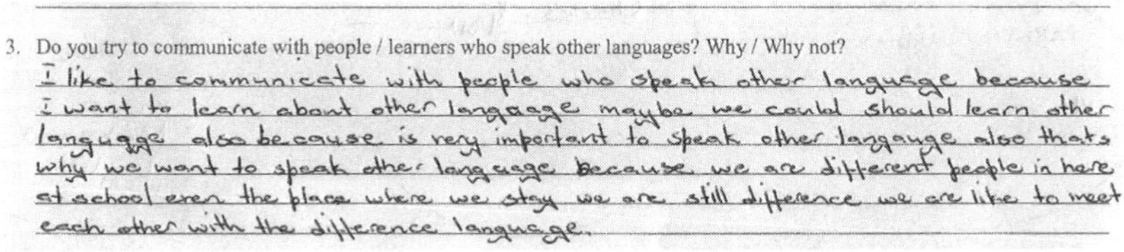

3. Do you try to communicate with people / learners who speak other languages? Why / Why not?

I like to communicate with people who speak other language because I want to learn about other language maybe we could should learn other language also because is very important to speak other language also thats why we want to speak other language because we are different people in here at school even the place where we stay we are still difference we are like to meet each other with the difference language.

Figure 3.5 'Communicate'

analyses. If, for instance, someone in a literacy-saturated environment writes 'luv', it is likely that they also know that there is an orthographically normative version, 'love', and that they would be able to write this orthographically normative version. Writing 'luv' then becomes an act of wit, skill and graphic creative display (as well as a display of some understanding of spelling conventions, e.g. in identifying the vowel in 'luv' as identical to the one in 'pun'), something that exists alongside normative writing and derives its indexical values of creativity and wittiness from the contrast with an (accessible) norm.

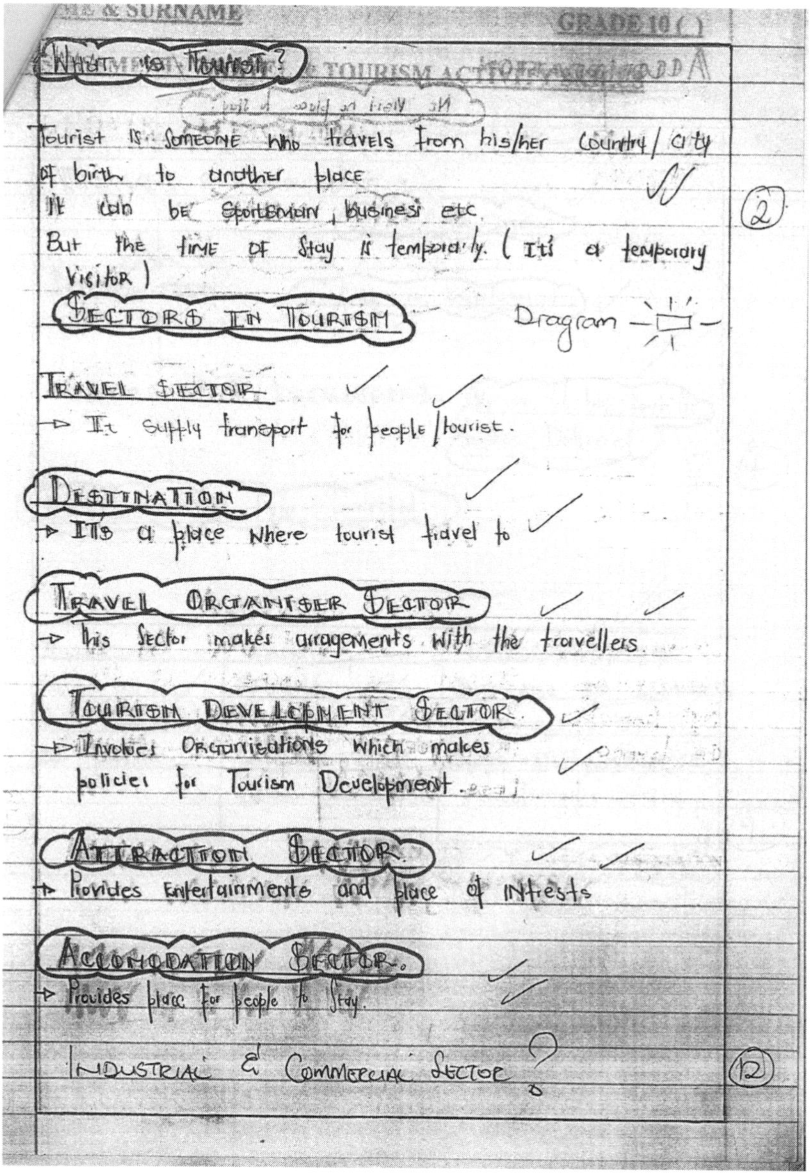

Figure 3.6 Decorated writing

What we are facing here is an interplay between two different literacies, both of which are within reach of the same user because both belong to the literacy repertoire of the user. In contrast, the learner who wrote 'dearist' instead of 'dearest' in her letter to the principal (figure 3.3) has no access to the orthographically normative version of the word; 'dearist' is her *best possible* graphic realization, because the orthographically normative version is not accessible in her particular literacy repertoire. Even if forms of writing in South Africa and the UK have a prima facie similarity, it is what lies beneath the surface that counts when we want to address the roles and functions of these forms of writing for those who employ them.

Summarizing, we have seen that the learners' writing in Wesbank High displayed features of grassroots literacy. The features are not group-specific but widespread features of a particular form of literacy, and they occur regardless of the linguistic backgrounds of the learners as well as of their average academic performance. They are, in other words, a level of shared literacy culture in an otherwise extremely heterogeneous community.

The teachers   The picture of a shared literacy culture becomes particularly intriguing as soon as we start looking at teachers' language usage. Many of the features we detected in the learners' writing also occur in the writing of teachers. Consider the following examples, taken from questionnaire responses:

(1)   English, being an international language would equipt learner to be able to communicate effectively internationally.
(2)   Learners feel shy to speak a minority languge. Mostly make youse of code switching. Also afraid of stereotyping.

In (1), we see a spelling error ('equipt') and a missing article or a problem with plural marking ('*the* learner' or 'learner*s*'); in (2) we also see spelling errors ('languge', 'youse') and two rather unexpected forms of subject and verb ellipsis in the two final sentences. The spelling errors in (2) are similar to those encountered in the learners' writing above. Figures 3.7 and 8 provide further examples; note again the typological similarity between the errors made by the teachers and those made by the learners (e.g. accent in 'avangelist' and 'galaries' in figure 3.7; unwarranted capitals and acoustic writing in 'Well Establish', figure 3.8).

So teachers and learners appear to share some of the features of writing and make typologically similar errors – both groups appear to different extents to be part of a particular hetero-graphic literacy complex, the sub-elite stratum of literacy. This is a sociologically realistic form of literacy in the sense that it mirrors the marginalized status of the community in which it occurs. It is a form of literacy that characterizes the place in which they operate, and in which access to elite (hyper-normative, homogenized) literacy is severely restricted. It is not the case

Personal Details/Persoonlijke besonderhede (optional/opsioneel)

1. Name and Surname / Naam en Van

   MRONKE HERBERT GJOAO-IYUJANA

2. Where do you stay? / Waar woon u?

   (illegible)

3. Where and when were you born? / Waar en wanneer was u gebore?

   CAPE TOWN   SOUTH AFRICA

4. What is your home language? / Wat is u moedertaal?

   XHOSA

5. What church denomination do you belong to? / Aan watter kerk behoort u?

   AVENGELIST CHURCH

6. What do you do for leisure ? / Wat doen u vir ontspanning ?

   PLAY (AN) MUSICAL INSTRUMENT
   (PIANO) VISIT GALARIES

Educational background / Opvoedkundige agtergrond

   DIPLOMA IN DANCE

1. Hoogste kwalifikasie (s) ? / Highest qualification ?

   UNIVERSITY DIPLOMA

2. By/Aan watter institut het u dit voltooi? / Institution obtained ?

   UNIVERSITY OF CAPE TOWN

3. Vir hoe lank is u al 'n onderwyser? / For how long have you been teaching?

   4 YEARS

Figure 3.7 Teacher's questionnaire 1

4. By watter skool (skole) het u voorheen geonderrig ? / At what school(s) did you teach before?

① Spine Rd SSS   (SA)   ⑤ Westbank
② Eisleben Prim (S.A)
③ Bower Park   (U.K)
④ William De Ferrers (U.K)

5. Hoe sien u die skool in 5 jaar se tyd? / How do you see the school in 5 years time?

Well Establish
Good Structure
Solid

6. Dink u dat die skool 'n sentrum van inligting vir die leerder is ? / Do you think that the school is a resource centre to these children?

Yes

7. Brei uit oor vorige vraag. / Elaborate on the previous question.

Due to the good infrastructure

Language / Taal

1. In what language do you communicate with the learners ? / In watter taal kommunikeer u met die leerders ?

Afrikaans

2. In what language do you communicate with your colleagues ? / In watter taal kommunikeer u met u kollegas?

Afrikaans and English

Figure 3.8 Teacher's questionnaire 2

that teachers incorporate an abstract, ideal and uniform literacy norm, which would set them apart from their learners. The reason is again a historical one. The teachers in Wesbank High all belonged to the same 'racial' groups as their pupils: coloured and black. And even if, in comparison with their pupils, they would be relatively well-off (they are a salaried professional lower middle-class), being black or coloured equalled structural disenfranchisement until very recently. In other words, the Wesbank High teachers come from a similar sub-elite stratum in society, in which the material and symbolic privileges of the elite were and are rare commodities. Traces of that structural marginalization can be found even today, and they provide a bedrock of shared culture between teachers and learners.

The teachers deploy this sociologically real local form of literacy as a normative tool in teaching practise. This becomes clear when we look at the way in which teachers correct and mark learners' assignments. Consider figure 3.9, an English writing assignment marked and corrected by the teacher. In discussing it, we shall use the term 'error' because we are addressing an evaluated exercise in orthographic correctness.

The teacher identifies and corrects eight writing errors and marks the assignment with 'excellent! 84%'. The teacher, however, does not spot the error in sentence 2: 'love *end* care', nor the two errors in sentence 4: '*somone*' and 'When you love her *our* him' (note that the teacher also let pass the division of 4 in two separate sentences). And in sentence 6, the teacher corrects two cases of phonetic writing ('all so spesiale'), but does not spot and appraise the initial intention of the learner (aborted while writing) to add a beneficiary to the syntax of the sentence ('fruits are *for someone* also very special'). A self-correction such as in sentence 6 reveals the learner's struggle with literate narrativity: the grammatical blueprint is there, but literacy obstacles prevent a smooth narrative realization of it. The teacher's encouraging marks and comments show that the form of literacy displayed by the learner is positively valued; the teacher's reading and assessment of it is less than punitive and overlooks several more errors as well as the general struggle with literate narrativity displayed in the learner's responses. Observe that the errors not marked by the teacher belong to the types we identified earlier: phonetic writing and 'accent' in writing – types of errors also present in the teachers' writing.

The teacher assessing the assignment in figure 3.6 overlooked several rather severe writing errors as well. For example, the missing articles are not identified as errors ('Tourist is someone …', 'It can be sportsman, busines etc.', 'provides place for people to stay' – note also the spelling error in 'busines'); and the inflectional error in 'It supply transport for people/tourist' is also not marked as an error. Turning to figure 3.3, finally (the letter to the principal), we again see that the teacher does not intervene in the general uneasiness of expression in the letter (the frequent use of 'but', for instance), and that very problematic expressions such as 'to thank you for *the doing us a big thing*' are also allowed to pass. We can

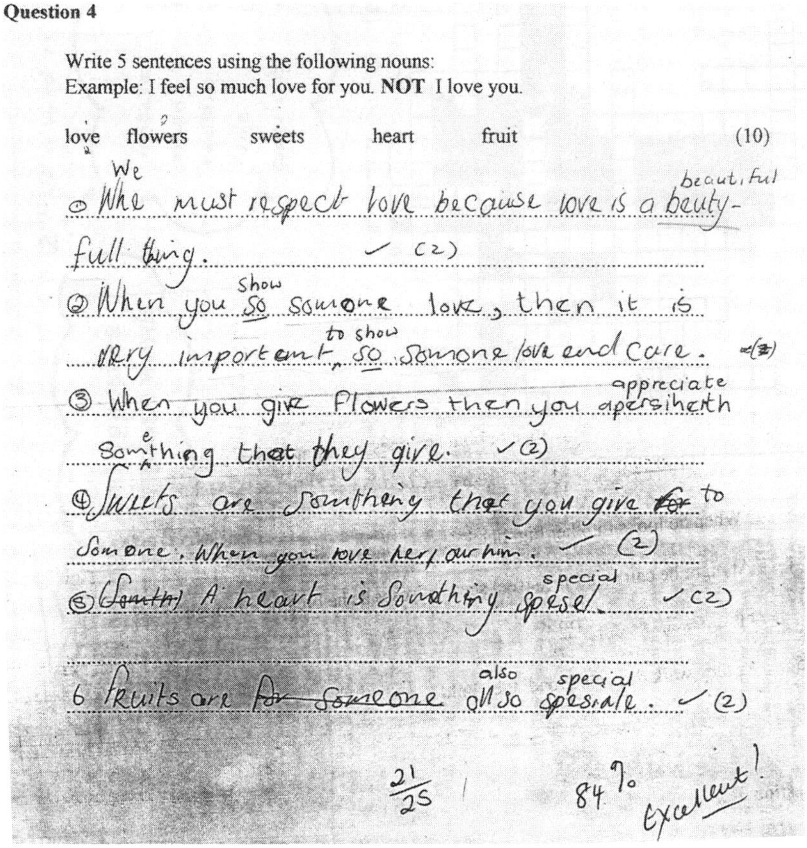

Question 4

Write 5 sentences using the following nouns:
Example: I feel so much love for you. **NOT** I love you.

love flowers sweets heart fruit (10)

① Whe [We] must respect love because love is a beuty-full [beautiful] thing. ✓ (2)
② When you so [show] somone love, then it is very importent, so [to show] somone love and care. ✓(2)
③ When you give Flowers then you apersihcrth [appreciate] somthing [something] that they give. ✓ (2)
④ Sweets are somthing that you give ~~for~~ to somone. When you love her/ our him. ✓ (2)
⑤ ~~(Somthi)~~ A heart is somthing spesel [special] ✓ (2)
6 Fruits are ~~for someone~~ allso [also] spesiale [special]. ✓ (2)

21/25 84% Excellent!

Figure 3.9 Corrected assignment

go on: our data contain numerous examples of teachers *partially* sanctioning and correcting learners' transgressions of 'general' English orthographic norms.

Peripheral norms The shared literacy culture thus affects systems of appraisal and marking by teachers. In other words: grassroots literacy becomes not only a practical code, a tool for expression, but also an *evaluative* and hence *normative* code, a code in which degrees of correctness and 'quality' can be distinguished. Thus a local system of differing 'qualities' of literate expression is created which does not pre-empt serious and consistent evaluation – see the teacher's marks and corrections and the diverging average scores of learners – but which shifts the yardstick of evaluation away from an unattainable presumed universal and singular norm to a local, realistic norm to which learners can aspire and towards which they can make improvements. This is not done on purpose – it is not the case that teachers perceive themselves as lenient towards learners (on the contrary, in our interviews with them, most teachers characterized themselves as demanding, strict and rigorous towards their learners). It is an effect of both groups being part of the same sub-elite literacy stratum in society.

This normative yardstick, consequently, is embedded in the local economies of semiotic resources. It is, in other words, a normative complex with at least some degree of sociological and cultural reality in terms of the levels of literacy prevalent in Wesbank, where (as we saw earlier) low levels of education are the rule rather than the exception, and where substantial diversity in linguistic, social and cultural backgrounds is the rule as well. Consequently, doing 'well' at school means doing well by local standards; it is about doing well *in Wesbank*, not in an abstract universe of learning. The sociolinguistic life of the community is dominated by this local normativity complex. Globalization can spread a language, but it does not spread the particular forms in which it occurs.

Undoubtedly, this has positive effects. The teacher's marks and comments such as 'excellent!' must have a stimulating effect on the learner, who, thanks to this realistic local normativity has the opportunity to perform better than if a punitive, external, perceived universal normativity was applied to their assignments. That this must have a positive impact on the self-perception of the learner, and on their motivation, is more than an educated guess. The localization of normativity probably also allows teachers to attain some degree of effectiveness in front of the large and very heterogeneous classes that characterize Wesbank High. Again, an 'absolute' (external, a-contextual) norm would most probably lead to no-passes for almost every learner, whereas application of the realistic norm allows for some degree of differentiation, some degree of identification of 'better' and 'worse' learners.

There is thus a pedagogical and moral case to be made for this procedure. Even though, from one perspective, it amounts to lifting 'errors' to the level of norms (and thus 'normalizing' errors in writing), another perspective suggests that it offers interesting pedagogical opportunities and is thus a productive, positive procedure. It can be seen as the *localization* of education standards – something which probably occurs everywhere (we have seen that all over the world, English is learned *with an accent*), but is rarely recognized and acknowledged. Education, certainly in literacy, is very often seen as developing with reference to indisputable and a-contextual codes and norms. What happens in Wesbank High is the 'downscaling' of education, bringing it down to the level of the local or regional community, borrowing its norms and expectations, and training learners in the local(ized) codes and norms. The norms in Wesbank High are used to *include*, not just to *exclude*.

Observe that this argument rests on an approach in which we see the English literacy skills of the learning community in Wesbank as a localized set of semiotic resources, which is organized in a particular way. Totalizing ideas of language and literacy are not helpful here; we need an ethnographic sensitivity to the ways in which in this community, people have organized their semiotic resources within local constraints and in view of creating locally valid opportunities for them. We shall consider the issue of how such resources are organized in repertoires in greater detail in the next chapter. The totalizing ideas of language and literacy are not wholly absent, however. They belong to a language-ideological layer of sociolinguistic realities, to which we can now turn.

Perceptions of the centre

In the practice of teaching and learning we see that Wesbank High has localized its normative complexes, adjusting its evaluative schemes and scales, and creating a viable, realistic pedagogy practice in which local varieties of literacy are valued. So far, so good – we have identified a set of practices which (perhaps counter-intuitively) is a *solution* to otherwise monumental obstacles to academic achievement: the unattainable nature of 'ideal' norms, the norms of the centre for people in the periphery. In so doing, we have encountered the core process of sociolinguistic globalization: a globalized language standard becomes transformed into relocalized vernacular varieties.

It is, of course, not only a solution but a problem as well, and in its most straightforward formulation the problem is this: while being able to develop a productive and stimulating learning environment which offers new opportunities to more learners in a 'difficult' social environment, the localization of norms also involves a move away from the norms of the 'centre'. And these norms, as we know, are hegemonic in the end. When Wesbank High graduates intend to move on to institutes of higher learning, the errors in their essays will not be perceived as tokens of local cultural creativity and peripheral normativity, but as indexes of poor academic literacy levels. The features that were instruments of inclusion and creativity at the local level of Wesbank, suddenly become objects of exclusion at a higher level. Their literacy skills are locked, so to speak, into one scale-level, the local one. This, too, is a core feature of sociolinguistic globalization: the relocalized varieties may get 'stuck' at a local scale-level and offer little in the way of mobility potential across scales for their users.

An overwhelming majority of learners and teachers saw English as the 'most important' language in South Africa – as the linguistic resource carrying most prestige and promise of social and spatial mobility (Dyers 2004a, 2008; see Bekker 2003 for an insightful historical analysis). Of course, 'English' – as a tool for social and spatial mobility – offers only a small margin of negotiability as to norms and codes: whenever we frame English in terms such as presented here, we are talking about *prestige varieties* of English. Wesbank High learners, however, expressed their belief in the mobility-endowing potential of English in strongly 'accented' varieties, varieties that displayed the peripheral normativity we identified in the previous section. Let us return briefly to figure 3.4 above. This is what the 16-year-old learner writes:

The language that I like at school to learn English because that Everybody they lean English because is a very nice language to Everyone that they want to speak English

Consider also this example from another learner's language-mind-map:

cause over race in this country can understand English and we can communicate with everyone whether in South Africa or in any other country.

It is clear that the 'English' both learners have in mind is not the 'English' they articulate in their answers; there is a gap between 'their' English and 'the' (normative and literate) English considered to be the most important language in South Africa.

This English is an object of considerable attention, and learners struggle to acquire it. What follows is a fragment from an interview between the researchers N and M and learners A and G:

1. N: the rest you don't like? .. afrikaans euhm .. life orientation: /
2. A: |no| i *don't want to learn afrikaans /. i already know . how to talk afrikaans / i want to learn *english like i can talk with you /
3. N: okay/ because you *can already speak afrikaans
4. A: | afrikaans yes
5. M: so you / you would prefer to .. learn english instead of afrikaans /
6. A: yes i've *got one english book /
7. M: | yeah
8. A: they .. they try to learn english and they .. they and=and afrikaans
9. M: yeah ..
   (...)
22. M: do you think it is important that you know . *many languages here in south africa / or .. / to learn many languages
23. G: {(lo) to learn many languages ... is important see::} [a lot of noise in the back, the learners are coming out of the classes]
24. A: but the *important language for me is *english
25. M: that's the most important language to you / and why /
   (3s)
26. A: i don't know why
27. N: is it maybe because most of the people can understand it
28. A: yes

Observe how A and G identify English as a *target*, as something to be learned, not as something already acquired (even though they responded to the interview questions in English). Note also that English is at the top of a local ideologically informed hierarchy of languages in which respondents usually distinguish three elements: English, Afrikaans and Xhosa. There is strong emotional affinity with Afrikaans and Xhosa (the 'mother tongues' of most children in Wesbank). English is usually specified as to domain – interaction with friends or outsiders (such as the European researchers), and class activities – and as a prestige resource it is situated *outside* of Wesbank: English (that is: the normative and literate variety of it) is the language that will allow people to 'get out of' Wesbank, to better and more prosperous environments (see also Dyers 2004a: 28, 2008). It is because of this connection between English and social and spatial mobility that English is given its (quite common) attribution of 'neutrality', a neutral medium allowing Afrikaans (coloured) and Xhosa (black) mother-tongue speakers to interact with one another without activating ethnolinguistic sentiments.

Dreams of 'moving out' are widespread. Many learners articulate explicit desires to move on to higher learning tracks, as in the next fragment where N and M inquire into D's plans after 'matric' (the qualifying exam after high school):

1. N: but do you wanna go to school *after matric? to: ehr
2. D: i want to go to a college
3. N: college
4. M: yeah
5. D: or omething
6. M: yeah
7. D: engineering

In the absence of such rather precise trajectories of further learning, the aspiration is usually 'to become rich':

1. F: you see my dream is to have a big house
2. N: mhm
3. M: that's your dream
4. F: yes: because .. i=i always grow up in those small houses
5. M: mhm
6. F: those shacks you see
7. N: mhm
8. F: i want i want to improve my *life /
9. M and N: yeah
10. F: to have a big house and those beautiful cars / you see

Or, in its most elementary form, just to get out of Wesbank:

1. N: do you have plans for the future? do you like . want to become something or a profession you would like to have /
2. E: ehr i have like two dif=different dreams / depends .. like my most dream is .to to=to=to=to move out with my family here in Wesbank you know /

3. M: yeah
4. E: and live ehr somewhere else / but *that i don't think *that .ehr is a good thing even though i'm still working on it you know /

All these dreams and imagined upward (and outward) trajectories are predicated on knowledge of the 'English' the learners described earlier as a prestige resource. There is an awareness of that, and this (sociologically very accurate) awareness explains the learners' desire to acquire 'English'. Thus, learners in Wesbank appear to have a rather precise idea of the 'centre' of society and of the way in which trajectories from the periphery to the centre require access to and control over specific symbolic goods such as ('standard') English.

It is in light of this that the localization of norms in teaching becomes slightly more problematic. The gap we saw between the 'English' identified as the resource of social and spatial mobility, and the 'English' in which they articulated this view, is what we call a *pretextual gap*: a gap between expected language competence and really available language competence (Maryns and Blommaert 2002). Such pretextual gaps are *systemic*: they do not depend on the individual efforts (or lack thereof), intrinsic capacities and possibilities of subjects, but they are elements of social structures of inequality and the reproduction patterns of such structures. Consequently, while the downscaling of normativity to a realistic local level of possibilities and norms is surely a productive and stimulating pedagogical instrument, it is at the same time something that reproduces systemic inequalities in society: the rift between centres and peripheries.

The production of locality

Peripheral neighbourhoods such as Wesbank display what Appadurai called 'vernacular globalization' – a grassroots dimension of globalization expressed, amongst other things, in dense and complex forms of neighbourhood hetero-geneity. This kind of grassroots globalization results, according to Appadurai, in more complex and unclear forms of locality, 'more than ever shot through with contradictions, destabilized by human motion, and displaced by the for-mation of new kinds of virtual neighborhoods' (1996: 198). Its effects include the destabilization and decentring of norms and the creation of spaces which, though they appear to operate within fixed sets of institutional norms (e.g. those of the education system), in effect operate with considerable autonomy. This autonomy, we have seen, may be extremely useful in solving *local* problems. In this case, it surely contributed to the construction of an adequate learning environment for the challenging school context of Wesbank High. But at the same time, it does not address problems that arise *translocally*, as soon as the locally acquired (and locally adequate) symbolic resources are 'exported', so to speak, to other places and spheres of society, crossing different scale-levels.

The dynamics of exclusion and marginalization in environments such as South Africa (but, by the same token, also elsewhere) involve complex scalar processes in which what counts as adequate and acceptable at one scale-level can be disqualified at another scale-level. Concretely, what counts as 'good English' in the township may be 'bad English' at the regional or state level. Inequality occurs on the boundaries between scales, the points of transition from strict locality to translocality, from a level defined by the rules and codes of one place to a level defined by the rules and norms of different places. At such points of transition, the issue is the *mobility offered by semiotic resources* such as language skills: some skills offer a very low degree of mobility while others offer a considerably larger degree of mobility and transferability across social and spatial domains. 'Standard' literacy usually falls in the second category, while 'non-standard' literacy falls in the first category, even if from one perspective it can be seen as 'full', developed, complex literacy within a restricted repertoire of literacy skills and resources.

Clearly, such a diagnosis casts a different light on issues too often caught in totalizing images of clashing languages, linguistic imperialism and oppositions between 'local' and 'international' languages. In analyses drawing on such images, the sociolinguistic process is reduced to a confrontation between a language from the outside (e.g. English) and people from the inside (old-style 'natives', to some extent) who are forced to use the outside language (e.g. Webb 1994; Mazrui 2004). The scheme thus drawn is attractively simple and it invokes moral and political frames of independence versus oppression, exclusion versus inclusion, respect versus rejection. Sociolinguistic reality – alas! – is considerably more complex and ambiguous. One of the main features of the language regime in Wesbank High, for instance, is the fact that 'English' is a multiplex item composed of at least two different objects: *English₁*, an ideologically conceived homogeneous and idealized notion of 'English-the-language-of-success', and *English₂*, a situationally and locally organized pragmatics of using 'English' in ways rather distant from English₁. This is a dynamics of re-appropriation, localization and relocalization in a repertoire, in which an unattainable English₁ is transformed into an attainable resource, lowering the threshold of access while maintaining its status, appeal and perceived transferability into upward and outward trajectories. English is thus both: it remains a language from the outside (English₁), but has simultaneously been made into a language from the inside (English₂). It is not just a 'foreign' language, but it has become 'our' language as well.

Ethnographic inquiry into such processes of locality and transferability opens up a wide range of issues and casts them in a fundamentally new light. The processes observed in Wesbank High cannot be understood when assuming the existence of one stable, singular and uniform perception of normativity in the field of literacy, nor in the field of 'language' in general. Instead, a more fragmented, contextualized and localized perception is required in which allowance is made for understanding practices in terms of repertoires, of a local play-off of structure and agency, of determination and creativity.

3.4   Images from the periphery

Ruhumbika as well as the people of Wesbank High articulated images of the world – images of their own peripheral position in the world as well as images of better places and of mobility, of trajectories towards these better places. In the case of Ruhumbika, such images were used ascriptively, as a way of defining and identifying characters in a novel. In the case of the learners and teachers in Wesbank High, these images were inhabited, they were the 'logic of practice' (in the sense of Bourdieu) that organized their worldview, learning procedures and aspirations. In both instances, the imagery was part of locality, it was a local imagery that was deeply embedded in the local conditions of life – those of the periphery of the world-system. And seen from the periphery, the world – and globalization – looks very different from how it is seen from the centre.

The world *is* very different too. People do not have the same resources everywhere, and scarcity of resources yields strange images of wealth of resources, and vice versa. The expectations people have of others, of people from other places, is very often not matched by the actual features and resources these people possess. People's resources reveal their place in the world, their resources are 'placed', so to speak, in that they betray the locality from where they are drawn and in which they fit. This raises issues of repertoires, and the next chapter will address them. For now, we can observe the particular kind of spatial determination that emerges from a sociolinguistic view of globalization. An American song sung by an adolescent in Finland acquires a Finnish accent; it acquires a Belgian accent when sung by a youngster from Belgium, a Nigerian accent when sung by a Nigerian, a Japanese accent when sung by a Japanese child, and so forth. Sociolinguistically, globalization is a strongly local and localizing phenomenon, in which strong features of local sociolinguistic regimes operate on the bits of globalized language that enter the local environments.

This to some extent qualifies existing views of cultural globalization as predominantly *globalizing*. The literature often emphasizes how local communities and places *change* because of globalization. They do, but overemphasizing change can obscure the importance of continuity in such processes, and certainly from a sociolinguistic viewpoint, continuity is as important as change, the persistence of patterns is as important as the transformation of patterns due to globalization.

4   Repertoires and competence

I argued in the preceding chapters that a sociolinguistics of globalization needs to be a sociolinguistics of mobile resources, not one of immobile languages. Our focus of analysis should be the actual linguistic, communicative, semiotic resources that people have, not abstracted and idealized (or ideologized) representations of such resources. Our focus should, therefore, be on repertoires, on the complexes of resources people actually possess and deploy. I already mentioned the 'truncated' nature of multilingual repertoires in super-diverse contexts such as those of a contemporary 'global' city. Multilingualism, I argued, should not be seen as a collection of 'languages' that a speaker controls, but rather as a complex of *specific* semiotic resources, some of which belong to a conventionally defined 'language', while others belong to another 'language'. The resources are concrete accents, language varieties, registers, genres, modalities such as writing – ways of using language in particular communicative settings and spheres of life, including the ideas people have about such ways of using, their language ideologies. What matters in the way of language for real languages users are these concrete forms of language, or, to go by Hymes' words:

> The place of language in the life of the community would be understood as more than a matter of sounds, spellings, grammatical categories and constructions. It would be properly understood as involving varieties and modalities, styles and genres, ways of using a language as a resource. (Hymes 1996: 70)

Shifting our focus from 'languages' (primarily an ideological and institutional construct) to resources (the actual and observable ways of using language) has important implications for notions such as 'competence', as I will try to demonstrate shortly. The question of what it is to 'know' a language, to 'speak it well' or to 'be fluent' in it will have to be reformulated, and some existing tools for measuring the answers to such questions (as in language testing schemes) will have to be critically revisited. A clearer understanding of repertoires, furthermore, may add detail and precision to analyses of communication processes in the world of globalized communication, where people often communicate with bits and pieces of genres and registers. Understanding that communication processes do not just proceed through 'a language' but through specialized and particular pieces of language may help us find a diagnostic for what, in a very vast literature, is called 'intercultural misunderstandings'. That, too, I will try to illustrate in this chapter.

4.1   Truncated repertoires

No one knows *all* of a language. That counts for our so-called mother tongues and, of course, also for the other 'languages' we acquire in our life time. Native speakers are not perfect speakers. Hymes emphatically warns us against the 'fallacy to equate the resources of a language with the resources of (all) users' (Hymes 1996: 213). There is nothing wrong with that phenomenon of partial competence: no one needs all the resources that a language potentially provides. We all have specific language competences and skills: we can use particular genres quite acceptably, speak in the registers that are typical of some social roles and identities, produce the accents of our native regions, and deploy the schooled literacy of our education trajectories. Our real 'language' is very much a biographical given, the structure of which reflects our own histories and those of the communities in which we spent our lives.

As an illustration, and with lots of reservations as to representativity and accuracy, consider the graphic in figure 4.1. It represents my own multilingual competences in four languages: Dutch (L1), French (L2), German (L3) and English (L4).

The four languages are ordered on the basis of the sequence in which they entered my repertoire: first Dutch, then (from the age of 8) French, then German (age 12) and English (age 13). In the graphic, I have set scores not for the languages, but for specific modes of usage of the languages: oral vernacular varieties (dialects, specific dialects and sociolects), oral standard varieties

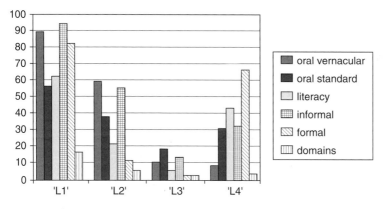

Figure 4.1 The truncated repertoire

(e.g. the varieties I should use in formal communicative situations), literacy level (specifically writing), competences to communicate in formal settings, in informal settings, and finally the range of domains in which I can successfully communicate. These divisions are just illustrative and indicative; a full-blown analysis of my repertoire would require much more in the way of distinctions. But with these rough indicators, perhaps the point may be made clearly.

We see that the range of competences and skills in Dutch is highest and most balanced. I am capable in Dutch of deploying oral vernacular as well as standard varieties; I can have informal contact as well as perform formal communication tasks, I can write complex formal texts in the language, and can communicate within a wide range of domains. If we compare this profile with French, however, we see some striking differences. My proficiency in vernacular varieties is higher than that in standard varieties, for instance. The reason is that the standard varieties I acquired were confined to classroom environments, while I acquired vernacular varieties as an adolescent growing up in Brussels, where vernacular French was the language of interaction with local friends and customers in my father's shop. Whenever I speak French now, it would have a distinct Flemish-Brussels accent. My literacy levels are not very well developed either. I can easily read French, but not write elaborate French prose. And while I can be a rather fluent communicator in informal contacts (using my vernacular French), lecturing or giving formal speeches in French would be tasks that exceed my resources.

German came into my life earlier than English, yet when we compare the profiles for both languages, we see sharp differences. German never rose above the level of a school language; English, in contrast, became a fairly developed tool, even if it entered my life at a relatively late stage. It entered my life as a professional tool, and this explains the absence of vernacular varieties (I do not know any dialects or slang varieties in English) and the very high level of literacy development. Most of my academic writing is in English, and I also lecture almost entirely in that language. The range of domains, however, is rather small. While I can pass for a fluent and articulate speaker in academic and professional domains, other skills in other domains are very underdeveloped. I am fairly inarticulate when I need to go shopping in a supermarket in the UK or when I need to explain a health problem to a doctor in English. I can, consequently, be seen as a very articulate speaker by some, and as a very inarticulate one by others – and all in the same 'language'.

This is where language tests often miss the point. In attempting to set average proficiency levels in 'languages', they overlook the very specific nature of language use, of the various chunks and pieces of language that we deploy for specific tasks. If we take, for instance, the terms of reference of the Common European Framework for Languages (the most authoritative measuring tool of the moment), and apply it to my English skills, we would see strange things.[1] As long as I can communicate within my formal, professional registers, I would not hesitate to qualify my performance in the terms of European Language Level C2 – the highest proficiency level:

Can understand with ease virtually everything heard or read. Can summarize information from different spoken and written sources, reconstructing arguments and accounts in a coherent presentation. Can express him/herself spontaneously, very fluently and pre-cisely, differentiating finer shades of meaning even in more complex situations.

If, however, I am asked to explain a technical problem in English to a plumber or an electrical engineer, or a health problem to a doctor, or a technical financial issue to an officer of the finance department of my university, my level of proficiency would more accurately be described as:

Can understand and use familiar everyday expressions and very basic phrases aimed at the satisfaction of needs of a concrete type. Can introduce him/herself and others and can ask and answer questions about personal details such as where he/she lives, people he/she knows and things he/she has. Can interact in a simple way provided the other person talks slowly and clearly and is prepared to help.

Which is the description of European Language Level A1, the most elemen-tary level of language proficiency. Testing systems, such as the European Language Levels, stand in a curious relationship to the real resources and skills that people have, because they believe they measure languages, while in fact they measure specific resources. If I were to be tested on the basis of test materials that fall within my range of highly developed skills, my score would probably be very high; if the test materials fall outside that range, my score would be very low.

   All of this is common sense and, as said above, a real analysis would require far more than what I have used here in the way of sophistication and argument. But the point deserves to be underscored, if for no other reason than because of the persistence of language-based views of competence in our fields of scholar-ship. The issue should be clear: we always have a determined range of specific competences, and some are very highly developed while others are consider-ably less developed. And there are always resources that we do not possess. The answer to the puzzle of our repertoires is in our biographies and the wider histories of the communities in which we live. If such communities are 'mono-lingual', in the sense that the available linguistic resources belong to what is conventionally defined as a specific language such as Dutch, then it is very likely that our repertoire will be composed of Dutch resources; if the available resources are derived from various conventionally defined languages, our repertoire is likely to be 'multilingual'. And acquiring these resources (a process usually called 'language learning') would in effect be the construction of a multilingual repertoire. We would acquire the linguistic features of these languages – their sounds, words, grammatical patterns of use – as well as some of their pragmatic features – ways of organizing interaction in such languages, communicative routines, registers that enable us to perform certain roles and identities – and cultural patterns – the use of genres, the language-ideological load of particular expressions, and so forth.

As argued in chapter 1, the super-diversity that arises from globalization processes results in communities of people whose repertoires are structured as such: as truncated complexes of resources often derived from a variety of languages, and with considerable differences in the level of development of particular resources. Parts of these multilingual repertoires will be fairly well developed, while others exist only at a very basic level. Immigrant children, for instance, may grow up in a family in which they hear their parents speak a language. They can understand this language, and respond adequately to utterances made in it, but they never learn to speak it. This does not mean that this language does not belong to the children's repertoire: it does belong to it, be it only in a minimal and receptive form. These children, conversely, speak the language of the host society, and will help their parents accomplish communicative tasks in that language. The language of the host society, thus, indirectly belongs to the range of available resources of the parents as well, because they can draw on their children's repertoire to achieve communication goals in it. The truncated repertoires of new immigrants often compel them to collaborative communicative work, in which the little bits of competence of some are added to those of others. The result is often something that has a very unfinished character: partial realizations of genres with partially 'correct' bits of languages.

We have seen several such 'unfinished' products in the previous chapters, and the 'unfinished' character of language and communication is probably one of the clearest objects of inquiry for a sociolinguistics of globalization. It is clear that mobility creates all sorts of challenges for people, while it of course also offers opportunities. Messages and people become more mobile, and this requires a stretching of the repertoires, often beyond their limits. Notwithstanding that, we see that some forms of 'unfinished' communication are quite successful, and I will now turn to one such success story: email fraud messages sent from the periphery of the world to the centre of the world. We will see that these messages, too, raise complex issues of competence.

4.2   Globalized genres of fraud

Dear, Sir
>
> I am writing following the impressive information about you through one of my friends who runs a consultancy firm under Nigeria Chamber of Commerce and Industry. He assured me of your Capability and Reliability to Champion a Business of great Magnitude

>
> I am Dr.Joseph Diara,The personal assistant to the newly appointed Accountant General Of The Federation (A.G.F)I and One of my colleagues are in custody of US$19.3MILLION,Which is an unclaimed foreign contract payment.This fund is currently in the suspence account of our paying ministry awaiting immediate claim.
>
> I have concluded every arrangement to make you clam this fund on our behalf as the true Beneficiary/Contractor.
>
> Please,If you are serious and interested in handling this transaction from your end, Do notify me by email or call me on my direct phone:234–80–452–15660.for further details.Please,send your response
> to:josephdiara@hotmail.com
>
> Yours Sincerely,
> Dr.Joseph Diara

(sample 1)

Here is a genre of contemporary globalized communication: an email spam, hoax message, originating presumably from somewhere in the periphery of the world and sent to a large number of addressees in the core countries of the world-system. This spam mail is associated with what has been tagged by the Federal Bureau of Investigation (FBI) as the 'Nigerian Advanced Fee Fraud', also known as '419 scams' after the section of the Nigerian Penal Code on financial crimes. The general pattern of the direction of 419 emails is a South-to-North run. The message is oriented towards a particular kind of subject in affluent societies: someone greedy enough to give in to the temptation of earning millions with an email reply. The 419 scams are quite successful. There are numerous reported and documented cases of these, sufficient for the Central Intelligence Agency and FBI to mention the scam on their official websites. The Central Bank of Nigeria has also published disclaimers in major newspapers around the world. Notwithstanding this prevailing South–North direction of interactions, the largest 419 scam on record is a South-on-South crime which led to the collapse of Banco Noroeste in Sao Paolo, Brazil, after Nigerian scam perpetrators siphoned US$242 million from the bank. It is clear that the messages appeal to many people: the orientations to particular subjects are effective, thus raising questions about the 'how' and 'what' of the messages.

In order for these orientations to be effective, the messages need to corre-spond to a wide variety of linguistic, stylistic and generic criteria – criteria that provide desired forms of presupposability, the right forms of indexical values to allow the message to be read as a genuine, bona fide business proposal. I would suggest that this complex of linguistic, stylistic and generic requirements projected onto a concrete textual artefact can be read as the lowest empirically observable level of globalization, as globalization-on-the-ground. I would, however, also suggest that such a conclusion cannot merely be drawn from prima facie characteristics of the document – for instance, the fact that it is distributed by the globalized channel *par excellence*, email – but that substantially more is required, and that we need in particular to address the minuscule linguistic, stylistic and generic features of such texts in order to arrive at a precise view of what language does in globalization contexts.

The reason, already emphasized a number of times before, is that we need to understand not only the simple fact of 'flow' but also the content and function of flows: the way, concretely, in which documents such as these can articulate or fail to articulate identities, intentions, contexts of intelligibility. In other words, the target is to understand how texts flowing through the channels of globalization can have textual functions. Such functions, sociolinguists have long assumed, are nested in sociolinguistic systems firmly grounded in the sociocultural and political fabric of 'speech communities', often seen as local. Globalization now clearly complicates the associative link between locality, speech community and communicative function. While we have some answers to the question about how to imagine translocal speech communities, we still struggle to come to terms with the idea of translocal functions. Texts such as these may offer us a glimpse into the potential and limitations of translocal functioning.

The theoretical drift of what follows is the tension between uniformity and diversity, which might be at the core of globalization processes. I want to establish the following points: (1) the authors of these email messages are fully inserted in the technology of globalized communication; (2) furthermore, there is very clearly also a significant degree of awareness of generic conventions for the messages; (3) however, the authors fail to produce 'complete', 'faultless' realizations of the genres. This then, I will argue, produces rich indexical messages which exclude some addressees and include others. In other words, incomplete instances of genre realization create peculiar translocal speech networks. This phenomenon may shed light on issues of communicative competence in a globalized environment: what we see is truncated competence, different competences co-occurring and together creating messages that might work or fail, depending on the degrees to which the different competences are developed. Before developing this argument, I shall have to introduce the data on which it is based.

The data: preliminary observations

Like many others, I receive email messages such as the above on a regular basis. The concrete analysis will be conducted on a small corpus of 56 messages between April and June 2005. Data collection proceeded indiscriminately, copying every message that reached my mailbox – about one per day. Apart from the fact that none of the messages is long (ranging between half a printed page and two printed pages), they all share a number of features: (i) almost all of them are written in varieties of English; (ii) they are all sent through international free providers; (iii) they all represent an attempt at a formal, official style of writing; (iv) the senders all pose as elite members in control of flows of money and knowledgeable about transfer procedures, and (v) they all offer to transfer sums of money into my account on a confidential basis. The amounts, stated in US$, Sterling or Euro, vary between 0.5 million dollars and 410.4 million dollars. The appendix to this chapter provides an overview of the corpus.

Types of offers   Typologically, we can distinguish four major types of offers.

1. Dormant accounts   Almost half of the offers made (25) are about what we could call 'dormant accounts'. Here is a typical story:

> **Ex. 1**
>
> > Dear Partner,
> > I guess this letter might come to you as a surprise since I had no previous correspondence with you, But with due respect I got your contact in my research for a reliable and honest person who will be capable and fit to assist me in handling a very confidential transaction involving the transfer of US75 million dollars only.
> > I want to transfer these funds to overseas(75.000,000.00USD) Seventy Five million United States Dollars).For our sharing and investment purposes in your country.
> > The above fund is not connected with arms, drugs or Money laundering; neither is it related to any terrorist sponsor of any sort.
> > I am Jumbo Williams Akunne,an accountant and Bank manager, The Executive and the Board of Directors have approved and accredited this reputed Bank with the office of the Director,International Remmitance/ Foreign Operation, to handle and transfer all foreign inherittance funds this final quarter of the year. I have my client involved who died in a plane crash with his wife and children,though i have tried to contact any of the relatives but to no avail and without any traceable next of kin,Hence the dormant nature of His account and if I do not remit this money out urgently it will be re-channeled into the bank's reserve.
>
> (sample 2)

The author often poses as a banking or insurance executive who has knowledge of and access to a large unclaimed sum of money, left in an account upon the tragic death of the owner, and often in danger of being appropriated by the state. The purpose of the transaction is money laundering: to get the sum out of the present account and country and funnel it into our bank account. (Note how in such messages, images of corrupt governments and inept bureaucracies are activated.)

2. Lottery rewards   About one quarter of the offers (13) assumes the shape of an announcement that I have won a substantial amount of money in an Internet lottery. Here is a typical announcement:

> **Ex. 2**
> We are pleased to inform you of the result of the Our Global Email Lottery programme held on the 26th April 2005.
> > Your e-mail address attached to ticket number 37511465899–6410 with serial number 4872–510 drew lucky numbers 7–14–88–23–3545 which consequently won in the 1st category, you have therefore been approved for a lump sum pay out of US$ 1,000,000.00 (One Million United States Dollars).
> >
> > CONGRATULATIONS!!!
> > Due to mix up of some numbers and names, we ask that you keep your winning information confidential until your claims has been processed and your money Remitted to you. This is part of our security protocol to avoid double claiming and unwarranted abuse of this programme by some participants.
> >
> > All participants were selected through a computer ballot system drawn from over 20,000 company and 30,000,000 individual email addresses and names from all over the world. This promotional programme takes place every three years. We hope with part of your winning you will take part in our next USD 50 million international lottery.
> >
> > To file for your claim, please contact our fiducial agent/attorney:
> > ======================================
> > BARRISTER. ROY HANS (ROYAL ADVOCATEN KANTOR)
> > Amsterdam-Netherlands.
> > Tel: (31) 617 792 760.
> > Fax: (31) 847 506 277.
> > E-Mail: RoyHansBVA@netscape.net
> > ======================================

(sample 28)

Lottery messages offer the lowest amounts of money (between 0.5 and 5.5 million $) but, as we can see, with promises of substantially higher gains in future rounds.

3. Rescue operations   Twelve offers suggest that I assist people who have got into trouble in their homeland to get their capital out of the country and made accessible to them, in return for a hefty reward. Here is an example:

Ex. 3

> My Name is MRS.SUZANA NUHAN VAYE from Liberia, a Country in West Africa. My late Husband is Issac Nuhan Vaye, Deputy Minister of Public Works in Liberia. My Husband was falsely accused of plotting to remove the then PRESIDENT OF LIBERIA CHARLES TAYLOR) from office. Without trial, Charles Taylor killed him. You can verify this from some of the international newspapers posted in the web sites below:
>
> (I)http://www.usatoday.com/news/world/2003–07–15-liberia_x.htm
>
> Before my husband was killed, he moved out the sum of $21.5 million through a diplomatic means, and deposited it with a Security Company Abroad. And this money was meant for importation of agricultural machineries.
>
> All that is needed is for my lawyer to instruct the company to transfer the funds to your account, I will remunerate you with 20% at the end, but most of all is that I solicit your trust and honesty in this transaction. I have been confined only to our country home and all my calls are monitored, so I will advise you contact my private Attorney Barr. P.O.Williams base in United Kingdom on his contact stated below for onward proceedings: -

(sample 41)

4. Charity A final type, of which my corpus has five examples, is a rather remarkable appeal to assist in charity. The author in all five cases poses as a devout Muslim who feels that the end of his life is near, and who tries to give his fortune to charities. Here is an example:

Ex. 4

> Now that God has called me, I have willed and given most of my property and assets to my immediate and extended family members as well as a few close friends. I want God to be merciful to me and accept my soul, I have decided to give alms to charity organizations, as I want this to be one of the last good deeds, I ever do on earth. So far, I have distributed money to some charity Organizations in the U.A.E, Algeria and Malaysia.
>
> Now that my health has deteriorated so badly, I cannot do this myself anymore. I once asked members of my family to close one of my accounts and distribute the money which I have there to charity organization in Bulgaria and Pakistan; they refused and kept the money to themselves. Hence, I do not trust them anymore, as they seem not to be contended with what I have left for them.
>
> The last of my money which no one knows of is the huge cash deposit in Europe whort eighteen Million US dollars (US$18,000,000.00) that I have with a deposit company abroad.
>
> Acknowledge this message so that I can introduce you to my lawyer who will handle the transfer of receivership by you of the above said funds.

>
> I will want you to help me collect this deposit and dispatched it to charity organizations. My lawyer shall put you in the picture of the funds, tell you where the funds are currently being maintained and also discuss modalities including remuneration for your services.

(sample 30)

In all four types, the story is different, and different moral frames are being invoked. There are offers that appeal to western liberal sentiments to invoke recipients' sympathy over the violation of human rights; offers which claim to have a philanthropic purpose, that is, the reason adduced for transferring the fund in question is to make a donation to a charitable or religious cause; and thirdly, some offers court reverse morality by claiming that they are 'saving' the funds they seek to transfer from falling into the hands of wayward establishment officials. But the patterns and procedure are identical in all cases: for unexplained reasons, I have personally been chosen as the preferred partner in a money transaction of considerable size and substance; I have to open a new bank account in which the money can be placed. And whatever the nature of the services I render to the authors of such messages, I shall be very generously rewarded.

Origin of the messages   From the email address we may be able to determine where a scam mail is from – each country (except the USA) has a registered node 'uk', 'ca', 'ch', 'hk', 'de', 'ng' etc. But there are neutral nodes on the free email services such as gmail.com, yahoo.com and hotmail.com which are more difficult for unschooled eyes to read. Also, it is possible to register an address in a country without being resident there through a falsification of personal details. The 56 messages in our corpus are sent by people claiming to write from 14 different countries. Table 4.1 presents an overview.

Table 4.1 *Claimed origin of authors*

Nigeria	11
UK	10
South Africa	7
The Netherlands	7
Benin	5
Ivory Coast	5
Dubai	3
Russia	2
China/Hong Kong	2
Liberia	2
Italy	1
Zimbabwe	1
Ghana	1
Senegal	1

The UK and the Netherlands are the sources of 'lottery' messages – seven and six messages respectively – and such 'lottery' items do not originate in other countries (with one exception, sample 19, which claims origins in the UK and South Africa). The other categories are dominated by Nigeria or, if we extend regionally, West Africa. Nigeria, Benin, Ivory Coast, Liberia, Ghana and Senegal together account for 25 out of 56 messages. South Africa does rather well with seven messages. If we discount the 'lottery' messages, Europe is the origin of a mere seven messages, and interestingly, three messages from European countries are 'rescue' messages. The two messages from Russia (samples 7 and 29) both claim to be part of an attempt to rescue some of Mikhail Khodorovsky's Yukos fortune while he does his time in jail; the message from Italy (sample 2) purports to protect the interests of Mr. Luigi Morgera, a Parmalat executive caught in fraud trials.

The messages, as a rule, offer an email reply address (about which I shall have to say more below), and in a number of cases also a telephone number. With one or two exceptions, the phone numbers corroborate the claimed place of origin. Authors claiming to be from Nigeria offer a Nigerian phone number, authors from the UK, a British phone number. The story of email providers, however, is considerably more complex and already offers us some insights into the patterns of globalization against which we have to interpret these documents.

Knowing your way around the globe: aliases, anonymous providers

All of the authors use open, anonymous commercial providers for sending and receiving messages. It is obvious that some attention has gone towards avoiding a recognizable trace of identity and creating opportunities for erasing one's traces and posing as an alias. A quick look at the selection of providers in the appendix yields a genuinely globalized picture.

Authors, without exception, choose commercial free providers of the Hotmail or Yahoo type, providers that offer free email addresses and some (limited) server space. These providers can be found all over the world, and authors in the corpus use providers based in Malaysia, Mexico, Spain, Italy, the UK, Russia, the USA, the Netherlands, the Philippines Turkey, China and Hong Kong, South Africa, Canada, France, Denmark, Uruguay, Poland, Argentina, Australia, New Zealand, India and Israel. With almost no exceptions, providers are based in countries other than the ones claimed to be the place of origin of the messages – messages are claimed to be sent from Nigeria, but they are sent through providers in the USA, Uruguay or the Philippines (note that none appears to be based in Belgium, the country of the addressee in this case). And often, the reply address is different from the sending address, indicating that probably, the authors frequently shift base, so to speak, from one provider to another.

The choice of providers is sometimes ingenious. Thus, sample 9 carries the message: 'mail sent from Webmail service at http://www.puk-en-muk.com'.

The latter is a second-hand clothing store in Hansweert, the Netherlands. Several messages are sent from http://yoursite.com, a US-based computer superstore. And sample 22 is sent from handbag.com, a women's e-zine based in the UK. The servers from which some messages have been sent no longer existed when I checked on them two months after receiving the message, perhaps suggesting that servers are being set up and dismantled repeatedly so as to prevent localizing efforts by others.

Add to this the capacity to do extensive and detailed searches for individual addressees on the Internet (emails are sent directly to one address and often also use the addressee's name in the text – the mails are personalized), and we can see that we are witnessing advanced computer skills here. The authors of these messages know their way around the world of virtual communication. In order to find providers such as the ones they use, thorough and well-targeted searches on the Internet are required; setting up email addresses, changing them, and keeping track of the complex flows of messages thus generated; knowing that providers can be accessed 24/7; and knowing that choosing far away, small providers can help create virtual anonymity – all of these are forms of highly developed computer literacy. The people authoring these messages are street-wise in the world of the Internet. They are fully competent users of the technology of globalized communication.

The complex forms of 'placing' – where the message is claimed to be sent from; where it is actually sent through, and so on – necessitate identity work, and authors make efforts to provide plausible aliases. Thus, for example, the lottery co-ordinator in sample 40 claims to be based in Britain and calls himself 'Simon Croft'; another one (sample 22) claims to be based in the Netherlands and calls himself 'Jan Van Klein' (not a very common, but also not an unlikely Dutch name). Sometimes, however, the use of 'placed' aliases (aliases that suggest a particular regional belonging) can backfire. The author of the lottery message in sample 51, based in the Netherlands, calls himself 'Van Bell' (to be contacted through a provider in Argentina); the one of sample 31 signs with 'Zack Sonnie' – both are highly unusual Dutch names. And the most unlikely one is that in sample 27 – a lottery message supposedly from the Netherlands and signed by 'Anton Geesink'. Anton Geesink is a good Dutch name, but it happens to be the name of a Dutch Judo legend, the giant who gained eternal Olympic glory when he won the gold medal in the heavyweight category at the 1964 Tokyo Olympics, defeating the Japanese favourite. And the authors of sample 28, again claiming to be from the Netherlands, refer to:

Ex. 5
> BARRISTER. ROY HANS (ROYAL ADVOCATEN KANTOR)

They overlook the fact that 'barrister' would be a very unlikely title in the Dutch legal system (where 'advocate', 'attorney' or 'lawyer' would be most common, and where the title would be 'Mr' – 'Master'), where 'advocaten kantor' ought to be 'advocatenkantoor' (one word, double 'o'), and where the title 'Royal' can only be carried by royal appointment, again a very unlikely qualification for 'Roy Hans advocaten kantor'.

In spite of these shaky examples, we see that, in general, authors display an awareness of degrees of isomorphism between names and places: British names when the author is supposed to be based in Britain, Dutch ones when in the Netherlands, and so on. There is an awareness of 'national' features across the world, and there is an awareness of the rest of the world. Authors mention other countries in their messages, sometimes so as to provide accounts of migration trajectories (of people or of money), or to display their international networking ability. I will come back to this feature below.

Let us take stock of what we have for the moment. Clearly, the messages are sent by people who are fully conversant with the technology of globalized communication. They know how to use the opportunities offered by the Internet to send personalized messages while remaining anonymous and untraceable, and they also know that the plausibility of messages can depend on 'placing' signs such as 'local' names. In other words, the authors are no Internet illiterates, quite the contrary: they possess advanced Internet skills, and they are fully inserted into the economies of global communication. This is a first type of communicative competence they display: they are fully competent in the technology of electronic communication. And this, remember, is the first point I wanted to establish.

Constructing genres

The second point is the awareness of genre conventions for drafting messages such as these, designed to travel through the globalized communication systems, crossing continents and time zones. There is a striking generic uniformity across the corpus. As genres, the messages are 'fully formed' (to use Hymes' 1998 terms); in the very least, they are in a process of stabilization. And in each of the cases, authors make efforts to deploy *registers of knowledgeability* in their messages, attempting to convey specific indexicalities of identity, purpose and truthfulness.

Two main genres can be distinguished: (i) the 'lottery' messages are by and large composed as *administrative and formal* texts, and they stand out by their deployment of 'technical' and procedural registers; (ii) the 'dormant', 'rescue' and 'charity' types are composed as *narratives of experience and trust*, and they are marked by registers of personal involvement, rapport and faith. We shall briefly discuss the first type and dwell somewhat longer on the second.

Administrative-formal genres   'Lottery' messages share a basic structural pattern. I shall use sample 31 to illustrate this.

i. A technical, businesslike subject line containing number references

Ex. 6

> 10TH GLOBAL PROMO-ORGANIZATION INTERNATIONAL PROGRAM, THE NETHERLANDS.
> ALFONSTRAAT B56, 1002 BS AMSTERDAM, THE NETHERLANDS.
> FROM: THE DESK OF THE PROMOTIONS MANAGER, INTERNATIONAL
> PROMOTIONS/PRIZE AWARD DEPARTMENT,
>
> REF: OYL /26510460037/02
> BATCH: 24/00319/IPD
>
> ATTENTION: RE/ AWARD NOTIFICATION; FINAL NOTICE

The tone and style are impersonal; there is no establishment of a personal form of involvement between sender and addressee. The messages also usually carry neutral terms of address: 'Dear Sir/Madam', 'Dear Winner', or in one or two cases a more marked 'Dear Lucky Winner'.

ii. An announcement of the award and of the procedure of selection

Ex. 7

> We are pleased to inform you of the announcement of winners of the 10TH GLOBAL PROMO-ORGANIZATION INTERNATIONAL PROGRAM, THE NETHERLANDS held the 23rd of april 2005. Having picked your email address by our electronic web site visitors collators in recognition of your patronage to the internet services, in the final draw, your name was attached to Ticket number 023–0148–790–459, with Serial number 5073–11 drew the Lucky numbers 43–11–44–37–10–43, and consequently won the lottery in the 3rd category. You have therefore been approved for a lump sum pay out of US$850.000.00 in cash credited to file REF NO.OYL / 26510460037/02. This is from total prize money of US$80,400,000.00 shared among the Twenty-nine international winners in this category.
>
> All participants were selected through a computer ballot system drawn from 25,000 names from Australia, New Zealand, America, Europe, North, Africa, America and Asia as part of International Promotions Programme, which is conducted annually.

Note the dense concentration of numbers, dates, references to institutional and technical items ('Global Promo-Organizational International Programme', '3rd category', 'credited to file REF NO.OYL/26510460037/02' etc.)

iii. A request for confidentiality and an invitation to initiate a procedure of claiming the award

Ex. 8

Your fund is now deposited with a Bank in Amsterdam, insured in your name.

> Due to the mix up of some numbers and names, we ask that you keep This award strictly from public notice until your claim has been processed and your money remitted to your account. This is part of our security protocol to avoid double claiming or unscrupulous acts by participants of this programme.
>
> To begin your claim, please contact our information centre at :
> infocentre@compaqnet.fr. For due processing and remittance of your prize money to a designated account of your choice.
>
> Note: In order to avoid unnecessary delays and complications, please remember to quote your reference and batch numbers in every one of your correspondences with your agent. Furthermore, should there be any change of your address, do inform your claims agent as soon as possible.

As can be seen, this part also contains the email address and phone number of a contact person. Note that the reply address operates through a provider in France.

iv. A closing formula
Ex. 9
Congratulations again from all our staff and thank you for being part of our promotions programme.
>
> Sincerely,
> Zack Sonnie.
> THE PROMOTIONS MANAGER,
> 10TH GLOBAL PROMO-ORGANIZATION INTERNATIONAL PROGRAM,
> THE NETHERLANDS.

Observe how generic features such as 'thank you for being part of our promotions programme' are directly borrowed from common commercial and promotional discourses. The lottery messages in general, and across the whole spectrum of the corpus, seek close generic identification with such widespread, recognizable commercial genres of communication, including the *cryptica* of jargon, reference numbers and comments on rules and procedures – things nobody understands but everyone instinctively interprets as signs of smooth professionalism, seriousness and really existent capitalism. Things, in other words, that have no referential value whatsoever but that operate totally at an indexical level, where they convey established and hence presupposable indexicals of professional, reliable, capitalist identity.

Narrative genres   The messages belonging to the 'dormant account', 'rescue operation' and 'charity' types mentioned in section 2 are more diverse in style, although they all assume *narrative orientations* to the genre, and all seek *personal rapport and involvement*. And like in the case of the lottery messages, there is a general template which can be summarized as follows:

i. Personal, direct address
ii. An apology and introduction
iii. A micro-narrative about the origin of the money
iv. An invitation to engage in a business transaction
v. Requests for confidentiality
vi. Closing formula

Stylistically however, they lack the smoothness and uniformity of the lottery messages; there are very diverse realizations of the narrative. Below are some of their peculiarities.

i. Terms of address   Authors use very different terms of address. The most neutral would be '(Dear) Sir', 'Attn: Sir', or 'Attn: Jan Blommaert', but many messages carry affective terms of address invoking strong personal involvement and rapport. Here is a list:

> Dear Friend (samples 3, 14, 16, 18, 29, 30, 42, 43, 56)
> Dear Partner (samples 4, 7, 46)
> Dear One (sample 44)
> Dearest One (sample 10)
> My Dear (samples 12, 39, 48)
> Dear (sample 19)
> Hello Dear (sample 50)
> Dear Respectful (sample 20)
> Attn: Please (sample 25)
> My letter to you (sample 26)
> ASALAM ALYKOM (sample 37)
> Good day (to you) (samples 36, 37, 38, 52)
> ATTN: MD/CEO (sample 41)
> For your kind attention (sample 49)

Needless to say, terms of address such as 'Hello Dear', 'My Dear', 'Dear One', or 'Dear Respectful' are slightly marked as choices within the context of what is supposed to be an inchoate business relationship. But *passons*.

ii. Apologies and introductions   The messages often contain profuse apologies for initiating contact. Interestingly, in doing so they often articulate an awareness of generic appropriateness conditions. In the next example, for instance, the author expresses his awareness that this kind of contact might not be the appropriate channel for a very sensitive transaction:

Ex. 10
> Forgive me for approaching you in this manner to discuss a matter, which is very sensitive indeed. Had I another alternative, I would have jumped at it. All I ask is that you take some time to hear me out.

(sample 2)

The tension between the personal nature of the message and the impersonal nature of email (spam) messages is a feature of a good number of such apologetic introductions. Explanations may be given as to how and why the addressee was selected as a potential partner. Interestingly in light of earlier remarks, some messages refer to Internet searches (or 'Internate' searches, sample 33). Here is a small selection; note the sometimes densely affective expressions referring to faith, trust and respect:

Ex. 11

> You may be surprised to receive this letter from me since you do not know me personally.

(sample 3)

Ex. 12

> I guess this letter might come to you as a surprise since I had no previous correspondence with you, But with due respect I got your contact in my research for a reliable and honest person who will be capable and fit to assist me in handling a very confidential transaction involving the transfer of US75 million dollars only.

(sample 4)

Ex. 13

> First,I must apologise to you for using this medium to communicate about this transaction,though it is my great pleasure in writing you this letter on behalf of my colleague and myself.I am Robert Chavez,the manager in charge of auditing and accounting section of a bank in London,UK.My colleague and I have decided to contact you on a business transaction that will be very beneficial to both of us at the end of the transaction.I would be brief and direct to ensure you understand everything properly.

(sample 9)

Ex. 14

> Compliments, I decided to bestow this trust on you, which I pray you will not ignore or betray.
I apologize in advance for any inconveniences this may cause you. I am Barrister Peter Iluo the Personal Attorney to late Mr George K.Marshal, who was a contractor here in Benin Rep.

(sample 39)

Ex. 15

> Kindly accept my apology for sending my mail to you. I am a true God fearing person, and I want you to trust me and help me out in this my condition. I believe you are a highly respected personality, considering the fact that I sourced your profile from a human resource profile database on your country in the Internet.

(sample 41)

Ex. 16

> This letter may come to you as a surprise due to the fact that we have not yet met. I humbly crave your indulgence in sending you this mail.
> I have to say that I have no intentions of causing you any pains so i decided to contact you through this medium. As you read this, I don't want you to feel sorry for me, because, I believe everyone will die someday.

(sample 43)

Ex. 17

> Permit me to inform you of my desire of going into business relationship with you.I got your name and contact I prayed over it and selected your name among other names due to its esteeming nature and the recommendations given to me as a reputable and trust worthy person that I can do business with and by the recommendation, I must not hesitate to confide in you for this simple and sincere business.

(sample 44)

The general tone is clear: this is a one-on-one relationship built on mutual confidence and supported by a realization of mutual material benefits or, in some cases, by the Almighty.[2]

Some of these fragments are almost formulaic, and textual reoccurrences suggest common authorship or extensive borrowing from each other. Compare the following fragments from samples 1 and 48. The author of sample 1 claims to be Nigerian and works through a Hotmail account; the author of sample 48 claims to be from Benin and works through providers in the UK and Denmark.

Ex. 18

> I am writing following the impressive information about you through one of my friends who runs a consultancy firm under Nigeria Chamber of Commerce and Industry. He assured me of your Capability and Reliability to Champion a Business of great Magnitude

(sample 1)

Ex. 19

> As it may interest you to know, I got your impressive information through my good friend who works with chamber of commerce on foreign business relations here in Cotonou-Benin, it is him who recommended your person to me to be viable and capable to champion a business of such magnitude without any problem.

(sample 48)

iii. Stories of origin   Offering an unknown correspondent a couple of millions is a rather unusual proposition, so almost all the messages in this genre offer small narratives about the origin of the money. Here are some samples.

Dormant accounts:

Ex. 20

> I am a branch manager in my Bank and Special Accounting officer to (Dr. Peter.Blommaert) who worked as an expatriate well Engineer with an international oil firm here. On the twenty-first of April 2001, my customer, his wife and their two children were involved in auto-crash along the ever busy Accra-Aflaho High Way. All occupants of the vehicle unfortunately lost their lives. Since then,the Board of Directors of my Bank have made several enquires to their embassy to locate any of my customer's extended relations but to no avail.hence the need to contact you since you share the same family name.I have contacted you to assist in repatriating the money and Property left behind by my client before they get Confiscated or declared unserviceable by the bank where this Huge deposits of US$45.5M was lodged.

(sample 8)

Rescue operations:

Ex. 21

> DURING THE CURRENT CRISIS AGAINST THE FARMERS OF ZIMBABWE BY THE SUPPORTER OF OUR PRESIDENT ROBERT MUGABE TO CLAIM ALL THE WHITE OWNED FARM IN OUR COUNTRY, HE ORDERED ALL THE WHITE FARMERS TO SURRENDER THEIR FAMRS TO HIS PARTY MEMBER AND THEIR FOLLOWERS,

>

> MY FATHER WAS ONE OF THE BEST INDIGENOUS FARMERS IN THE COUNTRY, WHO DID NOT SUPPORT THE PRESIDENT IDEOLOGY, THE PRESIDENT SUPPORTERS INVADED MY FATHER FARM LOOTED AND BURNT DOWN EVERYTHING AND CONFISCATED ALL HIS NIVESTMENTS,

>

> AFTER THE DEATH OF MY FATHER MY MOTHER AND I, ALONG WITH MY YOUNGER ONE DECIDED TO MOVE OUT OF ZIMBABWE FOR THE SAFETY OF OUR LIVES, WE TOOK ALONG WITH US THE MONEY MY FATHER KEPT IN THE SAFE IN MY MOTHER HOUSE WHICH AMOUNTED TO THE SUM OF US$10 M(TEN MILLION UNITED STATES DOLLAS) TO SOUTH AFRICA, THE FUN IS PRESENTL BEING KEPT IN THE SECRET VAULT OF A PRIVATE SECURITY FIRM BASED HERE IN PRETORIA-SOUTH AFRICA, THE OFFICIAL OF THE FIRM BELIEVES THEY ARE HELPING ME IN KEEPING MY PERSONAL VALUABLES NOT REALIZING THAT IT IS MONEY,

>

> MY MOTHER AND MYSELF HAVE DECIDED TO CONTACT ANY RELIABE OVERSEAS FIRM/PERSON WHO COULD ASSIST US TO TRANSFER THIS MONEY OUT OF THE PRIVATE SECURITY COMPANY BECAUSE WE AS ASYLUM SEEKERS HERE IN SOUTH AFRICA CANNOT OPEN A NON-RESIDENT ACCOUNT THROUGH WHICH THIS FUND WILL BE CHANNELED OUT OF SECURITY COMPANY TOAN OVERSEA ACCOUNT,

(sample 23)

Charity

Ex. 22

> Now that God has called me, I have willed and given most of my property and assets to my immediate and extended family members as well as a few close friends. I want God to be merciful to me and accept my soul, I have decided to give alms to charity organizations, as I want this to be one of the last good deeds, I ever do on earth. So far, I have distributed money to some charity Organizations in the U.A.E, Algeria and Malaysia.

>

> Now that my health has deteriorated so badly, I cannot do this myself anymore. I once asked members of my family to close one of my accounts and distribute the money which I have there to charity organization in Bulgaria and Pakistan; they refused and kept the money to themselves. Hence, I do not trust them anymore, as they seem not to be contended with what I have left for them.

>

> The last of my money which no one knows of is the huge cash deposit in Europe whort eighteen Million US dollars (US$18,000,000.00) that I have with a deposit company abroad.

(sample 30)

Despite the considerable diversity in origins provided in the messages, we can see recurrent features. Authors use a limited range of tropes in their stories, and here is a survey:

Money becomes available because of	Samples
Plane crash	4, 6, 9, 17, 24, 38, 48, 53, 56
Car crash	8, 12, 16, 33, 34, 37, 39
Civil war, political problems	3, 7, 10, 23, 29, 41, 55
Contract errors, fraud	1, 2, 25, 26, 54
Illness	30, 42, 43
Assassination	44, 52

Plane and car crashes, as well as stories of contracts and fraud, dominate the 'dormant account' stories; civil war and political problems as well as assassination are typically used in 'rescue operations'; the three instances of illness as a reason for the availability of money are all 'charity' cases.

Interestingly, some authors try to anchor these stories in recognizable contextualizing universes. Sample 14 talks of an Iraqi official who got killed by American bombs during the Iraq invasion of 2003. In sample 15, the money became available when its owners died in the Tsunami disaster of late 2004. The owner of the money in sample 17 died in the Concorde crash in Paris, while the owner mentioned in sample 56 was a passenger in the plane that hit the North

Tower of the WTC building on 11 September 2001. The authors of samples 3 and 23 both claim to be victims of Robert Mugabe's 'redistribution' policies in Zimbabwe, and those of samples 7 and 29 both pose as close collaborators of Mikhail Khodorkovsky, the Russian former Yukos oil mogul. The author of sample 2, finally, claims to be a collaborator of a senior executive of Parmalat, the Italian multinational that got caught up in serious fraud cases.[3] Thus, authors seek recognizable stories, which offer some prima facie plausibility, with a handful of them providing Internet links with information on the events in which they set their offer, to support (part of) their stories.

iv. Reassurances   Some authors go to some length in providing reassuring statements about their sincerity and about the risk-free character of the operation. The author of sample 4, for instance, tries to convince us that we should not have 'any atom of fear':

Ex. 23
> I will use my position in the Bank to do all the underground work and hasten the approval and release of the funds in your favour. I will not fail to bring to your notice that this transaction will be 100% risk free and will only take us 14 Banking days to finalize because as a banker, I know the Banking proceedures, so do not border or entertain any atom of fear as all required arrangement have been made to suit the both parties involved and to achieve success.

(sample 4)

He is echoed in this by the author of sample 37:

Ex. 24
I will not fail to bring to y our notice that this business is hitch free and that you should not entertain any fear as all modalities for fund transfer can be finalized within five banking days, after you apply to the bank as a relation to the deceased.

(sample 37)

The South African author of sample 32 (offering the staggering sum of US$126 million) is confident about the legality of the transaction:

Ex. 25
> I will apply for annual leave to get visa immediately I hear from you that you are ready to act and receive this fund in your account. I will use my position and influence to obtain all legal approvals for onward transfer of this money to your account with appropriate clearance from the relevant ministries and foreign exchange departments.

(sample 32)

And Barrister Malinga Yusuf (Alhadji), like some of his colleagues, actually claims to follow the orders of his superiors in the bank:

Ex. 26

> The sign legalised copy of her WILL is in my chambers, why the original copy is in the bank file. For four yrs now the bank has not seen any foriegn beneficiary presented by me due to my relaxation in law execution. Hence, the bank has called my attention to present a recomended beneficairy to process legal claim of this money and the estate without delay. otherwise the bank will deposit the money into the bank treasury as an unclaimed fund.

(sample 33)

In each of these cases, the reassurances are given on the basis of *identity*: the authors draw upon their influential positions in banks or industries, on procedural knowledge and financial and legal know-how to reassure us of their good intentions and of the guaranteed success of the operation.

v. Confidentiality, honesty and respect   Invariably, authors emphasize the importance of strict confidentiality – even if in the same move they reassure us of the legal and risk-free character of the transaction. They are also upfront about the actual details of the transaction, thus suggesting that the transaction can proceed without preliminary negotiation stages. It is immediately executed on the basis of confidentiality and sincerity:

Ex. 27

> I am Mr. Alex uju of the above address. I am sorry if I have intruded on your privacy or barged on you without your permission.
>
> I have a very rewarding business offer which I will want us to be involved in together with all trust, confidentiality and good brotherliness.

(sample 26)

Ex. 28

> This business itself is 100% safe, provided you treat it with utmost confidentiality. I have reposed my confidence in you and I hope you will not disappoint us. I have the authority of my colleagues involved to propose that should you be willing to assist us in this transaction, your share as compensation will be 20% while my colleagues and I recieve 70%, and the balance 10% for taxes and all other miscelenous expenses incured.

(sample 18)

Ex. 29

> May I at this point emphasize that this transaction is a successful arrangement, as an insider of the bank I have the capacity to monitor that everything is going well. On smooth conclusion of this transaction, you will be entitled to your own share of the total sum as gratification. This share of yours is negotiable as long as it is reasonable. Please, you have been adviced to keep this a top secret as we are still in service and intend to retire from service after we conclude this deal with you. I will be monitoring the whole situation here in this bank until you confirm the mon!

(sample 9)

Ex. 30

You must however NOTE that this transaction is subject to the following terms and conditions: Our convictionof your transparent honesty and diligence. That you would treat this transaction with trust, honesty and confidentiality. That as a foreign partner, you will heed to all instructions to the letter. Kindly commence action as we are almost behind schedule to enable this funds be included in the final quarter of this fiscal year's payment. When you receive this letter, showing your dedication and honesty to assist, I will like you to contact me immediately, so that we take the necessary steps immediately. I look forward to your response.

(sample 17)

Ex. 31

> Then you and me can share the money, 55% to me and 40% to you, and remaining 5% will go to expenses incured by both parties during the course of this transaction. I have all necessary legal documents that can be used to backup any claim we may make. All I require is your honest cooperation to enable this deal through. I guarantee that this will be executed under a legitimate Arrangement that will protect you from any breach of the Law. Please get in touch through my email and send to me your Telephone and fax numbers to enable us further about this Transaction.

(sample 8)

Thus, while the authors define their own reliability in terms of professional identity, competence and knowledgeability, the addressee's reliability is a matter of trust based on sincerity and a capacity to operate discreetly: the professional versus the Good Person. Expressions of respect for this Good Person are abundant throughout the corpus, and they sometimes culminate in very laudatory, slightly baroque closing formulae:

Ex. 32

>Finally, your reward for your noble assistance will be under negotiable. Thanks and remain bless. Waiting for your reply.
Yours sincerely.
Musa Jacob Kamara (JNR).

(sample 20)

Ex. 33

> When you receive this letter, kindly send me an e-mail signifying your interest including your most confidential telephone/fax numbers for quick communication. Respectfully submitted, Dr Dan Obi

(sample 37)

And on one occasion, the author (claiming to work for Lloyds Bank, London, but operating through an Italian provider) sketches the dangers of breaking the rules of confidentiality:

Ex. 34
> Remember this is absolutely confidential. My husband does not know about this risk taking. My family will be in shambles if it burst out and i will also be in trouble aswell as loose my precious job. Your contact phone numbers and name will be necessary for this effect.

(sample 5)

Structural stability and genre If we now take these insights together, we see that the authors of these messages clearly do not write from scratch. They all attempt to construct *specific types of text* from some conceptual templates, texts that produce certain, specific indexicals – texts that carry the message across. This message, let us recall, is that this is all about a genuine, honest business transaction of considerable size and benefit to all those involved in it. And such a message needs to be caught (iconically) in a recognizably 'serious' style, shot through by a wide variety of features that produce meanings that may convince the addressee. The texts, however, are *not explicitly persuasive*, but they are *indexically persuasive*: they try to convince the addressee of the authenticity of the offer through the deployment of generic and stylistic features that lock into existing, recognizable and presupposable indexical values. This is a restricted set of features, and a non-random one, and this explains the structural stability in the messages.

This was the second point I wanted to establish: that apart from being fully literate in the world of globalized communication technology, the authors of these texts are also culturally literate in the sense that they know that some messages, in order to be intelligible and convincing, require specific genre and stylistic characteristics. This is a second type of competence: let us call it cultural competence, the '*knowing what*' of communication. Many of the authors, especially those of the 'dormant account' messages, pose as businessmen, lawyers or bankers, and they adorn their names with categorizing labels such as 'Dr', 'Barrister' or '(Esq)'; they also refer to positions of influence and expertise, and they deploy semiotic emblems of such positions such as technical terminology for types of money (e.g. 'a *profiling amount* in an excess of US$100.5M' – sample 7; 'a *fixed deposit Amount*' – sample 12) and for legal and financial mechanisms of transfer (e.g. 'The bank is ready to release this money to any foreigner who stands as beneficiary and provides reliable information about the deceased owner' – sample 24). These are the *registers of knowledgeability* referred to earlier: authors make efforts to speak in ways that should reflect the particular position they claim to be in. Given the globalized nature of their communicative actions, they have to orient towards a restricted range of such ways of speaking: they have to convey meanings that can be picked up on the other side of the world. If we take the two points established so far together, the story is one of convergence, of the semiotic construction of similitude – I am like you, I am part of your world.

An orrery of errors

This is where things such as English and literacy come in: at the end of any ethnographic road, there are linguistic details. The examples given in the previous sections have already shown what this is about: many of the authors of the messages struggle with basic literacy skills and have an incomplete control over standard varieties of English. Both, as we shall see, are pre-requisites for a 'complete' realization of the genres. But incomplete realizations do not preclude communicative success – they result in more selective, smaller speech networks.

Whereas thus far I have tried to demonstrate processes of semiotic convergence in the messages, this point will lead us in an opposite direction, towards considering *diversity* under conditions of globalization. As we now know, globalization creates a heightened salience for the nature and structure of linguistic resources. As soon as linguistic semiotic products start travelling across the globe, they travel across different orders of indexicality, and what counts as 'good language' in one place can easily become 'bad language' in another; what counts as an expression of deference can become an expression of arrogance elsewhere; what counts as an index of intellectual middle-class identity in one place can become an index of immigrant underclass identity elsewhere. In other words, small details in linguistic structure – accent, writing style, politeness formulae, specific registers suggesting identities or relationships – grow in importance as objects of inquiry, questioning and evaluation of personality and case. Thus, the increase of mobility in globalization does not seem to have resulted in an increase of the acceptance of diversity. If anything, it has opened a new and wider space for measuring diversity *as aberrance* from newly reinforced or reinvented standards, customs and benchmarks, as we shall see in more detail in chapter 6. Rejection and exclusion on the grounds of features of one's linguistic resources are rife, although, as will be argued here, such rejections need not always be categorical.

Let us first have a closer look at the linguistic resources deployed by many of our authors in their attempt to convince us of the sincerity of their offer.

Grassroots literacy   Many of the messages display typical features of grassroots literacy: inconsistent punctuation, frequency of spelling errors, the unwarranted use of capitals and cross-register transfers (e.g. the use of informal styles in formal genres or vice versa). Consider some examples:

Ex. 35

> Through my internate search i got your mail address,that is why i am obliged to contact you to seek your interest and confiremation, and lay claim of this money with my legal backing and assistance ALLAH BLESS YOU AND YOUR FAMILY

(sample 33)

Ex. 36

> My names are George Tony. i'm a 65 years old man. i am Irish living in dakar (senegal). i'm a merchant and owned two businesses in Dakar. (…) please reply to this mail as i can only reply through my labtop can not talk very well: georgetony@fastermail.com sincerly,

(sample 34)

Ex. 37

Since then, I have made several contacts to His Countries Embassy in order to locate any of my clients extended relatives, which had also been unsuccessful.

(sample 39)

Ex. 38

> I am Tony Kobi the only son of late Mr and Mrs Christopher Kobi.My father was a very wealthy cocoa merchant in Abidjan the economic capital of Ivory coast, my father was poisoned to dearth by his business associates on one of their outings on a business trip. My mother died when I was a baby and since then my father took me so special.

(sample 44)

Ex. 39

Before The death of our Father on the 29th of June 2004 by 10.00am in a private hospital here in Abidjan. He secretly called me and my younger Sister and informed us that he has a sum of (US$6.5million) Six million five hundred thousand dollers. Which he Deposited in a Bank,in Cotonou. Benin repubilc.

(sample 52)

These few examples amply demonstrate the point: many authors deploy literacy skills that betray a position on the margins of global literacy economies. While they are fully literate as computer users and internauts, and while they appear to have rather clear and precise understandings of the cultural semantics required in this type of communication, many of them fail to accomplish the most basic task: the production of a degree of orthographic correctness sensed to iconicize the position from where they speak – a writing that matches their claimed identity as members of a highly skilled professional elite.

Grassroots English   The same applies to the varieties of English deployed by many authors: they reveal a struggle with norms, a series of orientations to stylistic conventions in local lingua franca varieties, and a lack of exposure to the normative codes of their addressees. This results in unexpected turns of phrase, misnomers, remarkable stylistic developments, as in the following examples:

Ex. 40

> I am writing in respect of a foreign customer of my bank with account number 14–255–2004/ASTB/123–99 who perished in an auto-crash with the whole passengers aboard.

> Since the demise of this our customer, I personally has watched with keen interest to see the next of kin but all has proved abortive as no one has come to claim his funds of US$32,000,000.00 (Thirty Two Million United States Dollar), which has been with my branch for a very long time. On this note, I decided to seek for whom his name shall be used as the next of kin as no one has come up to be the next of kin.

(sample 37)

Ex. 41

> BEFORE I INTRODUCE MYSELF AND MY PURPOSE OF CONTACTING YOU LET ME FIRST APPEAL TO YOU, TO KINDLY READ THE CONTENT OF THIS LETTER WITH KIND ATTENTION. I AM MR PATRICK MORRIS, A BANKER, I AM AN AUDITOR IN BANK OF SCOTLAND. I WANT TO TRANSFER OUT (FIFTEEN-MILLION POUNDS STERLINGS) FROM OUR BANK HERE IN LONDON. I HAVE THE COURAGE TO LOOK FOR A RELIABLE AND HONEST PERSON WHO WILL BE CAPABLE FOR THIS IMPORTANT BUSINESS TRANSACTION, BELIEVING THAT YOU WILL NEVER LET ME DOWN EITHER NOW OR IN FUTURE.
THE OWNER OF THIS ACCOUNT IS MR JOHN HUGHES FOREIGNER AND THE MANAGER OF PETROL CHEMICAL SERVICE HERE IN LONDON, A CHEMICAL ENGINEER BY PROFFESSION AND HE DIED SINCE 1995. THE ACCOUNT HAS NO OTHER BENEFICIARY AND MY INVESTIGATION PROVED TO ME AS WELL THAT HIS COMPANY DOES NOT KNOW ANYTHING ABOUT THIS ACCOUNT AND THE AMOUNT INVOLVED IS (15,000,000.00) POUNDS STERLINGS.
I WANT TO TRANSFER THIS MONEY INTO A SAFE FOREIGN ACCOUNT ABROAD BUT I DON'T KNOW ANY FOREIGNER, I KNOW THAT THIS MESSAGE WILL COME TO YOU AS A SURPRISE AS WE DON'T KNOW OUR SELF BEFORE, BUT BE SURE THAT IT IS REAL AND A GENUINE BUSINESS. I BELIEVE IN GOD THAT YOU WILL NEVER LET ME DOWN IN THIS INVESTMENT. YOUR FULL CONTACT PHONE AND FAX NUMBER, NAMES WILL BE NECESSARY FOR THIS EFFECT. HOPE TO HEAR FROM YOU IMMEDIATELY. THANKS MR PATRICK MORRIS N:B-YOU CAN REPLY ME THROUGH THIS BOX:Patrickmorris1@doramail.com

(sample 46)

Ex. 42

> Dear, we are honourably seeking your assistance in the following ways: To help us transfer the money out from Africa to your Country. since we don't have any idea about transction.

(sample 52)

The number of examples could again be multiplied: we find ourselves in a forest of Englishes with a bewildering range of varieties, and with very different degrees of proximity to linguistic and stylistic standards.

English is deployed for more than just operational reasons. It also serves as a powerful index of identity: it is through control over the globalized code of power and elite membership that our authors try to signal their claimed identities. Along with the choice of names that match the claimed place of origin of the messages, the choice of language is part of the creation of a trustworthy, recognizable persona. Examples 36 and 41 above provide us with interesting evidence for this. In sample 36, the author claims to be 'Irish' (written correctly, with a capital I) living in 'dakar(senegal)' (written without capitals and without space between the two words); he also stated that his 'names' (plural) are George Tony. In sample 41, our author claims to be 'A BANKER, I AM AN AUDITOR IN BANK OF SCOTLAND' – syntactically peculiar, and written with problematic punctuation and without the article delimiting 'Bank of Scotland'. Mr Patrick Morris, as he calls himself, has 'THE COURAGE TO LOOK FOR A RELIABLE AND HONEST PERSON', willing to engage in a transaction worth 'FIFTEEN-MILLION POUNDS STERLINGS' (with hyphen, and 'Sterlings' in plural).

Both Mr George Tony and Mr Patrick Morris claim to be native speakers of the language in which they write their message. In the case of Mr Morris (sample 41), the author's claim to being a Scotsman supported the claimed origin of the message – the UK (note that Mr Morris sends his message from a provider in Uruguay and expects us to reply through a free webmail provider on a cartoon fan site based in the USA). Of course, it is unlikely that a senior employee of the Bank of Scotland would write 'Sterling' in the plural – just as it is unlikely that our Irish Mr George Tony would conceive of his name as a plural construction. Non-nativeness shines through in every line of their messages. The point is, however, that in both cases the authors appear to assume that *their English is 'good' enough to pass as fluent, possibly 'native' speakers*. This can point towards differences in the values of particular linguistic resources in different places in the world – between different locally operating orders of indexicality: it is not implausible that both authors have no awareness of the difference between their variety of English and the normative varieties known to their addressees. The world-system, as we know, is not a continuum but a system riddled with disjunctures and discontinuities of various sorts, and linguistic normative complexes can be *perceived* to be global, but, as we saw in chapter 3, may in reality be very local and enclosed onto themselves, responding to local constraints and opportunities rather than to those operating in the 'centre' of language normativity.

The point here is that the particular realizations of English 'give off' all kinds of indexical information. In the case of Mr Tony and Mr Morris, they clearly provide abundant grounds for disputing their claimed Irish and Scottish identities – and by extension, for disputing the sincerity of the offer, the authenticity of the stories they tell. The non-nativeness of their English, in short, exposes their messages as cases of fraud; it destroys the whole indexical edifice they attempted to build in their message. This also applies to the numerous other examples in our corpus. To the extent that the authors invoke identities of professional elite membership and exhaust themselves in attempts towards convincing their addressees that they belong to the same stratum of the world, their orthographic, punctuation and linguistic difficulties give them away as someone else – as *poseurs*.

This is the third point I wanted to establish. The authors of these messages may be well inserted into the globalized communication technology networks, and they may have developed views of how to communicate in these networks, but they fail to realize the requirements for success in handling the complex and demanding genre tasks they engage with. The third kind of competence, linguistic competence, seems to be less well developed than the two previous ones. We are now ready to move on to some concluding reflections.

Truncated fraud

I would suggest that this little genre study can help us understand the complexities of linguistic processes in conditions of globalization. In its simplest form, the case I have tried to build can be summarized as follows.

The type of communication performed by the authors of these messages appears as a layered complex of requirements, deployed and deployable skills, and practices – as truncated repertoires in the terms developed earlier, with some resources that are very well developed and others that are less so. The authors of the messages participate fully in this communicative complex at some levels, while they fail to participate at other levels. They are fully competent users and manipulators of the technological and infrastructural aspects of globalized communication; in this respect they are 'matured' users (Baron 1998: 145). We have seen that they often display amazing degrees of expertise in detecting providers around the world capable of covering their tracks. They are also transcultural mediators, in the sense that they appear to have accurate understandings of the cultural genre conventions that dominate the particular kinds of communication they engage in. We saw how their messages display considerable amounts of structural uniformity and tightness, and how they sprinkle their messages with registers of knowledgeability, indexes of elite membership and trustworthiness, and stereotypical images of corruption and bureaucratic inadequacy in their countries. They know what the globalized customer wants, and they all display a tendency towards stylistic and generic convergence towards that point: a globally recognizable 'serious' letter written by sincere, serious business people. We can see some degree of awareness here about the communicative choices that need to be made in this globalized communication network. These authors are undoubtedly aware of the fact that their messages need to be specially designed for their target audiences, and they make choices that reflect this awareness.

But we also saw that at the lowest level of realization – the level where actual words, sentences and punctuation marks need to be organized into a text – the world-system re-emerged in full glory, with all its inequalities and differential speeds of development, collapsing into varieties of English that denied the accomplishments towards globalized generic recognizability at the two other levels. The 'knowing *what*' is not matched by 'knowing *how*', and examples like the ones by Mr Tony and Mr Morris reveal a disconcerting truth about language in the world-system: the fact that to many people, the 'English' they believe to be a symbolic vehicle for upward social mobility and the accumulation of wealth is something very different from the 'English' which is, in actual fact, required in order to have access to such upward trajectories. Many of our authors probably believe that their 'English' is not a problem because their addressees probably also use 'English' – and the common use of that word suggests compellingly that both varieties are the same.

They are not, and when their messages are read by highly literate elites in the First World, the *demasqué* will be quick and merciless. But the rule of diversity works in their favour as well. Internet communication is a space dominated by non-nativeness, and the same rules apply to inner London or Rotterdam as well as to Lagos or Johannesburg. There will be addressees whose varieties of English are as distant from the normative 'centres' as those of the senders. Some of them may not spot the rich non-native indexicalities of the messages. These readers may only perceive 'English' without interpreting variation as significant, and to them the proposed identities, relationships and activities may be fully credible – perhaps unusual, but maybe the best thing that ever happened to them. As mentioned earlier, email fraud actually *works*, and it makes victims, probably among those wide audiences whose competence in English is such that the peculiarities reported here pass unnoticed. And perhaps we should remind ourselves of the fact that there are a great many people (including fully fluent speakers of English) in that category. Thus, messages such as these, and their effects, offer us a glimpse of the growing diversification in the domain of globalized communication.

When the big things are all right, it is the small things that start to matter. The homogenizing ring of a word such as 'English' is the indexical trap of globalization: it leads people to believe that variety A is equivalent to variety B and so creates wide spaces for producing differences, at a time when such differences, however minimal, are read metonymically, in a densely indexical way, as evidence of fundamental differences. Instruments such as the Internet offer opportunities for homogenization and uniformization at one level of communicative structuring, and this process of homogenization further supports the perceived homogeneity of the linguistic resources we deploy in it; but precisely this process refocuses our attention on the things that cannot be homogenized: structural inequalities in the world.

4.3   A world of resources

The authors of the email fraud messages displayed the kind of chequered competence that I believe becomes more and more an issue in globalization. The different skills displayed by the authors entered their repertoires through very different historical trajectories, some short, some long, some collective, others individual, some through 'normal' (institutional) trajectories such as education, others through informal learning environments such as peer groups and non-institutional communities; some came into their repertoires on their own initiative and through their own efforts, others were offered to them by others. These differences are fundamental to an understanding of sociolinguistic reality, because a repertoire is never 'flat' and smooth, but always chequered and truncated, and thus reflective of the lives of real people in real social environments. The mobility of people and messages increases the visibility of the differences between repertoires. Since every aspect of human communication is always open to evaluative judgment, we see an expansion of the range of features in communication that trigger evaluation. The patchwork of competences and skills that the authors display offers a wide panorama, on which others can pass indexical judgments. We saw this already in our discussion of commodified accents in chapter 2, and we see it here again.

   This view of truncated multilingualism raises various theoretical issues and possibilities, and the issue of competence has already been addressed. In a very insightful paper, Charlyn Dyers (2008) analysed the repertoires of inhabitants of Wesbank, the township near Cape Town which was also the setting for some of our reflections in chapter 3. On the basis of a thorough analysis of the resources people use in a variety of domains, Dyers concludes that the multi-ethnic make-up of Wesbank, where literally everyone is an immigrant, creates truncated multilingual repertoires and language practices. Language resources get re-ordered and functionally specialized so as to cover specific tasks and functions, but not others. The pattern she observes, in which resources conventionally associated with a language get re-assigned to specific domains, would in a more traditional vocabulary be called language shift (with connotations such as language 'endangerment' or 'death'). Her use of truncated repertoires, however, shows that languages do not disappear at all, their resources become specialized and so locked into particular social spheres (to use Bakhtinian terminology). The 'languages' of the traditional vocabulary exist as 'registers' in a new and more productive vocabulary, and the real 'language' that the people possess is this patchwork of specialized multilingual resources. Such a view can have a deep impact on contemporary studies of language endangerment, because it removes the categorical aspect of such studies (a language is either 'vital' or 'endangered') and replaces it with a far more detailed and precise view in which shades of grey are allowed, and in which we can see that particular resources, even if they look obsolescent to the analyst, can have important functions for language users.

We might now also be in a position to start seeing patterns of oppression and dominance not so much in terms of languages as in terms of particular resources, some of which may (but do not have to) overlap with languages as conventionally understood. Perhaps it is not 'languages' that are oppressed, but their deployment over specific genres and registers – for instance, their use as a language of instruction in schools or of political debate in the public arena. And perhaps this insight can provide a more precise diagnosis of such phenomena, and (hopefully) better contribute to improvements. One thing looks quite certain: in a world in which patterns of mobility mean that more and more communication has the characteristics of an unfinished product, less and less analytic relevance can be attributed to conceptions of language that are based on the 'standard' varieties and images of it. More and more language will appear 'non-standard', not for reasons of the innate linguistic sloppiness or carelessness of people, but because of the complex play of truncated multilingualism and the problematic allocation of resources and functions which is an effect of mobility. A term such as 'non-standard' so becomes obsolete, because it covers far too much and far too diverse phenomena. Getting rid of it, and of related terminology, would be good for sociolinguistics.

Appendix to Chapter 4: The corpus

Nr	Name	Claimed location	Internet provider location	Phone number location	Other countries mentioned	Type	Amount
1	Dr. Joseph Diara	Nigeria	? (hotmail)	Nigeria		dormant	19.3M$
2	James Williams	Italy	Malaysia			rescue	Millions €
3	James Zulu	Zimbabwe	Mexico, ? (netscape)		Swaziland, South Africa, The Netherlands	rescue	9.5M$
4	Dr. Jumbo Williams	South Africa	Spain			dormant	75M$
5	Cynthia Wood	UK	Italy			dormant	20M$
6	Ben Okoye	Nigeria	UK			dormant	12.5M$
7	Olsom Berghart	Russia	Russia, ? (yahoo)			rescue	100.5M$
8	Lawal Sanusi PhD	Ghana	? (hotmail)			dormant	45.5M$
9	Robert Chavez	UK	USA, The Netherlands		Indonesia	dormant	14MGBP
10	Linda Koffi	Ivory Coast	Mexico			rescue	14.5M$
11	Simon Croft	UK	Philippines	UK		lottery	2.5MGBP
12	Hon. Nnamdi Chukwu Esq.	Benin	Turkey			dormant	10.7M$
13	Bill Scott	UK	Russia, USA			lottery	0.5M$
14	Josef Yun	Hong Kong	Hong Kong		Iraq	dormant	43.6M$
15	Adamu Yazid	Nigeria	USA	Nigeria	Indonesia	dormant	10M$
16	Tony Gawab	Nigeria	Argentina			dormant	10.5M$
17	Marcel Martin	South Africa	Spain, UK	UK	UK	dormant	?
18	Mukele Kelele	South Africa	Italy			dormant	31M$
19	Barr. David Mogwerane & associated (Esq.), Teresa Allan, Alexandra Davis	UK/South Africa	UK, South Africa	UK		lottery	0.82M$
20	Musa Jacob Kamara	Ivory Coast	Latin America		Sierra Leone	rescue	14.5M$, 100 kg gold
21	Lisa Jones, Forest Anderson	UK	USA	UK		lottery	5.5M$
22	Jan Van Klein	The Netherlands	UK			lottery	0.85M$
23	Yahaya Kumalo	South Africa	USA		Zimbabwe	rescue	10M$
24	Bruce Brand	South Africa	USA–UK–Canada		USA	dormant	26.9M$
25	Engineer George Ogbedi	Nigeria	USA			dormant	23.615M$
26	Alex Uju	Nigeria	Spain			dormant	5.2M$
27	Anton Geesink	The Netherlands	USA, UK	The Netherlands		lottery	1.5M$
28	Barrister Roy Hans, Susan Smith	The Netherlands	USA, ? (netscape)	The Netherlands		lottery	1M$

Nr	Name	Claimed location	Internet provider location	Phone number location	Other countries mentioned	Type	Amount
29	Mark David	Russia	UK		China	rescue	42M$
30	Shdak Shari	Dubai	USA, ? (netscape)		Europe	charity	18M$
31	Zack Sonnie	The Netherlands	France			lottery	0.85M$
32	Kethson Mour	South Africa	South Africa, ? (hotmail)			dormant	126M$
33	Barrister Malinga Yusuf (AlHaji)	Benin	South Africa			charity	28.562M$
34	George Tony	Senegal	Hong Kong		Europe	charity	12.5M$
35	Perry Graham	The Netherlands	USA, Hong Kong			lottery	1.8M$
36	Briggs Smith	UK	USA		USA, Europe, Canada	partnership	?
37	Dr Dan Obi	Nigeria	? (yahoo)			dormant	32M$
38	Martins Mulolo	Benin	Hong Kong, Italy		Lebanon	dormant	11M$
39	Hon. Peter Iluo Esq.	Benin	UK, Denmark		Togo	dormant	10.7M$
40	Simon Croft, Brian Hays	UK	USA	UK		lottery	2.5MGBP
41	Suzana Nuhan Vaye	Liberia	Spain (Biscayne), Hong Kong, Italy	UK		rescue	21.5M$
42	Ramesh Hassan	Dubai	USA, ? (netscape)			charity	18M$
43	Shehu Abdul	Dubai	USA, ? (netscape)			charity	?
44	Tony Kobi	Ivory Coast	Italy		Bulgaria	rescue	10.5M$
45	Rita Adams	?	USA	The Netherlands		lottery	0.5M$
46	Patrick Morris	UK	USA, Uruguay			dormant	15M$
47	Linda Green	UK	UK, South Africa	UK		lottery	3.5M$
48	Dr Tafik Dada	Benin	UK, Denmark			dormant	16.4M$
49	Mulan Qin	China	Hong Kong, PR China			rescue	410.4M$
50	Solomon Dike	Nigeria	Poland			dormant	'very big'
51	Van Bell, Lynn Rowlands	The Netherlands	Argentina, Spain, Australia, New Zealand	The Netherlands		lottery	1.5M$
52	Susan Dargbo	Ivory Coast	Latin America		Benin	rescue	6.5M$
53	Dafe Akene	Nigeria	India			dormant	25.5M$
54	Senator John Agoda	Nigeria	Argentina, Australia			dormant	29M$
55	Dan Pedro Vaye	Liberia	USA, Israel		South Africa	rescue	21.5M$
56	Barrister Ibe Festus	Nigeria	Denmark, India		USA	dormant	9M$

5   Language, globalization and history

5.1   Historical concepts

Understanding globalization is understanding a historical process, something that has considerable depth in time, and something in which we can discern different stages and moments of development. I underscored the importance of this point earlier in this book and now return to it. The difficulty we face was exemplified in Fairclough (2006): we can only observe globalization synchronically, while we can only understand it historically. Consequently, we must develop conceptual tools that are at least historically sensitive, that suggest and open a space of historical analysis and interpretation.

History, of course, is not the same as diachrony. It is not sufficient to specify a time-line along which sociolinguistic features develop and on which certain 'dots' mark important moments (a problem in some work on language policy and language planning). History means that time is filled with human activity, with actors who stand in various kinds of relationships to one another and whose actions influence those of others. Power, hierarchy, authority, normativity are central in understanding historical processes: history is filled with power and conflict (cf. Blommaert 1999a). Some works can be used as examples of historical sociolinguistic analysis. Bonfiglio (2002) reviews the genesis of 'standard American' accents and sets it against a panorama of race and ethnic relations, twentieth-century xenophobia and the emergence of new elites in the USA. We hear the voices of the ambitious in his study, and we see language ideology being articulated by identifiable actors to other identifiable actors. This is also the case in Collins and Blot (2003), where literacy in the USA is described as inextricably linked with histories of power and authority in language and beyond. There, too, we see identifiable actors at work and we can follow the debates they engaged in.[1] Fabian (1986) is a classic study of how language was 'planned' in the Belgian Congo by specific colonial and religious authorities in the context of particular phases of the colonial enterprise. And Bauman and Briggs (2003) provide an admirable historical account of the gradual development of a 'modernist' language ideology through an analysis of the writings of philologists, antiquarians, folklorists and early anthropologists. We see in their work the articulation of what became one of the key concepts of modernity: an ordered, pure and clean 'language' that could become the language of the modern nation state. All the works mentioned here (and there are more) contain a diachronic analysis. Language moves through time. But time itself is filled with actors, voices, moments of crisis, conflict and eloquent articulation; and power defines both the input and the output of the processes we can observe. This is what makes these works historical, and it is this kind of historical analysis that shows that language is such an eminently social and political object as well. We see in such works the various power tactics that are used *on* language and *in* language. We see how people define stakes for language in society, how they define social barriers and gateways for social mobility, how they regulate society through the regulation of language. Such work is important.

We are still stuck, though, with our initial problem: that a historical process such as globalization can only be observed synchronically. We can only witness the synchronic outcome of historical processes, and we need concepts that allow us to 'read back' from the synchronic manifestations towards the processes that produced them. Here, too, we can start from what we already have. Now widespread concepts such as intertextuality and interdiscursivity (e.g. Fairclough 1992) explicitly connect synchronic language objects with prior ones, and they sensitize us (or *should* sensitize us) to the intrinsic historicity of every language fact – something that Voloshinov (1973) had already pointed out. They emphasize that the interpretation of utterances in the here-and-now depends on retrieving elements from their history of use, and that in order to make sense of what utterances mean now, we must go back to what they meant before. Equally widespread notions such as contextualization (Gumperz 1982; Hanks 2006), affordances (Kress and van Leeuwen 1996) and indexicality (Silverstein 2003a, 2006a) do the same: they point towards the fact that meaning depends on inferences made from prior meanings, whereby such prior meanings are very often reflective of the social order. And this ordered nature of implicit (historical) meaning complexes is captured under terms such as genre and register (Agha 2007): enduring, relatively stable patterns of meaningfulness in language, the production of which triggers immediate connections between utterances in the present and in the past. Throughout all of this we see that normativity appears: the stable, intertextual and ordered aspects of language use are those aspects that we commonly label as 'norms' in language. Such concepts now belong to the stock and trade of studies of language in society, yet it is important to underscore that they are *historical* concepts, concepts that open a window from the present onto the past, and from products onto the processes that generate them. They make us aware of the fact that every act of language is an act that is grounded in historical connections between current statements and prior ones – connections that are related to the social order and are thus not random but ordered.

The concepts that I introduced earlier in this book also represented an attempt towards encapsulating this intrinsic historicity of language objects. The notion of orders of indexicality was explicitly aimed at describing the forms of social order that define normativity in language use. In that sense, the concept necessarily refers to historical patterns and processes, in which language-ideological perceptions of (desired) stability and predictability of language forms emerged (some of which are exemplified in Agha 2007). The same goes for the concept of polycentricity: it represents an image of a world in which power and authority are shared by various concrete actors – centres – from whom normative guidelines can be expected and are being adopted. The different centres operate at different scale-levels (another intrinsically historical concept) and thus represent different 'orders', some of which have long histories and are attached to relatively stable institutions, while others are momentary, flexible and ephemeral. In each case, however, there are connections between the present and the past, and people infer from past experiences and from their existing batteries of resources and skills what is useful for the present task. The latter, of course, already shows that even more widespread sociolinguistic notions such as 'repertoire' have an intrinsic historical dimension. Even if we can observe repertoires only in their synchronic deployment, we know that what is there in the way of resources and skills *was* there prior to the synchronic deployment, and we know that these resources and skills got there because of personal biographies and the histories of social systems.

I dwell on this point at some length because it is fundamental. Too often, the historical dimension of sociolinguistic phenomena is treated obliquely or is blandly overlooked, and this leads to the over-interpretation of synchronic phenomena. We then see similarities and differences that may not be explicable synchronically, or would receive a very different explanation if addressed historically. In the context of globalization, such issues become more and more difficult to manage, because there is a prima facie uniformity to many cultural globalization processes – the well-known 'McDonaldization'. We believe that we see similarities all over the globe (think of the spread of English or of the use of the Internet) and we start interpreting them *as* similarities, for instance as effects of one and the same process of colonialism and/or linguistic and cultural imperialism. The fact that similar effects may come out of very different processes is then lost, and the elementary sociolinguistic task of addressing the particular ways in which language regimes are shaped and constructed in actual societies and in actual language use is left to itself. We then end up with rather useless and misleading notions such as 'World English' (Brutt-Griffler 2002) that suggest a uniform object gradually but steadily developing from a tool on a 'national' scale to one on a 'world' scale. Such an analysis will not do because it overlooks the crucial differences that such processes display wherever they occur, and it also overlooks the foundational sociolinguistic task of describing actual resources (such as English) in relation to existing repertoires. Such things allow particular levels of generalization, not absolute generalizations.

This kind of over-interpretation of the synchronic plane of sociolinguistic phenomena is avoidable because, as we saw just now, we can start from a reasonably well-developed conceptual toolkit that allows and enables us to 'read back' from synchronic language use into historical backgrounds and historical patterns of meaningfulness. I will try to illustrate the potential of such analysis in the remainder of this chapter, starting with an analysis that addresses the prima facie uniformity of cultural globalization processes and attempts to delve a bit deeper into it.

5.2   The worlds of golf

Golf is one of Appadurai's (1996) 'ideoscapes'. Images of the sport have over the past decades become members of the category of 'indexical Viagra' (Silverstein 2003b): signs whose indexical arrows point up-up-up, signalling achievement, fortune and membership of Veblen's 'leisure classes', more popularly known as Yuppies. The suggestion is: golf is practised by wealthy and successful people – people who also drive expensive automobiles and wear Rolex watches and should therefore be seen as role models for the rest of society. Interestingly, golf is also a truly global sign. Golf players travel the world in search of good golf courses, and the membership of prestigious golf clubs is very cosmopolitan. Major golf tournaments are global mega-events, and golf stars such as Tiger Woods are global celebrities of the first order. Tapping into this imagery of golf thus opens this indexical world of success and achievement. Consider Figure 5.1 now.

This is an advertisement in which Siemens presents an electronic communication system. The advertisement appeared in the Belgian magazine *Knack* in 2006, and even though *Knack* publishes exclusively in Dutch, the text in the advertisement is in English. It is a global advertisement, one that aspires towards distribution on a global scale-level. It also contains some of the global discursive currency of business success. We read about the 'innovative HiPath real-time IP system', about 'service' and 'solutions'; and these upwardly pointing words are quoted from 'your IT Director' and your 'Director of Operations'. The addressees of this message are clearly people who hold senior positions in large (i.e. internationally operating) corporations, large enough to have an IT Director and a Director of Operations. An example of such a corporation is given: the Marriott hotel chain has adopted the 'innovative HiPath real-time IP system' and probably found it a solution 'as rare as a hole in one'. Marriott is of course a prestigious brand name, it stands for the kind of

Our **communication system**
needs to be as perfect as our service,
says your IT Director.
Solutions like that are as rare as a hole in one,
says your Director of Operations.

Only the innovative HiPath Real Time IP System
from Siemens was able to convince us, says Marriott.
www.siemens.com/network-success

SIEMENS
Global network of innovation

JW Marriott Grande Lakes, Orlando

Figure 5.1 Siemens advertisement

hotels and resorts that the globalized business elite tends to use. And that brings us to the dominant imagery in the advertisement: golf.

'Hole-in-one' is the golf term *par excellence* and it designates the ultimate (and therefore very exceptional) achievement of a golf player. And rather than the product (which remains invisible), the advertisement shows us a couple of handsome young people playing golf. The building in the background is

Figure 5.2 Golf poster, Beijing

identified as the Marriott resort in Orlando, Florida, and so the complex semiotics of the advertisement establishes a link between one of Siemens' customers
and a globalized imagery of success, elite membership and wealth, iconized in
the picture of the golfing couple. Every scale-jumping code is there now: there is
the globalized code of English, the globalized discursive code of successful
business and the globalized code of golf (the image and the jargon term 'hole-
in-one') with its dense symbolism. The advertisement is truly and fully global,
even if it is published in a local Belgian (and Dutch-language) magazine.

Now consider Figure 5.2, a picture of a poster taken in a street in Central
Beijing, April 2007. The poster is bilingual and it advertises a golf tournament
to be held in Beijing in that month. We see the same types of imagery as in the
Siemens advertisement: we see the global code English, we see the logos of
corporate sponsors, we get a bit of the jargon of golf ('teeing off') and we see an
image of a skilful golfer. The poster clearly draws from the same semiotic and
ideological wells as the Siemens advertisement.[2] This is the prima facie uniformity of globalization: there is a layer of manifest similarity between signs
that are being produced in very different places in the world. We have the
feeling that we perceive something very similar, something that taps from the
same sources and results in the same outcomes. It is this feeling that makes
globalization such a real experience for many people: the layer of similarity
creates its own intertextuality and, hence, familiarity.

But we should look somewhat deeper and beyond this superficial similarity. The poster is bilingual, and it is the product of professional design and manufacturing processes. A prestigious event such as the golf tournament, organized by a shamelessly elitist country club and supported by corporate sponsors, allows no shoddy communication work, and so we can assume that this product reflects considerable investment and attention from the ones who made it. We see beautiful lettering, a high-quality picture, a balanced composition of the overall poster and an attempt to make the poster appeal to international audiences as well by means of English. The two Chinese phrases at the top of the poster read: 'promote modern sportsmanship' and 'build a harmonious society'. The English underneath is not an exact translation; instead we get a reformulation in which we see some differences from the Chinese, a transition in style from Chinese 'political slogan' style to Western 'commercial' style. The two phrases that were separate in Chinese are now placed in a superordinate–subordinate relation in which the creation of new sportsmanship is done *for* the promotion of a harmonious society. And, of course, we get the golf jargon term 'teeing off' – only meant for people who are familiar with golf and who know English, mainly for the Beijing-based expatriates, in other words.

Such people would probably spot the rather dramatic typographic error in 'conciousness'. It is an error reminiscent of some of the examples discussed in earlier chapters of this book: the act of communication is 'unfinished' because of problems with access to the resources required for this act. For the one who typeset and proofread this poster, and for the printer, the English spelling error went unnoticed, it was not spotted as an error during its production process. Such people may also wonder about the connection between golf and 'a harmonious community'. The latter – building a harmonious society – is one of the main contemporary slogans of the Chinese Communist Party, and the phrase 'harmonious society/community' pops up non-stop in all segments of public life. The slogan can be found in numerous public inscriptions, and Chinese children hold essay-writing, speech and debating contests on the topic. So while we see that considerable effort has been spent in trying to make this poster into a globalized communication item – I gave a list of features above – the typo and the Communist slogan tie it firmly into the local and national scale-level.

If we now compare the two examples, we begin to see interesting differences beyond the similarities. While the Siemens advertisement can be said to have very little local flavour (e.g. it is in English while the magazine is in Dutch), and instead articulates a rather profoundly global style and message, the Chinese poster aspires towards the global scale-level but also displays important features of the local and national scale-level. The Siemens advertisement blends global currencies into a message that can be disseminated in identical form in Belgium, the UK, Switzerland, Argentina, and so on. Its potential for mobility is very high. The Chinese poster, while addressing a global (sub-)audience in English and with the icons of golf and corporate sponsorship, also addresses local and national audiences. And while the Siemens advertisement appears to draw its normative design from just one centre – global corporate enterprise – we see that the Beijing poster is decidedly polycentric. The organizers of the golf tournament orient towards the status groups that are usually targeted with such imagery, as well as to the world of corporate business; but they also orient towards the Chinese state by adopting one of the Party's most important political slogans. We hear the voice of the globalized elite of China, as well as that of the Chinese Communist Party.

We see two historically different faces of capitalism here, projected onto two different sets of representations. In the Siemens advertisement, the corporate world is a sphere of its own, very much free and unconstrained in its movements in the global marketplace. Its partners are other members of the same corporate world, and states are – ideologically at least – not direct participants in the processes of that world. In the Chinese poster, we see that similar imagery is being used, but that the message is polyphonic, and that the voice of the state appears alongside that of the new globalized elites (the 'business leaders' mentioned on Pine Valley's website). The state is an active partner in corporate culture in China, perhaps the most active one, and the priorities of the state need to be blended with those of the business elites, even if that generates rather strangely heteroglossic messages – like when China's most exclusive country club makes an appeal for a harmonious society.

The same images and semiotic materials are used in both examples. We see pictures of golf (carrying very much the same indexical values of success, elite membership, and so forth), we see English and we see golf jargon. But both examples instantiate different histories of becoming, and we see different forces at work in both. Golf appears as global currency, but in very different environments – historically different environments. And as a result, the semiotic outcome in both cases is very different. There are different worlds of golf.

5.3   Long and short histories

We saw very similar things in earlier examples in this book, for instance when I discussed the peripheral normativity that characterized English in a South African township school. The actual resources that were used there – the specific varieties of English and of literacy – had their own histories of arriving there, and they arrived there through a combination of the long history of apartheid (where Standard English and advanced literacy were firmly in the hands of white elites) and the shorter history of post-apartheid South Africa, in which English became a more democratically distributed item. The long history, however, influenced the shorter history, and so what became democratically accessible was the 'black', stigmatizing variety of English literacy, not the elite varieties.

When we now consider repertoires synchronically (and I said that we can only witness them synchronically), we see what we could call a *synchronized* repertoire. The different elements of the repertoire will appear as a relatively 'flat' juxtaposition of 'languages' 'language varieties' or concrete 'communicative skills', as when someone says that he 'knows English, French and Dutch' (or when, in a questionnaire, we ask 'which language people use at school/in hospitals/with friends/in court'). But when we discussed the truncated repertoires that characterize contemporary multilingualism in the previous chapter, we saw that such a flat juxtaposition hides tremendous differences between the actual resources that comprise the repertoire, and that such distinctions are of capital importance: they define when people will use specific resources and how they will then use them. They also explain why people do not use all of their resources at the same time, but appear to be experts in selecting the right bits of language for particular communicative tasks. Such distinctions between different resources represent, as I said, trajectories through which the resources became part of someone's repertoire; they are therefore also *historical* distinctions, distinctions that harbour different sociolinguistic histories.

Synchronization is the way in which repertoires offer themselves for inspection: as something which is not synchronic but is *made* synchronic during certain procedures such as metalinguistic interviewing or surveying. In sociolinguistic discourse we continually synchronize realities which, in actual fact, are multi-stranded and display multiple and very different leads into people's lives and the histories of the societies in which they dwell. It is an effect of the Saussurean legacy in sociolinguistics. The kind of sociolinguistics I have in mind here is one in which we de-synchronize and *historicize* sociolinguistic phenomena, looking into the very different leads that run from the object to the processes that produced it. Figure 5.3 can offer us a handy graphic representation of this procedure.

We see a forest of small wooden tablets, hung from a frame near a Shinto shrine in Tokyo. The wooden tablets are 'ex-voto' messages: requests or expressions of gratitude to the supreme being for certain favours. They are instances of a very old tradition in Japan, and the way in which they are written and displayed emanates tradition: they are not written on a piece of paper but on a wooden tablet, and they are displayed publicly in one particular spot in the shrine. We see different kinds of tablets too. While most of the tablets are in handwritten Japanese, some contain drawings of flowers, hearts or other emblems, and some are copies of old block-prints of deities or of episodes from legendary tales. And some of them are handwritten in English too (see Figure 5.4)

What we see here, I would suggest, is a synchronized sociolinguistic phenomenon, the components of which have very different origins. The phenomenon, thus, is actually a very layered one, in which we see very traditional items

Figure 5.3 Ex-voto tablets in Japan

Figure 5.4 Detail of ex-voto tablets

(e.g. the block-prints) as well as different forms of Japanese handwriting (traditional and calligraphic versus everyday and katakana writing) that find their origins in the circulation of Japanese orthography through the education system in different stages of its existence, which goes back to the nineteenth century. The English inscriptions have their origins in far more recent globalization processes that brought English within the realm of adolescents as a code of love and sweet talk. On the same tablet, however, the author's name is written in traditional and almost calligraphic writing. The different codes that compose this synchronized mosaic have different origins and arrived here through different paths. Decoding the mosaic involves tracing the origins of the composite parts, back into culture and society.

The distinction between long histories and short histories, of course, reminds us of Fernand Braudel's (1949, 1969, see also Wallerstein 2000, chapter 10) classic distinction between slow time, intermediate time and fast time in history. Slow time (the *durée*) was the time of the climate and of social systems; intermediate time was the time of empires, dynasties etc., while fast time was the time of events such as battles or revolutions (the *évènements*). Braudel noted that there was a correlation between these types of time on the one hand, and human agency and consciousness on the other. Few people are aware of the slow, long time of climate fluctuations (we now perhaps live in an era where people are quite conscious of it), and developments at this level are usually beyond the reach of individual agency. The time of empires has a higher level of consciousness and agency, and the fast time of events is within the reach of human individual agency and consciousness. People are more aware of a stock exchange crash than of the cyclical fluctuations of modern capitalism, for instance, and they have more direct impact on the former than on the latter. Braudel's claim was that the distinction between different types of time is essential for understanding historical processes, and I would say that it is essential for understanding sociolinguistic processes as well. We cannot understand change when we do not keep an eye on continuity as well, and the opposite is also true. We cannot, for instance, understand the patterns of super-diversity in the sociolinguistic and semiotic landscapes of current urban centres (as discussed in chapter 1) if we forget the more gradual changes that occur in the fabric of society and in the sociolinguistics of such areas.

This, too, is exemplified in the illustrations of the ex-voto tablets. We see different layers of historicity there, and each of them reflects a layer of change, from tradition to more modern to very modern. The examples, incidentally, can also be seen as examples of language contact and language mixing. We do see a juxtaposition of two languages: Japanese and English. We also see several modes of sign-making here: pre-printed images, little handmade drawings, handwritten calligraphic Japanese and 'normal' handwritten Japanese, and handwritten English. So the images represent a multilingual and multimodal complex, and the two dimensions are tightly intertwined. It is important to realize that, in considering such multilingual and multimodal complexes, the constituent elements – languages and modes – have arrived there via different historical trajectories, and that these trajectories have defined the 'affordances' of the elements (Kress and van Leeuwen 1996): they define what the different elements can contribute in the way of meaning and function. The fact that we see register-specific usage of English here – 'Love and Sweet' – is probably an effect of different affordances, whereby the English derives a lot of its value and possible meanings from its strong embeddedness in popular youth culture. It has become one of the instruments for expressing love and friendship in Japan, and this is a very recent development (one we associate with contemporary global-ization processes). Its occurrence is a translocal phenomenon: the same expres-sions could equally well occur in London, Brussels or Bangkok. It now occurs alongside religious and historical images that reflect a pre-globalization history (strongly connected to the emergence of the Shinto tradition and of Japanese national consciousness), the meaning and function of which is, consequently, strongly local: only people familiar with this kind of religious iconography have access to its meanings.

All of this has an effect on what we understand by indexicality. Indexicality is inherently intertextual: it connects previous utterances with current ones and grants an indexical load to present utterances that have their origins in the existing social order. This social order, of course, is in effect a polycentric patchwork of historically different elements, and its symbols – language and semiotic forms are important in this – carry traces of these histories. This is why we can see social processes through language and communication patterns. They are never 'flat' and smooth, but display small differences that lead us to big differences. In Bourdieu's words, '[e]very speech act and, more generally, every action, is a conjuncture, an encounter between independent causal series' (1991: 37). It is a nexus of different influences, some of which belong to individual trajectories, some to collective ones, and some have short histories while others have longer histories. This is why speaking a standard variety of a language indexically often and in many places flags membership of educated elites: the standard varieties are historically connected to social systems of elite production and reproduction, as Bourdieu (1984, 1991) demonstrated. And shifting from Standard Dutch into Standard English will consequently produce different index-ical effects than shifting from a strongly regional variety of Dutch into hip-hop English. While the first kind of shift will probably signal elite membership, the latter may signal peer-group coolness and anti-elite attitudes. The reasons for this, I repeat, are the different indexical loads of the elements that compose this particular communicative act; such differences relate the particular act to differ-ent forms of intertextuality, and consequently, to different histories. The accel-eration of historical processes in the context of globalization predictably leads to more complex forms of sociolinguistic change and thus requires a more sophis-ticated approach to such forms of change. Let us consider an example.

5.4   The chaotic shop

Mass tourism is one of the agents of rapid change in many places in the world, and it has fascinating sociolinguistic effects. Heller (2003) has shown how minority languages, previously threatened with extinction, can suddenly acquire a market value and thus a series of new functions (and a prospect for survival) due to heritage tourism. In many other places, we see how the sociolinguistic environment quite dramatically changes due to the presence of language materials designed for the tourist target audiences. These are new forms of multilingualism, often effectively minimal: in many cases, the announcement 'English spoken' is the only effectively available English in the shop or restaurant.

Typically, professionally made multilingual signs would attempt to provide a symmetrical pattern, in which everything which is announced in one language would also be announced in the other language (a menu would be a typical example). This is the modern, orderly conception of multilingual practices: A is equivalent to B. The speed of change, however, sometimes precludes such degrees of elaboration, and the effect is then often an 'unfinished' product – we have already seen several examples of that in the different chapters of this book. The town of Saariselka, located in the northern Finnish Samiland, has undergone just such a rapid change over the past decade.[3] From a small skiing resort mostly used by Finnish domestic tourists, it has rapidly become an internationally oriented, fashionable winter sports resort with hotels, restaurants and souvenir shops selling 'typical' Sami goods.

The town has several shops, but one in particular stands out. It is a huge shop which, apart from food, souvenirs and textiles, also harbours a restaurant, a liquor shop and an Internet café. The shop is abundantly and exuberantly multilingual. On the banner in Figure 5.5 we read English, Finnish, German, Swedish, French, Russian and Japanese.

Figure 5.5 The chaotic shop

Figure 5.6 Chaotic announcements

Figure 5.5 also gives us a flavour of the goods on sale there: the shop literally tries to cater for everything and for every taste, including exotic food. It is a truly globalized shop. In the shop, however, no attempt has been made at constructing the kinds of symmetrical and equivalent patterns of multilingual information. Some goods are advertised in Finnish only; others in Finnish and Russian, still others in Finnish, English and Russian, English and German, Finnish and Japanese, Finnish, English, German and French, or in English, French, German and Italian, and so forth. (Note that the Sami languages are not present in the shop.) Not a single object in the shop is advertised in all the seven languages that the shop itself uses to advertise itself. And while English would (apart from Finnish) certainly be the most widely used language, there is no clear hierarchy between the other international languages. In that sense, the shop presents us with chaotic multilingualism: the different languages are around, but in an 'unordered' manner.

Figure 5.6 provides an example of that. We see a billboard outside the shop, on which (some of) the shop's goods are listed. We can discern two 'international' words: 'restaurant' and 'souvenirs'. We also see one Finnish expression: *tekstiili sport* 'sport textiles', and the remainder of the billboard consists of co-ordinated English and German expressions. The 'unfinished' nature of this sign is visible in the haphazard organization of the multilingual resources here, as well as in the orthographic errors in *delikaties*. Several other expressions in international languages are somewhat shaky too, revealing quick translation work based on the available resources (such as dictionaries).

The rapid pace of change in emerging mass tourist centres such as Saariselka can be read from signs such as these. The many languages in the shops signal the presence of customers speaking such languages, and while there appears to be no symmetry and equivalence among the signs, the whole display probably reflects the shop owner's experience with particular groups of customers. For instance: the importance of German signs in the food section may reflect the fact that many German tourists rent a cottage and cook for themselves; the absence of such signs in the souvenir section may reflect the fact that most German tourists do not buy such goods there. The presence of Finnish–Russian signs in the canned fish section may reflect similar patterns of consumption among Russian tourists. The chaotic co-existence of the different languages, however, shows that the shop does not follow a seasonal or cyclical pattern, with, for instance, more Japanese signs when the Japanese tourist season is on, and more French ones when the French tourist season is on. Everything they had was in the shop, structured in a very unclear way – a juxtaposition of language resources reflecting the extremely rapid changes felt in a place like this, where sociolinguistic patterns may change with every new busload of tourists being offloaded in the town. The sociolinguistic ecology of the shop develops on the whimsical rhythm of international mass tourism.

We see something we have already encountered: the ways in which socio-linguistic environments follow and reflect the histories of places. Using a geo-logical metaphor, we see in the Saariselka shop the different sedimented layers of tourist presence, with a stratification in which Finnish would be the 'sub-strate' language, followed by a thick layer of English and then by the chaotic juxtaposition of several other languages. The third layer – that of the chaotic co-existence of languages – reflects the shop owner's willingness to move with the ultra-fast and changing rhythms of the tourist presence in Saariselka, while the presence of English reflects a more enduring layer of internationalization and that of Finnish, the national order and place. These different historical layers overlap in one space and time, and as before, what we see is a synchron-ized pattern of the diachronic emergence of multilingualism and multimodality, the constituent elements of which are of a different order. We can only under-stand the chaotic outcome if we examine the constituent parts' origins and trajectories, because the different parts do different things in the synchronic patterns we observe.

5.5   Conclusion

Mobility is not just a spatial term, it also applies to movement in time, and as I said before the two dimensions always occur together: a movement in space is also one in time. The mobility of certain sociolinguistic resources – think of English – resides in their invocative qualities: they invoke different histories of meaning and function, and intertextually project these historical features onto current acts of communication. When they are used in different places, they draw on locally available histories – English means something different in Dar es Salaam than in New York. And the co-occurrence of different languages and modes of semiotic production each time offer a synchronized juxtaposition of different histories of meaning and function that demands to be disentangled (cf. also Blommaert 2005, chapter 6).

The trajectory I have followed in this book so far has taken us from paradigmatic considerations in which I stressed the importance of resources rather than languages (chapter 1), to a view in which such resources were defined in terms of mobility, with all sorts of complex effects on their meaning and functions requiring new conceptual instruments (chapter 2), and a view of the structure of the world-system and of locality (chapter 3), to issues of truncated repertoires and the unfinished character of language in globalization, in which we saw how our traditional sociolinguistic conception of resources is affected by mobility (chapter 4). We now also know that we need to understand some of the complexity as reflecting different histories of resources. Most of the theoretical ground of this book has by now been covered, but we still need a perspective on sociolinguistic work. This perspective is that of inequality, and I will document it in the next chapter. It should be clear that inequality, as the main effect of power, is a historical product, just like all the other notions mentioned in this chapter. We will see how linguistic resources fall in historical regimes of inequality, and how this complex dynamics is being played out in the present.

6   Old and new inequalities

6.1   Globalization, the state and inequality

According to ideologues of this era such as Francis Fukuyama (1992), the post-Cold War processes of capitalist globalization produce more wealth for more people than any other era in history. It is also an era in which the modern nation state is on its way out, and its power (supposedly concentrated hitherto, which is highly questionable) is now dissipated and distributed over a wide variety of actors and networks (Castells 1996). Power is now held, and effectively enforced, by transnational capitalist ventures, international organizations, media empires and invisible, hardly visible (and otherwise free from democratic control) consortia of decision makers meeting each year in the Swiss ski-resort Davos and other places. There is truth in both propositions – Fukuyama's claim that the end of history would also mark an increase in global wealth, and Castells' and others' claim about the nation state now sharing its power with other actors. But both propositions also invite substantial qualification. I already quoted Hobsbawm in chapter 1, who affirmed that globalization 'has brought about a dramatic growth in economic and social inequalities both within states and internationally' (2007: 3), and the least we can gather from his work and that of many others is that globalization generates immense wealth for some and *also* immense misery for others. Hobsbawm (2007) also emphasizes the importance of traditional state structures in globalization. The nation may be on its way out, but the state is not; according to Wallerstein, contemporary capitalist globalization is heavily dependent on the existence of states:

Capitalists need a large market … but they also need a multiplicity of states, so that they can gain the advantages of working with states but also can circumvent states hostile to their interests in favour of states friendly to their interests. Only the existence of a multiplicity of states within the overall division of labour assures this possibility. (Wallerstein 2004: 24)

And this 'overall division of labour' is based on inequality between states, not equality. Wallerstein, consequently, sees a perpetuation of existing inequalities in the age of globalization: generally speaking, those who were already poor will remain poor, while those who were (almost) rich will become richer.

153

These developments occur internationally as well as within the boundaries of states, as Hobsbawm argued. And the new patterns of 'super-diversity' mentioned in the opening chapter of this book are likely to breed such accentuated inequalities between different groups within one society, as an effect of new migration combined with a weakening of that segment of the labour market conventionally described as the working class. High unemployment in that social stratum and rising commodity prices push people to the margins of society or keep those already marginalized in place, and the gap between the haves and have-nots widens. Such forms of 'hard' socio-economic marginalization are often accompanied by forms of 'soft' marginalization: the marginalization of particular cultural features, identities, practices and resources such as language. The globalized state is, as we shall see, an important actor in such processes of marginalization.

In this chapter I will first present an analysis of an asylum application case in the UK. Such cases, I believe, illustrate much of the real-world dynamics of globalization, and the analysis will bring out the power of the late-modern state in the domain of migration. Inequality is the main product of power: power stratifies, categorizes and divides people in contemporary societies. And language, curiously, repeatedly crops up as a core ingredient of the mechanisms of state power in the field of migration. In that sense, globalization processes now strengthen state power effects in the domain of language; they perpetuate old forms of linguistic inequality and create new forms in their stride. We will also see this in the second set of examples I shall offer, from Belgian language immersion classes in which migrant children learn Dutch. There, too, we will see how a state-organized instrument such as education (an 'ideological state apparatus' in the terminology of Althusser) imposes a punitive, excluding and exclusive language regime on children whose presence is an effect of super-diversity. Both examples are intended to illustrate that globalization, along with people who benefit from it, also counts many losers; that the modern nation state very often functions as the instrument of selection and exclusion in this respect; and that language is becoming an extremely sensitive and critical feature in such processes. Language is at the heart of power processes in environments characterized by super-diversity.

6.2   Language, asylum and the national order

In *The Age of Capital* (1975), Eric Hobsbawm describes the paradox of the late nineteenth century, where the classic nation states of Europe were formed at a time when capital became effectively globalized. While the state became less and less of a relevant scale-level economically, it became the most relevant political scale-level, and the expansion and solidification of a transnational economic infrastructure went hand in hand with the expansion and solidification of a national infrastructure: new political systems, education systems, communication systems and military systems. High modernism set in. The development of standardized national languages was, of course, an important part of this nation-building process, and when the discourse of trade and industry started conquering the globe, it did so in newly codified and glorified national languages.

Processes of globalization acquired that name about a century later, and while globalization contributes little new substance to the processes of world-wide economic expansion, it adds more intensity, depth and velocity to these processes, and it expands the range of objects involved in these processes to include people. The phenomenon of refugees and asylum seekers is a key ingredient of the present stage of globalization. I will argue that globalization phenomena again appear to trigger an emphasis on the national order of things. In the context of asylum application procedures, the imagination of language, notably, is dominated by frames that refer to static and timeless national orders of things. So while asylum seekers belong to a truly global scale-level of events and processes, the treatment of their applications is brought down to a rigidly national scale: a very modernist response to post-modern realities and something we have already encountered in previous chapters of this book.

I will discuss at length one particular case of an asylum application in the UK. The case is that of a young man I shall call Joseph Mutingira, a refugee from Rwanda, whose application was rejected largely on the grounds of the particular sociolinguistic profile he displayed. This profile, the Home Office argued, disqualified him as someone 'from Rwanda'. Joseph appealed against this ruling and provided a very long written testimony documenting his life, the incidents in which he was involved and his escape, rebutting the arguments that supported the ruling. This document will be the main data I shall use; in addition, I also have the written records of the two interviews Joseph did in the context of his application (dated, respectively, November 2001 and June 2004) as well as a copy of the official decision by the Home Office of November 2005 on Joseph's case.[1] I will argue that Joseph's life history provides all sorts of clues about his belonging and life trajectory. However, taken together, these clues construct a new sociolinguistic profile, one that does not fit the traditional national imagination of Rwanda, but one that fits the realities of Rwanda during and after the 1994 genocide.[2] The main point here is that the sociolinguistic repertoire displayed by Joseph is indicative of *time*, not just of *space*: it connects to the *history* of a region over the last two decades, not just to the region. Thus, sociolinguistic repertoires index full histories of people and of places, not just institutionally genred 'origins', and the analysis I provide here offers some additional substance to positions submitted in chapters 4 and 5.

Joseph's life history

Joseph's long affidavit reads like a horror story and it grimly testifies to the profound distortion of the social fabric in Rwanda in the 1990s leading to the genocide of 1994. Here comes a very elementary point: we must read his life history against the backdrop of what we know about that dramatic period in that region of Africa.[3] We must try to imagine his life history as set in a real context, and imagine his life as a possible trajectory followed by people in that region at that time. If we do not, his life history makes no sense – and this fundamental disbelief in the possible realism of such descriptions was what lay behind the rejection of Joseph's asylum application in the UK. I suggest we accept, and use as an assumption, that in thoroughly distorted conditions of life, thoroughly distorted lives can be realistic.

Joseph says he was born in Kigali, Rwanda, in November 1986. This was disputed by the UK authorities, and we shall come back to the issue of Joseph's age further down. He says he is a Hutu, even though his mother was Tutsi. His father was a politician and his mother a businesswoman whose activities were mainly deployed in Kenya. She took young Joseph with her to Kenya, where he attended an English-medium nursery school and, in between visits home, often stayed with a friend of his mother's in Nairobi, with whom he spoke English. He picked up a few words of Swahili from classmates. At home in Kigali, his parents insisted that the children speak English too. The family lived in a compound surrounded by walls, and the father forbade them from going out and socializing with other children. The family had a servant who spoke Kinyarwanda; Joseph learned some Kinyarwanda from him. Visiting friends spoke English, Kinyarwanda and French.

In 1992, at the age of five, Joseph returned to Rwanda with his mother. Shortly after their return, his mother was murdered in circumstances unknown to Joseph. She was buried in their garden, and shortly afterwards the servant left the house. About six months later, the house was attacked at night. Hearing shouting and noise of people breaking things, Joseph jumped out of the window and ran away. His father and the other children in the house were all killed during the raid. Joseph ended up in a group of other people trying to escape from the area where they lived. He told them that he had an uncle living in Gisenyi, a town on the border with the Democratic Republic of Congo (DRC) and next to the Congolese town of Goma. They took him on board a lorry and, after several hours, dropped him off in Gisenyi, where he found his way to his uncle's house. In that house, French and Kinyarwanda were spoken most often, but Joseph's uncle consistently spoke English with him. His uncle told him that his father was a politician, that his father killed his mother because she was a Tutsi, and that Tutsis murdered all the members of his family out of revenge. In his uncle's house, Joseph slept in the basement, and hardly communicated with anyone (remember, he was a small child). But Joseph saw many people visiting his uncle and heard them speaking 'Kinyankole' (Runyankole), a language similar to Kinyarwanda. Joseph picked up a bit of Runyankole, and started speaking it with his uncle. Given his uncle's proficiency in English, French, Kinyarwanda and Runyankole, Joseph suspected that his uncle had lived in another country, and given the proximity of Gisenyi to Goma he believed it must have been the DRC. (Runyankole is, in fact, spoken mainly in Uganda and the border areas of Uganda, Rwanda and DRC, but as we shall see it is also a diasporic language among Rwandan migrants and refugees.) After some time (Joseph was six years old), his uncle started sending Joseph on errands. He had to carry a bag to a certain place, where someone would tap on his shoulder and take the bag from him. Joseph later came to believe that his uncle was involved with 'people from another country', with whom he was plotting something. Gisenyi is adjacent to the Congolese town of Goma, which was the gateway to the Interahamwe rebel-dominated Maniema and Kivu regions in DRC, so this scenario (in 1992–1993) is not unthinkable (see, e.g. Vlassenroot 2000, Vlassenroot and Raeymaekers 2004).

Joseph did this 'for several years' until 'one day in 1996 (I think)' he was stopped by Rwandan Patriotic Front (RPF) government soldiers. They challenged him in Kinyarwanda, but since his Kinyarwanda was still very basic, he answered them in Runyankole. The bag was confiscated and proved to be full of weapons and ammunition. One of the soldiers then interrogated him in Runyankole, and they suspected that Joseph came from the other side of the border and was a child-soldier of the Interahamwe. They arrested him and took him to his uncle's house. They called his uncle out, exchanged some words, and then summarily executed the man in front of the (now 9- or 10-year-old) boy. Joseph was brought to a detention camp where he was beaten every day and interrogated about his involvement in rebel activities, about other members of his group, and so on. The interrogations were held in Runyankole, and the fact that Joseph did not have a fluent proficiency in Kinyarwanda was held against him, as grounds for suspicion of being a foreign 'infiltrant'. After some weeks, he was brought to a prison, presumably in Kigali. He found himself in a cell together with another, older, boy named Emmanuel. The latter had been an Interahamwe member, and he spoke Runyankole as well as Kinyarwanda. Like the prison guards, Emmanuel first thought that Joseph came from another country, given his proficiency in Runyankole. Joseph was routinely and very brutally tortured; in addition, he was repeatedly raped by Emmanuel. 'After some years' Joseph was put on a forced labour regime; given that the guards' orders were in Kinyarwanda, he learned the language to some degree, and he also learned the Kinyarwanda and Swahili songs they would have to sing during work.

After four years in prison, in 2001, he received a visitor: a lady he vaguely remembered. A short while later, during work, a guard told him to go in the bush, and there he met the same lady. She urged him to follow her, together with another boy in prison uniform. They got onto a bus; after a while the other boy got off. The lady and Joseph continued their journey to a coach station, where they caught a bus that took them 'to another country'. There people 'were speaking languages I couldn't understand'. They got to an airport, and the lady produced travel documents for Joseph. Together they boarded a flight that took them to the UK, where the same travel documents enabled Joseph to enter the country. During the whole journey, the woman discouraged Joseph from speaking or asking questions, and in order to gain and reaffirm his trust she repeatedly mentioned the name of Joseph's mother (Joseph afterwards thought she was the Kenyan woman who took care of him in Kenya during his early infancy). They took a bus, got off at some place (presumably central London), and the lady vanished.[4] After several hours of waiting for her, Joseph started walking around, asking people for help. One man took him to the Immigration Service. Joseph was now about 14 years old. When he stated his age to the official ('an Asian lady who spoke Kinyarwanda'), she called in a medical officer who, after the briefest and most summary of examinations, concluded that Joseph was over 18 and should, consequently, be treated as an adult. Here lies the origin of Joseph's 'disputed' age.[5] One week later, a first 'screening' interview was conducted, and Joseph describes the event as intimidating: the officials insisted on short and direct answers, did not make notes of some of his statements (especially on his linguistic repertoire), and threatened to throw him in prison, something which, given his background, was to be avoided at all costs. When the interviewer asked him about his 'mother tongue', Joseph understood this as his 'mother's language' and answered 'Kinyarwanda'. A Kinyarwanda interpreter was called in, and in spite of Joseph's insistence that he would be more comfortable in English and notwithstanding his explanations for his lack of proficiency in Kinyarwanda (not recorded in the verbatim account of the interview), the interview started in Kinyarwanda. Joseph's restricted competence was quickly established, and after he declared that he also spoke Runyankole, an interpreter fluent in Kinyarwanda and Runyankole was called in and the interview was continued in Runyankole. Interestingly (and an implicit acknowledgement of Joseph's linguistic repertoire), supplementary questions were asked and answered in English and noted down in the verbatim account. Joseph's case was dismissed as fraudulent, and both his age and his nationality were disputed.

In November 2003, Joseph's case was reopened by the Home Office, and a second interview took place in June 2004. This interview yielded the usual set of 'contradictions' in comparison with the first, notably with respect to Joseph's language repertoires. In addition, Joseph was not able to give details about Rwanda and Kigali (he could not, for instance, describe the nearest bank to his house in Kigali). He was also asked to provide the numbers from 1 to 10 in

Kinyarwanda; since no interpreter was around, he was asked to write these words 'phonetically'. He produced a written list which was half Kinyarwanda and half Runyankole. The result was easy to predict: his application was rejected again. Joseph was ascribed Ugandan nationality and was to be deported to Uganda.

From a strange life to no life

Towards the end of his affidavit, Joseph writes 'I may have an unusual history, but this does not make me a citizen of a country I have never been to'. Certainly, what transpires from the summary above is that his life was dominated by a kind of Shibboleth-predicament, in which his linguistic repertoire continuously played against him. When he was arrested, his proficiency in Runyankole suggested to the soldiers that he was an agent of the Interahamwe from neighbouring DRC; to Emmanuel, that proficiency suggested the same affiliation; and in the UK his knowledge of English and Runyankole were taken as strong evidence that he was from Uganda, not from Rwanda (where proficiency in Kinyarwanda and French would be expected). So his linguistic repertoire – both positively through what is there and negatively through what is absent from it – perpetually gives him away, categorizes him and creates confusion and suspicion about the veracity of his story. Joseph's language repertoire is continuously seen as indexical of certain political and historical positions, defined from within the synchronic universe of meanings, social categories and attributive patterns in which his interlocutors operate. His proficiency in the particular languages and language varieties he knows continuously 'gives off' information about him, it allows his interlocutors to make quick interpretive jumps from speech to society, to provide contextually loaded readings of his words, and to build an image of Joseph on the basis of how he communicates.

Life on an exit strategy   The key to Joseph's 'unusual history' lies in his early childhood. Sociolinguistically as well as in more general ways, Joseph's life becomes 'unusual' right from the very beginning. As said from the outset, we shall assume that Joseph does not lie about the main lines of his story. And if we follow that story, what becomes very clear is that his family was somewhat aberrant. His father was 'a politician but I have no knowledge of what he did'; in terms of the essentialized categories of ethnic politics in Rwanda, he was identified as a Hutu as well. The father shielded his family from the outside world by prohibiting the children from playing outside their compound, and by insisting on an English-only policy at home. According to Joseph's statement, their father was very strict on the use of English at home, and actively forbade the use of other languages by his children: the father 'thought that speaking

English set us apart from other people and showed that we were more civilised'. In his affidavit, Joseph suggests the following:

Looking back, I wonder whether my parents had lived abroad when they were younger and that is why they spoke English.

Given the troubled history of that region, and given his father's prominence and visibility in public life, this may very well be true. It is not unlikely that his parents had lived abroad as exiles or refugees for a while during one of the many periods of crisis in Rwanda since independence. The fact that Joseph's mother appears to have had business interests and networks in Kenya could be further circumstantial evidence for that. Mamdani (2000: 307–312) shows that large numbers of so-called 'Banyarwanda' (Rwandans, both Hutu and Tutsi) were present as labour migrants in Uganda from the 1920s. Many of them were employed in the cattle-herding Ankole region, where Runyankole is spoken. Refugees of the 1959 and 1964 conflicts also found their way to the same region. A number of these refugees got UNHCR scholarships for schools in, among other places, Nairobi, which became a centre for Rwandan exiles (the exiled king of Rwanda resided in Nairobi). Given the envy this generated among the local population in Uganda, refugees often had to 'pretend to be what they were not: Banyankole, Baganda, Banyoro' (Mamdani 2000: 312). So-called Banyarwanda were also prominent in Museveni's rebel army (and prior to that in Idi Amin's secret police): up to a quarter of the Museveni rebels who marched into Kampala in early 1986 were Banyarwanda (Mamdani 2000: 321). The point is: the history and politics of Rwanda have since long been entangled with those of Uganda, Kenya and other neighbouring countries. That Joseph's family had some involvement in neighbouring countries, and that Runyankole may have entered the family repertoire (e.g. his uncle's) should not be seen as something exceptional. In fact, many Rwandans (Hutu as well as Tutsi) who have a diaspora background are fluent in Runyankole, and that includes the current Rwandan President Paul Kagame, who grew up in the Ankole region.

It is, thus, also not unlikely that the family lived on an exit strategy. The father – a politician – must have been aware of the volatility of the political climate in Rwanda and (given Joseph's uncle's involvement in the Interahamwe) may have been active in particularly sensitive and dangerous (radical Hutu) politics: the kind that could have warranted a permanent readiness to escape from Rwanda and settle elsewhere, in a country such as Kenya where English is widely spoken. Remember: the timeframe described by Joseph (from 1986, the year of his birth, until his arrest in 1996) covers the victory of Museveni in Uganda (1986), the RPF invasion in Rwanda (1990) and the genocide of 1994: an extremely tumultuous period in the region. The fact that Joseph was put in a nursery school in Kenya adds weight to that suggestion.

And the fact that, as Joseph later learns, his Tutsi mother was killed with at least the passive involvement of his Hutu father also bespeaks deep and active involvement in Hutu radicalism. The Tutsi raid on Joseph's house, during which the whole of his family was murdered and the house was set alight, also fits this picture – we see a foreshadowing of the genocide of 1994 here, and radical Hutu are already pitted against radical Tutsi groups in murderous incidents. Joseph's story makes enough sense to be plausible.

When Joseph escaped to his uncle's place, the pattern of political involvement of course becomes clearer. His uncle kept Joseph out of sight and continued the English-only policy with him, but he also received many visitors who spoke French, Kinyarwanda and Runyankole. We know that both Hutu (Interahamwe) and Tutsi (RPF) rebels had their bases in the neighbouring countries Uganda and DRC (Mamdani 2000, Vlassenroot 2000). Runyankole, as we know, is spoken in Uganda (and is part of the 'Runyakitara' cluster, along with Kinyarwanda, Runyoro and other languages), and with the perpetual movements of groups of migrant, exiled or refugee Rwandans, its spread to particular pockets in Rwanda and DRC is a given. It explains why Joseph met so many people in Rwanda who spoke Runyankole: apart from the people in his uncle's house, some of the RPF soldiers and prison guards also spoke the language; so did Emmanuel (an Interahamwe militant), as well as later in the UK the second interpreter in Joseph's application interview, who was fluent (like the Rwandan soldiers and guards) in Kinyarwanda and Runyankole. Thus, the 'foreignness' of Runyankole is not a matter of spatial distribution of the language. Joseph's proficiency in Runyankole is interpreted, quite systematically and by all the people he describes in his narrative, as a sign of being from another country *as well as* a sign of membership of a radical Hutu movement. The language is, by those who in interaction with Joseph project synchronic indexical meanings onto it (the soldiers, Emmanuel, the interrogators, the prison guards), understood as a sign of Hutu rebel involvement imported from neighbouring countries. The geography of the language is a *political* geography, something which does not come as a surprise now that we know something about the history of migration and rebellion in the region. We shall come back to this below.

Joseph's childhood is likely to have been spent in a family living on an exit strategy and acutely aware of the danger of their times. Let us not forget that most of the critical period described by Joseph was indeed his childhood, and that this childhood was spent in a deep political crisis in Rwanda. As a toddler, he was raised in Kenya; at the age of five (too young to enter school, where French and Kinyarwanda would be the dominant languages) he returned to Rwanda. Shortly afterwards, and after an interval in which he informally learned some Kinyarwanda from the family's servant, his mother was killed, his family murdered, and he fled to his uncle in Gisenyi where he lived in hiding and, thus, did not enter school at the normal age of six. For all practical purposes, he was dead, and his uncle probably banked on this when he started sending him on errands providing arms and ammunition to rebel groups from Goma. His communicative network was extremely narrow. He still did not socialize with other children, and only met his uncle's fellow rebels, with whom he interacted in Runyankole. His uncle gave him some books to read, in English mostly and some in Kinyarwanda (this provides evidence of reading skills, not of writing skills). Language learning, however, proceeded exclusively through informal channels. The bit of Kinyarwanda he already knew allowed him to start picking up some Runyankole, and the English he spoke was solely deployed with his uncle. The reading of books provided some back-up to these learning trajectories, but overall they were informal – that is, they developed outside the collective, regimented and literacy-based pedagogies of the classroom. The latter may be part of the explanation for why he failed the number writing test (and thus had to revert to 'phonetic' writing) during his second interview: in all likelihood, Joseph never acquired full literacy in either of the languages he speaks, and during the interview he was asked to write a language which, in his experience, has had very limited functions and is quite close to the language which had more extended functions, Runyankole.

Joseph was arrested at the age of 9–10, and at that age he has not had any formal schooling. His multilingual repertoire is constructed through informal learning processes, and is highly 'truncated', i.e. organized in small, functionally specialized chunks. We shall return to this topic below. For the moment, suffice it to note that Joseph has had indeed 'an unusual story', but that such a story may not have been all that unusual in the Rwanda of the early 1990s. This is not how the Home Office saw it.

The grounds for rejection   The Home Office, in its rejection announcement letter of November 2005, saw Rwanda in a very different light: as a relatively stable and relatively uniform nation state characterized by 'national' features such as a relatively stable regime of language (Kroskrity 2000).

The letter begins by describing the linguistic operations governing the interview procedures (in giving these examples, I shall not be concerned with the grammatical or rhetorical consistency of the text):

(1) It is noted that you claim you were born in … Kigali and that your principal language is English. However, you say you also speak Kinyarkole [sic] and a little Kinyarwanda. It is noted that when you were substantively interviewed, it was conducted in English [reference to the 2004 interview] and when you were interviewed by an Immigration Officer [reference to the 2001 interview], you started the interview speaking in Kinyarwanda then after ten minutes, the interview was continued in the Kinyarkole language…

This description is followed by an authoritative statement about language in Rwanda:

(2) Although English (and Swahili) are spoken in Rwanda, English is spoken by the Tutsi elite who returned from exile in Uganda post-1994. The BBC World Service, however, advises that a genuine Rwandan national from any of the ethnic groups will normally be able to speak Kinyarwanda and/or French. Kinyarwanda, the national language, is the medium of instruction in schools at primary level while French is used at secondary level. Kinyarwanda is also spoken in the neighbouring countries of DRC, Tanzania and Uganda (Rwanda country report April 2004). Whereas, Runyankole is a dialect mainly spoken in the West and South of Uganda (Uganda country profile April 2005). … Based on the information above, it is considered that the language called Kinyarkole used at your screening interview is more widely known as Runyankole, therefore, Runyankole will be referred in the rest of this letter.

Observe for the moment (a) the reference to formal and institutional language regimes, such as the dominant languages in the education system (which, as we know, was unknown to Joseph); (b) the way in which languages are seen as distributed over *countries*; (c) the sources of evidence used here: the BBC World Service and two unidentified country reports; (d) the fact that the Home Office states that the language (or 'dialect') 'Kinyarkole' is more widely known as 'Runyankole'. Several of these points will be addressed more fully in the next section. Now as to Joseph's own performance as a subject set in this tight and stable nation state institutional language regime, this is what the Home Office observes:

(3) Reasons to doubt your nationality can be drawn from the fact that you are unable to speak Kinyarwanda and/or French. As already stated … you were screened for the main part in the Ugandan dialect [sic] and then were substantively interviewed in English. It is noted that you were able to answer a few questions asked in Kinyarwanda at the start of your screening interview. However, in your substantive interview you were asked to state the numbers one to ten in Kinyarwanda … and also asked for the phrases 'Good Morning' and 'Goodbye', you wrote your answers down phonetically because you could not write in the language … [I]t has been decided that although written phoneti-cally you did not get all of them correct … Your lack of basic knowledge of the Kinyarwanda language suggests that you are not a genuine national of Rwanda.

Joseph had written some words in Kinyarwanda and others in Runyankole. The Home Office continues hammering away at Joseph's linguistic repertoire and performance during the interviews:

(4) When asked how you were able to understand Kinyarwanda if you were never taught it and only taught to speak English … you did not answer the question directly, instead you said that you wanted to speak English, but you can also understand Kinyarwanda and Runyankole as well. It is believed that if you were able to pick up and speak fluent Runyankole from your uncle with whom you alleged to have stayed for

four years in Gisenyi yet unable to pick up Kinyarwanda, even though you claim to have lived in Rwanda for thirteen years [sic]. Your inability to give the correct (phonetic) translations for the general greetings in Kinyarwanda, damages the credibility of your claim … Based on this assessment, it is not accepted that you are a genuine Rwandan national as claimed.

Language is the key element in the argument of the Home Office. But it is not the only one:

(5) It is noted that you were able to describe the old Rwandan flag … however, when you were questioned about the basic geography of your home in … Kigali, you were unable to give any information. For instance, you were unable to state any well known land-marks, sites, places, and buildings to your home … You did not know of the nearest bank to your home … You were also unable to name any of the major roads nearest to your home in … Kigali … It is not accepted that you have sufficiently demonstrated your knowledge of the basic country and local information regarding your alleged place of birth, as such, it is not accepted that you were born and have lived in Rwanda as claimed.

This, then, leads to the following conclusion:

(6) It is the opinion that a Rwandan national should be expected to know something about their country of origin and place of birth. Moreover, it is believed that you could be a Ugandan national as result of your knowledge and use of the Runyankole language at screening … Or, you could possibly be a national of a different East African country where English is much more widely spoken. Your true nationality, however, cannot be determined at this point in time.

There we are: Joseph's 'unusual' life has been reset in a different country and in a different time frame, because the Home Office doubts his age as well. From someone with a strange life, Joseph has now been redefined as someone with no life at all.

Defying the monoglot ideal

In a seminal paper, Michael Silverstein (1996: 285) distinguished between a 'speech community' characterized by 'sharing a set of norms or regularities for interaction by means of language(s)', and a 'linguistic community'. The latter is described as

a group of people who, in their implicit sense of the regularities of linguistic usage, are united in adherence to the idea that there exists a functionally differentiated norm for using their language denotationally … the inclusive range of which the best language users are believed to have mastered in the appropriate way.

Consciousness of a standard (the 'best' language) would typically be something that falls within the realm of linguistic communities, and while speech communities are characterized by bewildering diversity, linguistic communities as a rule pledge allegiance to a single norm, and define subjects as '(ab)normal' depending on their degree of fit with that single norm. This pattern of categorization, in which subjects are placed 'in' or 'outside' normalcy depending on how 'normal' their language repertoire is, belongs to what Silverstein calls a 'monoglot ideology'. A monoglot ideology makes time and space static, it suggests a transcendent phenomenology for things that define the nation state, and presents them as natural, neutral, a-contextual and non-dynamic: as facts of nature. Such a monoglot ideology is applied by the Home Office in judging and categorizing Joseph as a language-using subject, and it is the fact that Joseph defies this monoglot ideal that serves as the basis for disqualifying him and his claims.

In what follows I shall try to decode this process in which two 'profiles' are opposed to one another. In order to do that, I shall have to give sociolinguistic-analytic attention to two different phenomena: the language-ideological work of the linguistic community used as a conceptual backdrop by the Home Office, and the practical, pragmatic repertoire displayed and narrated by Joseph, and the speech communities we can see through that.

The national sociolinguistic horizon   Let us now return to some of the fragments from the Home Office letter above, and observe how strongly they define languages in terms of national circumscription. In fragment (2) above, for instance, we read

(7) The BBC World Service, however, advises that a genuine Rwandan national from any of the ethnic groups will normally be able to speak Kinyarwanda and/or French. Kinyarwanda, the national language, is the medium of instruction in schools at primary level while French is used at secondary level.

In fragment (3), we encountered

(8) Your lack of basic knowledge of the Kinyarwanda language suggests that you are not a genuine national of Rwanda.

In fragment (4), we saw

(9) Your inability to give the correct (phonetic) translations for the general greetings in Kinyarwanda, damages the credibility of your claim (…). Based on this assessment, it is not accepted that you are a genuine Rwandan national as claimed.

And in fragment (6), finally, we read that

(10) it is believed that you could be a Ugandan national as result of your knowledge and use of the Runyankole language at screening (…). Or, you could possibly be a national of a different East African country where English is much more widely spoken.

The space in which languages are situated is invariably a *national* space, the space defined by states that have a name and that can be treated as a fixed unit of knowledge and information (as in the 'country reports' quoted by the Home Office). It is also a unit of power, control and institutionalization, as is evident from the frequent references to formal institutional environments (such as the education system) for the proliferation and distribution of the languages here mentioned.

We have also seen how language itself is totalized and strongly associated with levels and degrees of proficiency: Joseph does not speak *enough* Kinyarwanda, or does not speak it *well enough*, his answers were *not correct*.[6] Even if part of the first interview was done in Kinyarwanda, and even if Joseph wrote some words down in Kinyarwanda, that level of proficiency is deemed to fall below the expectations of normalcy associated with nationality. As affirmed by the BBC World Service (reliably, one assumes), 'a *genuine* Rwandan national from any of the ethnic groups will *normally* be able to speak Kinyarwanda and/or French', and that means a *lot* of *correct* Kinyarwanda and French. And given the assumption that a 'normal' Rwandan national would have gone through the national education system (and would thus have had exposure to formal learning trajectories for the national languages), 'speaking' a language equals 'speaking and writing'. Joseph is asked to *write* numbers in Kinyarwanda, as part of an assessment of whether he *speaks* the language. The highly regimented nature of literacy is simply overlooked, regardless of the fact that Joseph had clearly stated that he had not attended any schools in Rwanda, and regardless of the fact that his problem with literacy had led the interviewer to ask him to write phonetically. The Home Office should have known that they were facing a young man for whom literacy was a hurdle.

As the argument continues, since Joseph knows Runyankole *well enough*, and since that language is 'officially' spoken (as a 'dialect', according to the Home Office) in Uganda, Joseph could be a Ugandan national. The fact that, in Joseph's account, many other Rwandans were reported to use Runyankole, and given the fact that even in the Immigration Authorities' offices the Home Office had no problem finding an interpreter fluent in both Kinyarwanda and Runyankole – all of this is overlooked or disregarded. Languages can spill over borders, and such phenomena are rife in regions where a lot of cross-border traffic exists; such cross-border traffic is frequent in regions such as that of the Great Lakes where there are large numbers of 'old' and 'new' refugees (Mamdani 2000, also Malkki 1995). People there, consequently can have densely mixed, *poly*glot repertoires. These are elementary sociolinguistic facts that are not taken into account in the Home Office's use of language as an analytic of national belonging. This is why we need to shift our focus now from language to speech, and towards the real, practical resources that Joseph has.

A polyglot repertoire   All of the above is of course reminiscent of Pierre Bourdieu's observation in *Language and Symbolic Power* (1991: 45):

To speak of *the* language, without further specification, as linguists do, is tacitly to accept the *official* definition of the *official* language of a political unit. This language is the one which, within the territorial limits of that unit, imposes itself on the whole population as the only legitimate language, especially in situations that are characterized in French as more *officielle*. (italics in original)

And he continues, 'this state language becomes the theoretical norm against which all linguistic practices are objectively measured'. The political unit that is the target of the Home Office's 'objective measurement' is Rwanda, and 'the' languages of Rwanda are (normative, standardized and literate varieties of) Kinyarwanda and French. The Home Office overlooks the fact that when a state is in crisis (like Rwanda for most of its postcolonial history and certainly in the period covered in Joseph's story), symbols of the state and its power such as the national language may be questioned, as many nationals may no longer live by the ideology of the state. This can be heavily contested as well. In fact, since speaking the national language may in itself be an expression of political allegiance, it may, in circumstances of violent conflict, require dissimulation or denial for one's own safety. As mentioned earlier, speaking a 'rebel' language such as Runyankole induces a political semiotics.[7]

Joseph did not have a repertoire that accords with the expected 'official' and 'national' one. But what was his repertoire? It appears to have been a 'truncated multilingual' repertoire, composed of functionally specialized 'bits' of language(s) which he had picked up in informal learning trajectories during his life. Remember, of course, that given the particular chronology of the events in his life, Joseph did not attend school apart from the nursery school in Kenya. The linguistic repertoire he reports in his affidavit is the repertoire of a child or an adolescent who grew up in extraordinary conditions, outside any form of 'normalcy'.

Joseph provides lots of information, very detailed in fact, on how he acquired and deployed the multilingual resources he had. In fact, given the prominence given to language issues by the Home Office, his affidavit is replete with descriptions of how and why he acquired his linguistic resources, and how he relates to them. Here is a little selection of statements on language, following the biographical line reported in the affidavit.

(11) My first language is English. This is the first language I can remember speaking. Ever since I was a small child, as far back as I can remember, my parents spoke to me in English.

(12) It was very important to my father that we children always spoke English as he thought that speaking English set us apart from other people and showed that we were more civilised.

(13) The servant would speak Kinyarwanda. I remember sometimes when my parents were both out, the servant would tell us little Kinyarwanda poems and sayings, and so I picked some Kinyarwanda up from him. He also understood and spoke a little English, but he was not fluent.

(14) At school in Kenya we were taught in English. All communication was in English and if you spoke to the teachers you had to talk to them in English … Some of the children did speak to each other in Swahili or Kikuyu in the playground…

(15) When I had been to my uncle's house with my parents they had spoken French and Kinyarwanda, but mostly Kinyarwanda. However, my uncle had always spoken English to me and my brothers.

(16) My uncle spoke lots of languages. He was very good in English, French, Kinyarwanda and Kinyankole … When I first got to his house I couldn't understand the languages he was speaking and I thought he spoke a different language with every person that came to his house.

(17) I did not have a lot to do, and so I would listen to my uncle and his friends talking and I began to learn some of the words they were speaking. The language [Runyankole, JB] is quite similar to Kinyarwanda, and so it wasn't difficult to learn more, since I already understood some Kinyarwanda … Eventually I knew enough to speak a bit of Kinyankole to my uncle. I think he was surprised about this. At that time I didn't know the name of the language that my uncle spoke. I knew he had lived in another country because my parents had told me that he lived in another country. I guessed that this is why he spoke that language. I didn't know where the language come from [sic] as I had never heard the language before. I assumed it was from a nearby country. I thought maybe it was a language from the DRC (Zaire) but I had no reason for this except that I knew it was a country which was next to Rwanda.

(18) After I had been there a while I told him [Joseph's uncle] that I wanted to learn, and so he brought me a few books. Mostly the books were in English. Sometimes they were in Kinyarwanda, and some had both languages in them.

(19) [The soldiers] started questioning me in Kinyarwanda asking me what was in the sack. I understood what they were saying to me, but I couldn't reply. I was very shocked, and I didn't have good enough Kinyarwanda to explain, and they were all talking at once so I just froze. I spoke to them in Kinyankole to reply to their questions because that was the language I was using most commonly at the time. The soldiers called another soldier over. This soldier spoke to me in Kinyankole and asked me questions… I now think that they thought that I was a child who had been brought up abroad, and was part of the Interahamwe who was training to come back to Rwanda and fight … The soldier who spoke Kinyankole would translate for the others and tell them what I said.

(20)   I kept telling them [the prison guards] I didn't know, but they said that the fact that I didn't speak good Kinyarwanda was evidence that I was a rebel.

(21) He [Emmanuel] spoke Kinyankole and Kinyarwanda very well ... He told me that he had been working for a Hutu rebel group and had been a soldier in a different country. I thought that this was DRC or Uganda ... I think that is how he learned Kinyankole.

(22) We would be given orders in Kinyarwanda. My Kinyarwanda was good enough to understand what they said and so I would know what to do. There was no talking to each other so I didn't get to learn any more Kinyarwanda or talk to anyone ... The prisoners would sometimes have to sing songs on the way ... Usually the songs were in Kinyarwanda, but sometimes they would sing Swahili songs.

(23) I have bad associations with the Kinyankole language. I feel that learning Kinyankole has been a disaster for me. I wish I had never learned that language ... I want to keep myself apart from that language. Anyway, I do not speak Kinyankole as well as I speak English. I can communicate at a much more basic level. I can make myself understood, and I can understand what someone else says in Kinyankole, but it is not like speaking in English which I find much easier, and which allows me to express myself more clearly ... My Kinyarwanda is not a good language for me to communicate in either. I do have basic Kinyarwanda, but I cannot speak it fluently. When someone talks to me in Kinyarwanda I can understand what they mean, but not every word that they say. However, I cannot reply easily.

Joseph is generous with information on how he acquired languages (fragments 11, 13, 14, 17 and 18), as well as on the particular skills he acquired in these languages (fragments 22 and 23). But he also gives us rather precise micro-descriptions of sociolinguistic environments, in which different people use different languages and use them in different ways, often including reflections on how people acquired the languages they mastered as well as elements of the specific genres in which the languages were deployed (fragments 13, 14, 15, 16, 17, 19, 21 and 22). And finally, Joseph also appears to be quite aware of the indexical values of some of these languages: English sets them apart and suggests a superior level of 'civilisation' (fragment 12), Runyankole suggests an identity as a foreign Hutu rebel (19, 20 and 21), and he himself has very negative attitudes towards that language (fragment 23). Here is the political geography of the language again: Runyankole, in the crisis-ridden Rwandan context in which his story is set, naturally signalled enemy identities to those whom he encountered on his way.

Observe how specific and precise Joseph is in all of this. He specifies that he can 'understand' people but not 'reply' to them in Kinyarwanda; that he has a 'basic' active knowledge in Runyankole; that Swahili was used in RPF songs sung in prison (but not for commands, which were in Kinyarwanda), and so on. Joseph articulates a fairly well-developed ethno-sociolinguistics, in which various highly specific resources – 'bits' of languages – are assembled into a truncated repertoire, the 'best' language of which is English (which 'allows him to express himself more clearly' than Kinyarwanda or Runyankole). We see how Joseph specifies lines 'into' particular languages, genres, registers. These lines are situational and dependent on the highly specific communicative networks in which he gets inserted. He grew up 'outside' Kinyarwanda, except for the poems and sayings he picked up from the servant; he acquired English in a schooled and rigorous home context; his Runyankole came into existence by eavesdropping on conversations between his uncle and visitors in the house, and was later used in interactions with the soldiers and with Emmanuel. And his Kinyarwanda (as well as bits of Swahili) developed when he got into prison. As already mentioned before, there are hardly any formal learning trajectories here (except, minimally, for English), and he learns the particular pieces of language in the context of a deeply distorted life. The result is a very distorted repertoire, but a 'normal' repertoire can hardly be expected under such conditions. Let me underscore that this repertoire is not tied to any form of 'national' space, and neither to a national, stable regime of language. It is tied to an individual's life and it follows the peculiar biographical trajectory of the speaker. When the speaker moves from one social space into another, his or her repertoire is affected, and the end result is something that mirrors, almost like an autobiography, the erratic lives of people.

Runyankole or Kinyankole?   We have seen that the Home Office bases its arguments for rejecting Joseph's claims on his partial knowledge of Kinyarwanda and his (unqualified) knowledge of Runyankole. It is the latter language that situates him in Uganda according to the Home Office (and in spite of evidence that shows that the language is also used by Rwandans, including the Home Office interpreter). In fragment 23 above, we saw, however, how strongly Joseph qualified his own proficiency in Runyankole: 'I do not speak Kinyankole as well as I speak English. I can communicate at a much more basic level'. He can 'make himself understood' and understand what other people say. In addition to the fact that he (rightly) considers that language to be one of the severe problems in his life, he self-qualifies as a non-native speaker of Runyankole.

This is further evidenced by something that the Home Office failed to pick up, in spite of the fact that they themselves mention it. We read in fragment 2 above:

(24) Based on the information above, it is considered that the language called Kinyarkole used at your screening interview is more widely known as Runyankole, therefore, Runyankole will be referred in the rest of this letter.

The use of the term 'Kinyarkole' in the Home Office's letter is strange, and it does not reflect Joseph's own consistent use of 'Kinyankole'. The point, however, is that the Home Office redefines what is named in the reports as 'Kinyankole/Kinyarkole' as 'Runyankole' – using a different prefix to the stem '-nyankole'. *Ru*nyankole is the official name of the language, and it is the name used for the language by its native speakers.[8] Using the prefix 'Ki-' for the language would mimic the use of that prefix in language names such as

'Kinyarwanda', 'Kirundi' and 'Kiswahili', and would rather obviously mark non-native, diasporic usage and identification of that language. It would be a rather predictable *Rwandan* way of identifying Runyankole. The upshot of this simple observation (but one missed by the Home Office) is that Joseph's consistent use of the name 'Kinyankole' places him outside the national socio-linguistic order of Uganda, where the language would be called Runyankole.[9]

It is, in a way, an elephant in the room, but such elementary errors disqualify Joseph as a native speaker of Runyankole, and thus (in the logic of the Home Office) would rule out Uganda as his place of origin. The use of Kinyankole, in addition to Joseph's account of his limited proficiency in the language, would clearly point towards a position as a speaker of a local (Rwandan or cross-border) lingua franca, diaspora, variety of the language. It would in effect be evidence for a totally different sociolinguistic image of the region, in which languages and speakers do not stay in their 'original place' but move around on the rhythm of crises and displacements of populations. That image, needless to say, corresponds far better to the historical realities of the Great Lakes region after independence.

Modernist responses

We have reached the conclusion of the disturbing story of Joseph's life and his asylum application, and what remains is to observe how in the face of post-modern realities, such as the globalized phenomenon of international refugees from crisis regions to the West, governments appear to formulate very old modernist responses (see also Maryns 2006). We have seen, in particular, how in Joseph's case, the Home Office relied on a national sociolinguistic order of things in assessing his linguistic repertoire.

To begin with, his repertoire was seen as indicative of *origins*, defined within stable and static ('national') spaces, and not of biographical trajectories that develop in actual histories and topographies. The question as to which (partic-ular and single) language Joseph 'spoke' was a question that led to statements about where he was born, about the point in the world where his origins lie. The fact is, however, that someone's linguistic repertoire reflects *a life*, and not just birth, and it is a life that is lived in a real sociocultural, historical and political space. If such a life develops in a place torn by violent conflict and dislodged social and political relations, a pristine image of someone being born and bred in one community with one language as his 'own' is hardly useful. In fact, using such a pristine image is unjust. If we accept that Joseph led the life he documents in his affidavit, then very little in the way of a 'normal' sociolinguistic profile can in fact be expected. In other words, if the Home Office had assumed that Joseph *might* have been a genuine refugee, deviance from a 'normal' socio-linguistic profile would have been one of the key arguments in his favour.

Imposing such sociolinguistic normalcy (with the deeper implications specified by Bourdieu above) amounts to an a-priori refusal to accept the possible truth of his story. In fact, it creates a catch-22 for Joseph. If his sociolinguistic profile had been 'normal' (to the Home Office), that would have been strong evidence that the life history he told was untrue. If he had had a command of schooled and literate varieties of Kinyarwanda and French, this would naturally have meant that the account of his troubled childhood was a concoction.

As we know, such imageries of sociolinguistic normalcy belong to the instrumentarium of the modern nation state. In fact, in the sort of Herderian twist often used in nationalist rhetoric it is at the core of modern imaginings of the nation state, and it revolves around a denial or rejection of what Bauman and Briggs (2003) call linguistic hybridity: impure and mixed systems, non-standard forms, transformed language resources. (About this, see also Zygmunt Bauman's 1991 discussion of the relationship between modernity and ambivalence.) It comes with the monoglot package described by Silverstein (1996, also 1998), in which language testing and emphases on literate 'correctness' assume a prominent place – witness the little literacy test administered to Joseph in order to ascertain his 'knowledge' (totalized) of Kinyarwanda (see also Collins and Blot 2003). The paradox of this modernist reaction to post-modern realities is sketched above: injustice is almost by necessity its result. Imposing a strictly national order of things on people who by their very nature are de-nationalized and trans-nationalized, is not likely to do justice to their case. In particular, it produces tremendous difficulties with coming to terms with

the logical intersection between mobile people and mobile texts – an intersection no longer located in a definable territory, but in a deterritorialized world of late modern communication. (Jacquemet 2005: 261)

It is far too easy to rave about the ignorance or absurdity displayed by the Home Office in this case. The point that needs to be made is wider and graver than that. It is ultimately about the way in which anomalous frames for interpreting human behaviour – the modernist national frames referred to here – are used as instruments of power and control in a world in which more and more people no longer correspond to the categories of such frames. This problem is not restricted to asylum cases; we can also see it in the field of schooled instruction (e.g. Collins and Blot 2003), media regimes and various forms of language policing therein, and so many other places and events where institutions have to address cultural globalization. The dominant reflex to increases of hybridity and deterritorialization, unfortunately, too often appears to be a reinforced homogeneity and territorialization. We will see very similar phenomena in our next example as well.

The theoretical questions this raises are momentous, and we should pause to consider one of them. It is clear that a sociolinguistics of languages does not offer much hope for improvement. It is precisely the totalizing concept of language which is used in cases such as these to disqualify people, often on the basis of the flimsiest of evidence. What is needed – and here I reiterate one of the main theoretical points of this book – is a sociolinguistics of *speech* and of *resources*, of the real bits and chunks of language that make up a repertoire, and of real ways of using this repertoire in communication. Sociolinguistic life is organized as such: as *mobile speech*, not as static language, and lives can consequently be better investigated on the basis of repertoires set against a real historical and spatial background. It is on the basis of such an analysis of resources that we were able to answer the language-based claims of the Home Office about Joseph's national belonging. In work on these topics, we should keep track of the strong definitional monoglot effect of the modern state – of the way in which time and space are made (literally) 'static' (i.e. a feature of the state) in relation to language – and part of any post-modern phenomenology of language and culture should be devoted to understanding the very non-post-modern ideologies and practices that shoot through post-modern, globalized realities. We need to balance both and to understand that a totalized, modern concept of language is very much part of post-modern realities.

6.3   Mainstreaming the migrant learner

Joseph's life was measured against a 'mainstream', which was a reflection of the national order. The linguistic resources he had brought with him during his escape and move to Europe lost weight and value during the journey, and by the time he offered them for inspection in Britain, they had been turned into arguments that could be used against him. This was done by a state apparatus, the immigration authorities, and we saw that their response to Joseph's deterritorialized and mobile existence was a very modernist one, stressing the national order of things as if he had never migrated. In the face of super-diversity, governments appear to return quickly to the safe fortresses of modernism, emphasizing homogeneity and uniformity across the population, and using tools to categorize and discriminate in the process. Language has become such a critical tool.

Joseph's presence in Europe was part of the new migrations we have already repeatedly mentioned, and, as we know, such migrations involve a wide range of nationalities, driven by a wide range of motives and using very different modalities of migration. Children of such new migrants go to school, and let us now consider what happens there. I will draw on work done in Dutch immersion classes in the Flemish part of Belgium in 2002–2003. Newly immigrated children are defined as 'other-language newcomers' (*anderstalige nieuwkomers* in Dutch) and are brought into at least one year of Dutch immersion prior to being 'mainstreamed' in regular classes. Note that there is a very strong political–ideological undercurrent that supports this immersion tactic: in the

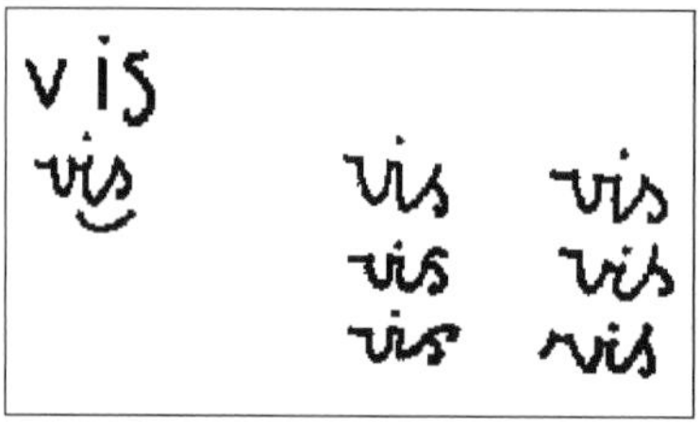

Figure 6.1 'Vis'

context of migration, the Flemish Government increasingly emphasizes the importance of Dutch as a prerequisite to 'integration' into the host society (see Blommaert and Verschueren 1998 for a general discussion). This phenomenon is another face of globalization: while the flow from centre to periphery is characterized by international resources such as English, the flow from the periphery to the centre is trapped in localism and regionalism. In Belgium, immigrants have to learn Dutch and French, not English; they need to learn Swedish in Sweden, German in Germany, Spanish in Spain, and so on.

In an earlier publication (Blommaert, Creve and Willaert 2006) we pointed out that immigrant children are being declared 'language-less' and illiterate when they enter such immersion classes. Their often intricate multilingual repertoires are not recognized and certainly not used as existing and valuable linguistic-communicative instruments, and pupils find themselves in an 'A-B-C' environment in which language and writing need to be learned from scratch. The procedure and motivation are simple. When a child does not speak Dutch, its linguistic resources are considered to be without value 'to live in our society', and children, so to speak, have to un-learn their languages and literacy practices, replacing them with Dutch-only ones. A strong 'monoglot' image of linguistic and cultural homogeneity transpires from these practices, which are very often executed by highly motivated and well-meaning teachers, whose goal is genuinely to promote the well-being of their migrant pupils in Belgian society and to improve their 'social integration' in Belgian mainstream society. Teachers very often believe that writing is the best way to 'correctly' learn a language. But writing is interpreted in a curiously restricted way: as the production of particular *forms of writing*. Consequently, tremendous efforts are spent in acquiring highly specific formal writing skills such as the graphic shape of the 's' symbol in figure 6.1 (the underlined form is the teacher's instruction).

The climate in such classes is hardly stimulating. Pupils painstakingly repeat the writing exercises in attempts to 'get it right', and very little other learning goes on. Language – Dutch in this case – has become an oppressive monolith, something that is so centre-stage in the learning process that differences

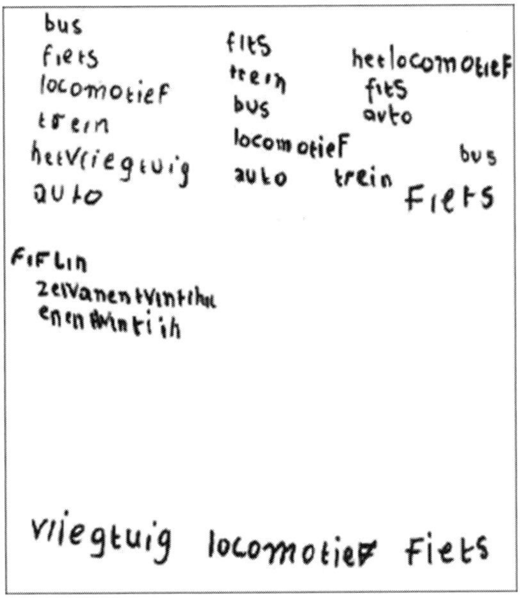

Figure 6.2 Vladi's copybook

between 'right' and 'wrong' define the learning trajectories. Doing it 'right' will quickly lead to qualifications of educationally successful (i.e. 'intelligent', 'smart') children, while doing it 'wrong' leads to qualifications of learning problems (i.e. the 'not-so-smart' or 'struggling' learner). This regime obscures, backgrounds or overlooks the many other learning processes that children effectively display in such classrooms. And in that sense, they very often miss the ways in which migrant children deploy the totality of their linguistic and semiotic repertoires in creative and productive blends that reveal real progress. The child who wrote the 'vis' example above was already literate. He already knew how to write. These writing skills were brought along from previous learning experiences, and the child writes, in effect, a perfectly adequate version of 'vis'. His writing skills are, however, disqualified and he is now facing the task of writing the word *precisely* in the way the teacher did. The point is: the child already knew how to write, but he was confronting a task replete with ideological perceptions of 'right' and 'wrong', in which 'right' stands for *exactly* the way a Belgian child would write 'vis'. The real learning that the child already possessed, and which he deployed in this task, were back-grounded. I want to focus now on one particular piece of writing, produced by a 12-year-old boy from Bulgaria whom we shall call Vladi (a pseudonym). Figure 6.2 is a page from his copybook in which he practised his writing of dictated words.

Figure 6.3 Two words from Vladi's notes

Vladi's writing shows signs of unfamiliarity with the writing conventions of Dutch. We see the unwarranted use of capitals ('Fiets', 'locomotieF') and difficulties in sequencing the graphic symbols into one uninterrupted string (as in 'vis' above): he writes separate symbols. Notwithstanding that, Vladi's writing is largely correct, even when it comes to realizing some of the more tricky peculiarities of the Dutch orthographic system such as the double symbols *ui* and *au*. More interesting are the errors. Vladi provides two versions of the Dutch word *fiets* 'bicycle': *fiets* and *fits*. And he also writes the two very peculiar forms seen in figure 6.3. Transliterated, these would read as *zeivanentvintihi* and *enentwintiih*. These are realizations of what in standard Dutch orthography would be *zeventwintig* 'twenty-seven' and *eenentwintig* 'twenty-one' respectively.

These forms are intensely interesting, because what Vladi writes here is a very accurate graphic approximation of the *local Dutch accent of the teacher.* Vladi's school was in Antwerp and his teacher was an Antwerp native. In the teacher's local accent, the distinction between long and short [i] sounds is unnoticeable, even if they are represented by two different graphemes, *i* (short [i]) and *ie* (long [i:]). So in the teacher's accent, the [i] in *vis* and in *fiets* would sound identical ([vi:s] and [fi:ts]), and this inaudible difference is reflected in Vladi's use of both graphemes *i* and *ie*. This is even more outspoken in the case of *zeivanentvintihi*: in the teacher's local accent, the word *zevenentwintig* ([ze:vənəntwɪntəɣ]) would be pronounced as [zævənəntwɪntəɣ], and this is precisely what Vladi writes: he writes the Antwerp dialect accent that he hears from the teacher, using the conventional grapheme *ei* for [æ]. Vladi is freewheeling here. While most other forms he writes (e.g. 'locomotief') are the result of formal learning, he also experiments in his copybook, noting down new words he has heard – *zevenentwintig* and *eenentwintig* – or attempting to combine words with articles as in *het locomotief* (which should be *de locomotief* 'the locomotive'). In making these brave attempts, we see that Vladi exploits what he has already learned in the way of orthographic logic and that he simultaneously ventures into the many places where such logic is absent. In his *enentwintiih*, he writes the initial long [e:] as *e*, orthographically wrong, but understandable because long [e:] can also be written as *e*. In the same word, the [w] is correctly written as *w*, while in *zeivanentvintihi* he wrote the same sound as *v*. Together with the final soft [ɣ], the [w] is notoriously hard to acquire for many non-native speakers of Dutch; the orthographic errors are thus understandable.

Vladi produces voice here: the voice of an eager and enthusiastic learner who pushes the limits of his learning by experimenting with the resources he already has. Even if his writing skills suffer from basic imperfections – his use of capitals etc. – we see that it offers him a capacity to start reproducing and expanding the things he knows. His voice is, however, that of an immigrant: he records the local accent probably without an awareness that it is not a standard form of Dutch. Any Dutch is Dutch for those who do not know it (like any English is English for those who do not know it). The orthographic errors he produces, consequently, reveal his particular position vis-à-vis Dutch: that of a non-native learner in Antwerp, surrounded by local native accents and confronted with the compelling normativity of a standard orthography. His writing, in short, defines the immigrant learner.

The tension is easily sketched. Vladi's writing reveals 'social integration' in a real sociolinguistic environment. He picks up, perhaps also reproduces in speaking, the local accent of Dutch. He does that very well, and in that sense his writing skills are excellently developed. But his performance as a language learner will be judged not on the basis of the sociolinguistic reality in which he finds his place, but on the basis of a normative standard that only exists, for him, as a set of formal writing conventions (which can be seen from his alteration of /fits/ and /fiets/). Simply put, while his writing of *zeivanentvintihi* is absolutely accurate as a replica of sociolinguistic reality, it is just an error when seen from the normative standard ('monoglot') viewpoint. And so while from the first perspective Vladi is fully integrated, he is not integrated from the second perspective. Unless we see his writing skills as skills for producing an experiential voice, we will be tempted to disqualify them as just 'bad writing'. Entering the mainstream, here, means being able to reproduce a strictly regimented set of skills, the function of which is just reflexive: to demonstrate that one can reproduce them.

What we see in these examples is how pupils construct voice under severe constraints on linguistic choice. The pupils had to work in a medium that was not theirs, and they all clearly struggled with some of the basic skills they had to use. The effects of literacy and language, when perceived as normative and as vehicles for just a small set of stereotypical 'linguistic' functions, is that linguistic products are silenced and made invisible. The texts discussed in both examples are all very unremarkable and easy to dismiss as just trivia documenting a particular stage in a learning trajectory. I prefer to see them as little sites of struggle – a struggle to make sense and to make oneself understood under exacting and restraining conditions. Such conditions characterize much of what we understand by globalization for many people who are part of globalization processes: they are disabling rather than enabling, excluding rather than including, and repressing rather than liberating. Producing voice under such conditions is possible, but detecting it requires a tactic of examination that focuses on implicit patterns, on the poetics of semiotic form rather than the linguistics of structure. It requires, in other words, a demanding and complex form of analysis – one, however, which I believe to be very necessary if we believe in equity and equality.

I am not the first to define schools as sites of struggle; indeed, this view is far from original and shared by generations of educational researchers. But we also need to understand schools as institutional environments in which the elementary processes of subjectivity – making yourself heard and understood by other people – can be and are problematic in an age of globalization. People use all there is to use in making sense; they use explicit linguistic resources as well as implicit, sociocultural ones. If we solely focus on the explicit resources and deny the existence of the implicit ones, chances are that their voices are not identified, recognized and heard.

6.4   The end of the state and inequality?

In the discussion in chapter 2 of commodified American accents, I pointed out that the state had to share its normative authority in the field of language with new commercial providers who use the Internet for their language teaching business; I also pointed out how this created particular tensions between different orders of indexicality, operating at different scale-levels. In the preceding analysis, however, I hope to have shown that such a division of labour does not mean that the state is 'out'. The fact that the state does not hold *absolute* power over everything does not mean that the state does not have any power at all. It does have close control over, for instance, immigration, and language plays an increasingly important part in that dynamic of power. In the field of immigration, we see that the state as a scale-level is still of crucial importance for an understanding of contemporary globalization processes. Exclude or forget the state from an analysis, and the analysis will be incomplete. Migrants are drawn, reterritorialized and firmly locked into a *national* scale-level. This shift between scale-levels, we have seen above, involves a wholesale reordering of the frames within which migrants are treated and their stories analysed. The histories they draw upon in trying to make sense to immigration interviewers are cast aside and replaced by a stable, uniform bureaucratic TimeSpace horizon, in which they often do not make sense. The resources they brought along, which have their origins in different TimeSpace frames, are subject to disqualification or 'misrecognition' in the sense of Bourdieu. It is with the static and timeless image of *the* language – the Saussurean synchrony of language – that state authorities go to work on the super-diversity that now characterizes their urban centres. The instrument, needless to say, is fundamentally flawed, and there is little hope that good things will happen with it.

This insight, I hope, is sobering for those who believe that globalization only offers opportunities. It does to some people – think of this author – who can deploy their mobile resources across different spaces and scales. But it is seriously constraining for many others who do not possess such resources or whose resources do not match the orders that are imposed upon them in the punishing formats of immigration applications. It is also sobering, I hope, to those people who believe that globalization means that the state becomes less and less relevant as a level of political and economic agency. It becomes less and less relevant for people like the present author, who can surf the web and travel the world on the strength of his solid European passport and his middle-class highly educated class features. It is extraordinarily relevant for those lower on the social ladder, whose well-being (and indeed, sometimes their life) depends on the goodwill of state systems for immigration control and the control of poverty, unemployment, unsafe housing, and so on. The bottom line is that we see how inequality becomes an engine of a system of globalization, of which the state is one highly relevant scale-level. The fact that states all over the Western world these days employ very similar tactics for immigration control (see Blommaert 2001a, Maryns 2006) does not represent a fundamental problem here: each state operates within the particular confines of its national boundaries, and it acts there with absolute, oppressively absolute, control.

People such as Joseph are mobile people who, in many ways, epitomize globalization. Their lives are globalized lives, and this should teach us a lesson about what globalization is about. If we compare him to the customers of the American accent courses, or to the authors of the email fraud messages in the previous chapter, we see that Joseph belongs to a specific stratum of globalization – to the bottom of the globalization market, so to speak. He is not wanted or targeted as a customer for new Internet business, and neither is he the savvy guy who sends out clever messages to credulous Western addressees. He is not someone who makes the most of globalization. His position in the processes of globalization is very vulnerable, even if his position is definitional of globalization. He is a victim of globalization, and it is good to devote some attention to people such as him too.

7   Reflections

7.1   Sketch of a road map

In the previous chapters I have developed some conceptual tools for a socio-linguistics of globalization. I argued that such a sociolinguistics ought to be a sociolinguistics of mobile resources and not of immobile languages. I showed how mobility affects the phenomenology of language, and how we need to think about it in terms of scales, orders of indexicality and polycentricity. I then tried to develop a perspective on locality, arguing that the sociolinguistic world needs to be seen in terms of relatively autonomous complexes, obviously influenced by global factors but still firmly local. I argued that through all of this, we need to think of truncated repertoires rather than of 'complete' languages in the traditional sense of the term, and that we need to see communication in global-ization as often 'unfinished', as a deployment of incomplete communicative forms. And I offered inequality as a perspective on all of this, arguing that, paradoxically perhaps in a so-called post-modern age, the modern state is very often the engine behind much inequality. Together, these arguments and con-cepts form a kind of cosmology for the sociolinguistics I have in mind; they should offer us a sketch of a road map for the poorly charted waters in which we now find ourselves.

The shift from language to resources is crucial in all of this. This is not a new idea: abandoning structural notions of language for more phenomenological ones, in which language events and experiences are central rather than language-as-form-and-meaning, has been a key ingredient of what is called pragmatics (e.g. Verschueren 1998); it also underlies contemporary linguistic anthropology and several branches of discourse analysis (Blommaert 2005; Johnstone 2008), and recent sociolinguistics has explored it as well (Rampton 2006; Makoni and Pennycook 2007). The consequences of that shift, however, are not yet deeply understood. We must, for instance, accept that abandoning a structural notion of language (a linguists' construct, as we know) compels us to replace it by an ethnographic concept such as *voice*, which embodies the experiential and practice dimensions of language and which refers to the way in which people actually deploy their resources in communicative practice.

Traditional notions related to multilingualism, such as code-switching, then become moments of voice in which people draw resources from a repertoire that contains materials conventionally associated with 'languages'. The 'language' dimension, however, is not of paramount importance for understanding what such people do, and multilingual practices such as those would be better seen as heteroglossic practices in which different voices are being blended. And this can be done in conventionally defined 'monolingual' as well as 'multilingual' speech. Heteroglossia is the default mode of occurrence of communication, and differences in language materials do not present a fundamental complication for this: it is just heteroglossic speech. The occurrence of the truncated resources described in chapter 4 – the default mode of occurrence of multilingual speech, I would suggest – would then be describable in terms that are far more sensitive to immediate, and distant, historical context. We then see how the authors of the fraud email messages attempt to construct the voice of a trustworthy business partner out of the resources that they have at their disposal: technological resources and skills, and cultural and linguistic knowledge. And we see that as a result of the particular configuration of these resources, several voices are being produced: that of the trustworthy business partner *along with* that of someone from Africa writing English with an African accent (a historical context-feature), the voice of a crook trying to lure us into a tricky deal, and so forth. We get, in short, a clearer image of the real communication that is attempted in these messages.

So the shift from language to resources in our perspective should not pose any serious difficulties. But there is a second shift, one from a view in which language is narrowly tied to a community, a time and a place (the Saussurean synchrony also precipitated into notions of the speech community and related ones), and in which language is primarily seen as having local functions, to a view in which language exists in and for mobility across space and time. This shift, I would say, is conceptually far more momentous than the previous one, because it forces us to consider linguistic signs detached from their traditional locus of origin (in a speech community, and with a specific set of local functions), and instead re-placed, so to speak, in very different loci of production and uptake – where the conventional associative functions of such signs cannot be taken for granted. We saw examples of this in chapter 2, when we discussed Nina's Derrière, and I argued there that such shifts force us to abandon the conventional connections between language and its linguistic functions: the French was not linguistic French in Japan, it was emblematic French, and it only became linguistic French when someone with a degree of linguistic competence in French walked by. The upshot of this is that we need to think of language *semiotically* and not linguistically if we intend to capture what goes on in such cases. More particularly, we need to think of linguistic signs as being *indexically* organized, where indexicality stands for the projection of sociocultural function onto semiotic form. Such projections of functions may be widely diverse, and the range of possible functions for linguistic signs is far larger than just their conventional linguistic functions. Thinking about such signs linguistically, as language, obscures many of these functions and puts us on an unproductive track of (conventionally understood) multilingualism. It is only when we think of linguistic signs as being very much 'open' signs, onto which several functions (simultaneously) can be projected, that we can start to find answers to the complex and often bewildering phenomenology of language in globalization (see Silverstein 2003a; Agha 2007 for a broad discussion of these themes).

What I want to do next is to show how the conceptual tools I have developed here can be used to productively recast hotly debated sociolinguistic issues, and I will take the hottest possible one: English in the world. The topic of English, its spread and its many modified varieties worldwide, defines the sociolinguistics of globalization in its current form. And as we have seen repeatedly, one very dominant paradigm in addressing this issue is that of linguistic imperialism (Phillipson 1992) and linguistic rights (Skutnabb-Kangas 2000). This paradigm subscribes to a sociolinguistics of immobile languages – I have discussed aspects of this in chapter 2 – and assumes that where English occurs, indigenous (and especially minority) languages are threatened, first with attrition and eventually with language death (the so-called 'linguicidal' hypothesis within the linguistic-rights paradigm, henceforth abbreviated as LRP). I have already repeatedly emphasized that this paradigm misses the point of what such new globalized language hierarchies mean (e.g. Blommaert 2001b). Let me now try to apply the instrumentarium of a sociolinguistics of globalization to this question.

7.2   English in the periphery: imperialism revisited

I will do so by revisiting some of my own research on the regime of language in Tanzania (East Africa). I will divide my discussion into three subsections. In the first, I shall summarize the main findings of a previous study on state ideology and language in Tanzania (Blommaert 1999b). The outcome will be a paradox: the state's attempt towards the generalization of Swahili at (almost) all levels of society was a huge success; its attempt towards ideological hegemony, how-ever, was a failure. The two subsections to follow will offer explanations for this, first, by examining the position of the state vis-à-vis developments both at higher and at lower scale-levels, and second, by looking at some grassroots language practices that may reveal some of the dynamics that caused the para-dox. Finally, I will address the way in which this case may inform a different approach to linguistic rights and inequality.

Throughout this discussion my aim is to clarify the theoretical reflections made elsewhere in this book and to demonstrate that they may have some analytical purchase. More specifically, I hope to demonstrate that the usual LRP assumptions can be supplanted by the ones outlined above and that this might lead to better, more precise and more empirically sustainable outcomes. In LRP, the argument of linguistic rights (a) almost invariably involves the promotion of indigenous languages as status languages at all levels of society, and (b) it usually identifies the state as a crucial actor in this process, both negatively (the state denies rights to people) and positively (the state is the actor that should provide and secure rights for people). Tanzania is a case in point.

The Tanzanian paradox

The case is easily summarized. The postcolonial Tanzanian (then still Tanganyikan) state was one of the first to declare an indigenous language, Swahili, the national language of the country. Swahili also became an official language alongside the former colonial language English. Swahili was immediately introduced as the medium of instruction in primary education. The real boost for Swahili came when the state embarked on a massive campaign of nation building in the mid-1960s. This nation-building campaign was an attempt towards establishing socialist hegemony, and Swahili was given a crucial role in this. The language was defined as the language of African-socialist (*Ujamaa*) ideas, and the generalized spread of Swahili would be a measurable index of the spread of socialism across the population.

A few qualifications are in order here. First, the ideal situation envisaged by the architects of the campaign was monoglot. The campaign would be a success when the population used *one language imbued with one set of ideological loads*: those of *Ujamaa*. Homogeneity was the target, and the spread of Swahili-and-*Ujamaa* would have to go hand in hand with the disappearance of other languages-and-ideologies. The first target, obviously, was English – the language of imperialism, capitalism and oppression; but the same went for the local languages, which were seen as vehicles for traditional, precolonial cultures, as well as for 'non-standard' varieties of Swahili (e.g. code-switching, the use of urban varieties), that were felt to indicate the incompleteness of the process of hegemony. The 'better' and 'purer' one's Swahili, the better a socialist Tanzanian patriot one would be. We have here a typical Herderian cocktail of one language/one culture/one territory as an ideal organization for society.

Second, not only the conception of language as a vehicle for a specified (politically defined) set of Herderian ideological values, but the whole *operational* conception of language was inherited from colonial predecessor regimes. We see a long history at work here. Swahili was standardized and its main vehicle was (normative) literacy produced through formal education systems. Scholarly efforts concentrated on standardization, language 'development and modernization', purism, and so forth; in short, on the construction of Swahili as an artefact of normativity focused on referential functions. There was a model for such a degree of 'full languageness': English. Throughout the history of postcolonial linguistics in Tanzania, scholars kept referring to English as the kind of level of 'development and modernization' that needed to be attained for Swahili. And pending that 'full languageness' of Swahili, English would *have* to be used in higher education in order to produce a class of top-notch intellectuals needed for specialized service to the country. Thus, while Swahili was spread to all corners of the country, and was used in almost every aspect of everyday life, post-primary education remained (and still is) a domain where English was hegemonic.

Decades of concentrated efforts towards the goal set forth in the early 1960s resulted in the generalized spread of Swahili. Sociolinguistically, Swahili and its varieties have become the identifying code of public activities throughout Tanzania. But what did not happen was the ideological homogenization of the country – while Swahilization was manifestly a success, the monoglot ideal was a failure. Neither English nor local languages and 'impure' varieties of Swahili disappeared. And the spread of Swahili did not galvanize the hegemony of *Ujamaa*: the one-party system collapsed in the late 1980s and it was replaced by a multiparty, liberal capitalist state organization which, ironically, adopted Swahili as its vehicle for nationwide communication (just as the postcolonial state had adopted Swahili as an interesting instrument for propaganda and grassroots organization from the British colonialists before them).

In sum, Tanzania is a case where the state granted prestige status to an indigenous language. It also granted its citizens full rights to acquire that language. And it was a state where the formal colonial language was, certainly during the 1970s, a stigmatized language that should ultimately be completely replaced by Swahili. In terms of LRP, everything seemed to be in place. So, what went wrong?

The state in space and time

Let us begin by looking at how Tanzania fitted into larger pictures. As said earlier, we have to conceive of the state as one scale-level in a stratified polycentric system. So what the state did needs to be placed in a wider dynamic of events at other levels. Furthermore, all of this is caught in different historical processes, and every ingredient of the process will show residual elements of these historical processes as well. From this vantage point, several observations can be made.

1. Tanzania was a space of its own, and the nation-building attempt was a typical state activity the range of which was the territory controlled by the state. But we clearly see a lot of moments where the state oriented towards

higher-level, transnational centres. At the most general level, the construction itself of a national space was a factor of the international world order of
the day, which imposed the adoption of colonial boundaries onto the postcolonial states and which also offered models for organizing the state
bureaucracy and administration. Tanzanians oriented towards a number of
transnational ideals: *panafricanism* and African liberation (which spurred
the unification of Tanganyika and Zanzibar and which also fortified socialism as a state ideology); the kind of *socialism* championed by the organization of Non-Aligned States (in turn something which strongly oriented
towards the Cold-War framework); *development* ideals that evolved around
sustainable grassroots development (an influence of Maoist China); and
standard Western models of formal *education* as crucial both to development
and nation building.

2. Tanzania also oriented to transnational models of language and communication. As mentioned earlier, the state is often the level where a modernist,
static, homogeneous and reified notion of language is constructed and used
as something to which others need to orient (Bourdieu 1991; see also
Ferguson and Gupta 2002). Tanzania adopted earlier, existing models of a
monoglot regime of language focused around standard, purified and literacy-
driven varieties of Swahili (cf. Fabian 1986; Errington 2001). It also adopted
a classic nationalist model of language-and-ideology, the Herderian one.
And it offered these models as normative to groups in Tanzanian society,
both in everyday life, in administration, in education and in scientific work.
Next to this, it also adopted existing world-wide linguistic hierarchies in
which 'fully developed languages' such as English or French stood at the top
and were the model for Swahili (defined, in the same move, as somewhat
lower on the ladder of language development). In short, Tanzania adopted a
regime of language which was transnational (and which also defined the
colonial era in the country) and inserted Swahili into that regime.

3. Most of what is said in (1) and (2) represents the *durée* dimension of the
Tanzanian language regime: general conditions under which the Tanzanian
state operates, and which often become invisible as soon as they are 'repatriated', brought into the national space as part of a national project (that of
nation building). The transnational models to which the state orients are
transformed into national models and offered as points to which sub-national
groups ought to orient. The world-system disappears out of sight as soon as
the state brings it into the national space.

4. At the same time, this is not a static phenomenon, and we need to consider
the different histories here. The position of the Tanzanian state vis-à-vis
higher levels shifts repeatedly throughout the postcolonial period. In general – and generalizing – three periods can be defined: (1) the shift out of the
colonial world order, something which takes the Tanzanian state a few years

after independence; (2) the Cold War, i.e. the global world order prior to 1990; and (3) the post-1990 world order, i.e. the era of contemporary globalization and capitalist hegemony. In each of these periods, changes in the relative indexicalities occur. For instance, with regard to the 'value' of English, it is clear that it shifts from an ambivalent stance in the first period (being the language both of the former oppressor and the model for organizing the independent state) to a markedly negative stance during the Cold-War period and again to a moderately positive stance in the post-1990 period. English in each period (but also Swahili and any other language or variety) receives value attributions that derive from scales valid transnationally, and the development of language evaluations testifies to the shifting alignments of the Tanzanian state in the world-system. Note too that the three periods are not to be separated: rather than breaks between one period and another, we see how residual aspects of the value system in previous periods still occur in later ones. New orders of indexicality are built out of the rubble of earlier ones.

5. But the state also responded to grassroots and civil society forces, notably with regard to the relationship between Swahili and local minority languages. Within the normative frame for which the state as a (strong) centre stood, various groups in society developed counter-hegemonic discourses and practices. In its most visible form, people were unwilling to *replace* their existing repertoires with the monoglot complex of Swahili. Nobody actually disputed the importance of national linguistic unity, but only a few people accepted the idea of individual monolingualism. Most people allocated specific functions to the Swahili varieties they had adopted into their repertoires and enthusiastically shifted between various ingredients in their repertoires (Mekacha 1993; Msanjila 1998, 2004). Furthermore, while usually strongly supporting Swahilization, the emerging class of professional intellectuals in particular launched themselves into debates about *what kind of (socialist) values* the language was supposed to disseminate. The state was forced into such debates, and the general assessments of language policies were effects of such debates between state and civil society. To be precise: the way in which the state's actions were seen as either successes or failures was an effect of a national dynamic in which the transnational dimension was hardly visible – in itself evidence of the way in which the state functions as a centring institution creating a 'national' space and thus effecting closure to aspects of the issue that transcend the national space. For local intellectuals in such debates, the only centre to which they oriented was the state; for the state, it was both the world-system and civil society.

6. The bottom line to all of this is: the state was an intermediate institution responding both to calls from above and from below, and the state to some extent got stuck between these two levels. The state was not an autonomous

actor, but an embedded one, one that invited very different approaches dependent on the level from which one approached it. Add to this the heritage of models of language and language infrastructures – the monoglot, purist, standard, Herderian complex – handed down as part of the way in which Tanzania had to fit into the world order (and developed for Swahili by colonial linguistics), and we end up with a strangely contradictory general image. The state was extremely powerful, as the actor that defined the national space and some critical ingredients of it, and as the actor that had absolute control over an infrastructure that led to generalized language spread. But at the same time, it was extremely weak, because the instruments with which it could work were both deficient in scope and capacity (Tanzania was, and is, a very poor country) and were hand-me-downs from transnational levels that could never answer the ambitions of the state itself nor those of local groups in civil society. To put it in its crudest (and hence overstated) form: the state had adopted sociolinguistic models and ideals that were recipes for inequality wherever they were applied, while these models were at the same time always offered as recipes for progress, modernization and development. The state adopted crucial orders of indexicality of a capitalist society and attempted to apply them in the construction of a socialist state.

Fooling around with language

We have now described the awkward position of the state. Let us now move down the temporal and spatial scale-level to that of everyday life in urban Tanzania, and ask: what did people effectively do with language? Again, we have to keep the general model in mind: a stratified polycentric system in which people orient to a variety of (hierarchically ordered) systemically reproduced indexicalities. The state provided such a set of indexicalities, and it did so with considerable force, aplomb and determination. But let us not forget that

> [i]t is entirely possible … that in the ordinary course of their history communities will come to differ in the degree and direction in which they develop their linguistic means … The same linguistic system, as usually described, may be part of different, let us say, *socio*linguistic systems, whose nature cannot be assumed, but must be investigated. (Hymes 1974: 73, emphasis in original)

To the extent that we require evidence to back this up, Ben Rampton's work on 'crossing' and 'styling' (1995, 2006) is a ready candidate. Rampton demonstrates how London adolescents of a variety of ethnolinguistic backgrounds create ways of speaking that orient to new, peer-group or popular youth-culture indexicalities, and thus allow 'crossing' into ethnolinguistic indexical spaces not customarily theirs (e.g. white Anglo kids adopting Jamaican Creole). In practise, 'customarily' here stands for indexicalities that are valid at higher levels and are produced by other centring institutions such as education, neighbourhood norms, or national norms of 'standard' and 'substandard' or prestige and stigma. Thus, what counts as a prestigious language variety from the point of view of the school system may be a stigmatized variety from the point of view of the pupils, and vice versa (e.g. Rasta slang can be a prestige code). Linguistic resources can indeed function in very different sociolinguistic systems, to adopt Hymes' terms, and they can do so simultaneously.

This, I would argue, is the level at which we have to look if we want to understand what people actually do with language, what language does to them, and what language means to them, in what particular ways it matters to them. And if we want to make linguistic rights more than just a trope in political-linguistic discourse, this is where we should start. Invariably, alas, we end up with a rather complicated image. Let me give a few examples from Tanzania.

Public English   Years ago, I started noticing the often peculiar varieties of written English used in all kinds of public displays in urban Dar es Salaam. Such varieties would come to me in the form of signs on doors and walls of shops, bars and restaurants, inscriptions on the small, privately operated buses that provide mass transportation, advertisements in newspapers or on billboards, road signs, and so forth. The most striking aspect of these publicly displayed forms of English literacy was the density of 'errors' or rather unexpected turns of phrase in them.

Here is a small sample:

- *Fund rising dinner party* (on a banner in central Dar es Salaam)
- *Disabled Kiosk* (the name of a 'kiosk' – a converted container that serves as a small shop – operated by a disabled man)
- *Whole sallers of hardwere* (sign at a hardware shop)
- *Shekilango Nescafé* (the name of a café on Shekilango road in suburban Dar es Salaam)
- *new Sikinde tea (room)* (the name of a café, note the brackets)
- *Sliming food* (in an advertisement for a health shop)
- *Con Ford* (written on a bus)
- *Approxi Mately* (written on a bus)
- *Sleping Coach* (written on a long-distance bus)

Clearly, these inscriptions are packed with information. They reveal a problem with the distribution of linguistic resources: standard English with its codified referential meanings on the one hand, normative literacy conventions for English on the other. Seen from the angle of monoglot normativity, the people who wrote and used these inscriptions display incomplete insertions in economies of linguistic forms. In that sense, they testify to some of the crucial problems of language policy in Tanzania: the lasting prestige functions attributed to English combined with the extremely restricted access to its prestige-bearing, standard varieties (the latter being completely conditioned by access to post-primary education).

But there are other aspects to this. It is clear that the producers (and consumers) of these signs orient towards the status hierarchy in which English occupies the top. This is an orientation to a transnational, global hierarchy, reinforced by the state's ambivalent and meandering stance on English. There is an orientation to English as a code associated with core values of capitalist ideas of success: entrepreneurship, mobility, luxury and female beauty. The use of English is sensed to index all of this. But at the same time, it indexes this not in terms of internationally valid norms (e.g. standard varieties of written English), but in term of *local* diacritics. The man who commissioned the *disabled kiosk* sign probably did not imagine himself as an international businessman, but he did imagine himself as a businessman in Dar es Salaam (or even more specifically, in the Magomeni neighbourhood of Dar es Salaam). And at this point, a new space of meaning attribution is opened. We have an act of communication which at the same time orients towards transnational indexicalities and to strictly local ones, and the effect is that the English used in these signs has to make sense *here*, in Magomeni – but *as English*, i.e. as a code suggesting a 'move out' of Magomeni and an insertion into transnational imaginary networks.

This is a repatriation of sign-complexes which offers a tremendous semiotic potential for users: they can produce strictly local meanings of great density and effect. The man who wrote *Con Ford* on his bus was simultaneously advertising the brand of his vehicle, alluding to the folk-category of 'conmen' – smooth talkers and ladies' men – and boasting the standards of comfort in his bus, while also displaying his wit and capacity to perform word play in English. The same goes for the owner of the *Shekilango Nescafé*: an anchoring in the local geography goes hand in hand with a display of knowledgeability of prestigious, European brand names (Nescafé), a suggestion of a degree of sophistication and European-touch-of-class for his business, and a flair for finding good-sounding names for things. And as for the authors of *fund rising* or *sliming food*: they target an audience who would perceive the total value of the English display rather than its normative correctness, and so offer them a space for identifying with high-class, internationalized categories of activities. It is the value of English and of literacy *in Dar es Salaam* that has to be made central.

So contrary to what a certain literature would suggest, we are not really witnessing an invasion of an 'imperialist' or 'killer' language here. What we are witnessing is a highly complex, intricate pattern of appropriation and deployment of linguistic resources whose values have been relocated from a transnational to a national set of indexicalities. It is a *Tanzanian* bourgeois (or bourgeois-aspiring) resource.

Tough talk and its norms In the mid-1990s, I started to note the emergence of a hip-hop scene among youngsters in Dar es Salaam. One thing led to another, and I soon found myself in the company of young people willing to initiate me into their ways of life. It started with a girl telling me that her brother now spoke *Viswahili*, i.e. the plural of 'Kiswahili' – multiple Swahilis at the same time. The boy was called and he produced some phrases to me in the presence of his father, who disapprovingly said that 'this is not Swahili' and told me that the boy *anaongeza chumvi* – 'added salt', exaggerated, went too far. Rules had been broken. (Note that at this point we already have two metapragmatic qualifications for the talk of the boy: one that refers to a plurality of 'languages', another marking 'eccentricity'.)

The girl and her brother brought me in contact with a group of approximately fourteen young people, all living in the neighbourhood and all between 14 and 20 years old. The group consisted of six male core members and a second circle of boys and girls. In terms of ethnic background as well as social class, the group was highly heterogeneous: some of the members were poorly paid waiters or messengers, one worked as an aide to a shoe repairman, while some others were children of middle-class families and had access to prestige goods (clothes, shoes, music cassettes) and cars. Yet, there was clearly a 'group' here:

- Despite class differences, all of the members defined their outlook on life in terms of deep frustration – an awareness of being on the margins of the world expressed through mottoes such as *jua kali* 'burning sun' or 'hard heat' (a metonym for the general condition of poverty and misery in Tanzania) or *machungu sana* 'much bitterness' (i.e. frustration), and marked references to places, displaying an awareness of situatedness in a world-system: *majuu* 'the West' (literally 'the things up there'), *Jahanam* 'the third world' (literally 'Hell') or *motoni* 'the third world' (literally 'in the fire').
- Furthermore, the core members had adopted nicknames and insisted on being called by these names in the context of the group. The names again reveal various orientations to status complexes and/or identity categories. Some were modelled on African-American acronyms: *Q*, *KJ*, another copied the name of a well known Reggae artist: *Toshi* (Peter Tosh), another was called *blazameni* – a local version of 'brother man'. Yet another was called *msafiri* 'the traveller' (the boy had spent some time in South Africa working in the mines – an experience conferring considerable prestige), and finally, the oldest member of the group was called *jibaba* 'little father' (he had fathered a child).
- The group also identified themselves as belonging to a larger category of urban youngsters: *wahuni* 'crooks', 'bandits', the Swahili equivalent of the 'Gangsta' of American hip-hop culture. It was quickly pointed out to me that this label should not frighten me, for there were several categories of *wahuni*. They reassured me with statements such as *sisi hatuibi* 'we don't steal' (in other words, 'we are not real criminals').

- The group had its own meeting places: a container converted into a bar, in front of which the shoe repairman who employed one of the members had his small shop (a small stall with one bench). Another hangout for the group was a soccer field a few hundred metres away, where they could meet *in plenum*. There was a distinct locality to the group – a *barrio* awareness.

Already we see how the group organized itself in reference to multiple centres: the world-system and their own marginalized position therein was one such very salient focus of orientation; it provided a frame of reference in which English, hip-hop slang, Rasta slang and travelling could acquire particular emblematic values to be exploited in naming and qualifying practices. They shared some aspects of their groupness with other *wahuni* in Dar es Salaam – a generic *wahuni* scene being another centre, the focus of which were the star rap groups of Dar es Salaam (groups with names such as *II Proud* and *Da Dee-plow-matz* and with colossal prestige). Capitalizing on the stardom of the rap groups, two weekly tabloid magazines had started to use bits of *kihuni* in their attempt to reach the young urban readers. This level was in turn superimposed by transnational (but essentially African-American) 'Gangsta' culture notably focused on international rap stars such as Tupac. And finally the neighbourhood – their *barrio* – was a powerful focus of orientations. Other *wahuni* groups were all identified in reference to Dar es Salaam neighbourhoods: the *wahuni* of Manzese, of Magomeni, of Ubungo, and so forth.

The group of *wahuni* spoke *kihuni*, the language of the bandits, and the *viswahili* earlier mentioned to me. I started recording conversations with the group, and invariably, such conversations took the shape of unilateral displays of *kihuni* in the form of single words or phrases. The group, unsurprisingly, was deeply committed to the creation and maintenance of an 'antilanguage' shared by the whole of the Dar es Salaam *wahuni* scene. It consisted of baffling instances of linguistic mixing, borrowing and relexification in Swahili, English and other languages, and sound play. Consider the following examples, loosely categorized as English (relexified) borrowings; relexifications from Swahili; borrowings from other languages; sound play, *vifupi* (shortened forms) and so on:

English borrowings:

- *kukipa* : to leave, to take off (< 'to keep')
- *kutos*: to leave alone (< 'to toss')
- *macho balbu*: eyes wide open in amazement or fear (*balbu* < [light-]bulb')
- *mentali*: friend (< 'mental', refers to 'mental fit')
- *Krezi*: friend (< 'crazy')
- *kumaindi*: to want something (< 'mind')
- *kukrash*: to disagree (< 'to crash')
- *dewaka*: man-of-all-trades (< 'day worker')
- *bati*: blue jeans (< 'board', corrugated iron roof plates)
- *pusha*: drugs dealer (< 'pusher')

Relexifications from Swahili (SS = standard Swahili):

- *unga*: cocaine (SS 'maize flour')
- *mzigo*: marijuana (SS 'bag', 'luggage')
- *chupa cha chai* (also *thermos*): small plane (SS 'tea flask', 'thermos flask')
- *pipa*: big plane (SS: 'oil drum')
- *kukong'otea*: to stalk (SS: *kukong'ota* = 'to hit', 'to beat')
- *kupiga bao*: to have sex (SS: 'to overtake a vehicle')
   Borrowings from other languages:
- *mwela*: policeman (< Maasai)
- *kulupango*: jail (< Luba, *ku lupango*)
- *ganja*: marijuana (< Jamaican Creole, Rasta slang)
- *kaya*: marijuana (<Jamaican Creole, Rasta slang)
   Sound play etc:
- *kupasha* = kupata: to receive
- *zibiliduda*: a girl who plays hard to get (also *gozigozi*)
- *kibosile*: a rich man ('boss')
- *kishitobe*: a girl with a large backside (refers to the name of a Greek cargo vessel)
- *K'oo*: Kariakoo (a neighbourhood)
- *Zese*: Manzese (a neighbourhood)
- *Migomigo:* Magomeni (a neighbourhood)
- *Jobegi*: Johannesburg

The dynamics of *kihuni* are not exceptional: very similar phenomena will be met elsewhere in similar kinds of groups. Neither is the domain distribution of *kihuni* surprising. Terms cover domains such as: crime, drugs, sexual intercourse, female genital morphology, travel, poverty vs. wealth, the city, the group and its networks.

But more interesting is the *normativity* in which all of this is couched. *Kihuni* had its own centres, its own bodies of codified norms: the rap stars and the tabloids that used *kihuni*. The group spontaneously formalized its sessions with me, turning them into a kind of formal instruction into the language. I audio-recorded what went on, but they also insisted that I should *make notes* of the words and phrases they offered me. And while I was making notes, they would watch carefully how I noted the words and phrases, and they would occasionally – rather vigorously – correct me whenever what I wrote down did not correspond to what they thought it should be. I reverted to a pattern of explicit checking what I had written, asking *hivyo?* ('like this?') and showing them my notes. Orthography mattered. For instance, a frequently used term was *toto* – a sexualized term for 'girl' derived from Swahili *mtoto*, 'child'. The plural of *toto* is *totoz*: instead of adding a Bantu plural prefix (*wa-toto*), the group used a hip-hop slang plural suffix '-*z*', tying the use of the term firmly to transnational Gangsta culture by exploiting the morphology and orthography of Swahili.

What this means is that, remarkably, *kihuni* is a *literate* code – or at least that written images of *kihuni* terms mattered in the process of transfer/initiation in which I was involved. The code transferred to me needed to be *correct*, and in their view of what a language should be, this meant that it was subject to standards of written form, for control over written varieties of *kihuni* offered opportunities for semiotic alignment with the local and the translocal. This flexible, hermetic, sub-cultural code dismissed by parents and others as 'not Swahili', was conceived of as a 'full language' by its users – as one of the many *viswahili* controlled by apparently quite strict ('peripheral') norms and rules.

Just like in the case of the English inscriptions discussed earlier, the picture we get here is one of relocation and appropriation – in other words, of semiotic opportunity – rather than of deterioration of standards, language loss or any other simple metaphor of English imperialism. There is not one single complex of indexicalities attached to the highly 'impure' blend of whatever linguistic material these kids could get hold of. The indexicalities are multiple and again, like in the cases discussed earlier, revolve around the capacity to suggest the transnational while firmly remaining within the national, the regional, even the strictly local: it is a repertoire that allows them to 'get out' of Dar es Salaam *culturally*, to culturally relocate their local environments in a global semiotics of class, status, blackness, marginalization. And if we look for the value the code has for the kids themselves: it is their *language*, captured in normative perceptions and activities as soon as someone from the outside intends to acquire it. It is treated as if it were a 'full' language, with a name (*kihuni*), a set of spoken norms and registers, and even an orthography.

What went wrong?

If we now combine the elements discussed in this section, we can begin to see what went so dramatically wrong in Tanzania – in the eyes of its own language planners. The key to understanding this is the fact that Tanzania was not an autonomous space, but was encapsulated in divergent processes both at a higher and at a lower level. The state was not an autonomous actor, and it could not operate in total freedom: it had to operate under conditions that were both historically and synchronically constraining. At the same time, it was the actor upon which everything converged: it was *the* centring institution in the process. The failure of its own definition of hegemony lies in the fact that the state was so weak *because* it was so strong. The crucial centre did what it had to do: be the crucial centre; but it had to do that under constraints that precluded success.

The effect was the creation of a space in which a hugely unequal pattern of distribution of linguistic resources occurred and started to operate (very different from Bourdieu's unified linguistic market). Vernacular Swahili was generally spread, with some degree of literacy in Swahili for a rather large group of the population. In a different stream, English continued to be a prestigious resource because of its embeddedness in a class-organizing system of reproduction: higher education, which for a long time was the only ticket to the elites. This order of indexicalities, in which English, standard and literate language varieties stood on top, and vernacular Swahili and local ethnic languages were way below, was a national order, but it was obviously permeated by transnational orders. And the various scale-levels at which such indexicalities operated – the transnational, the national, the regional, the strictly local – could all be oriented to by speakers. By using one way of speaking versus another, they could 'place' themselves in relation to images culled from the various levels, the combination of which was a strongly local semiotics of identity, probably only fully understandable – fully 'social' – to people from that place, as we saw in chapter 3.

This surely is a feature of inequality: the capacity to 'move out' by means of specific semiotic resources is definitely one of the elements of what we understand by 'empowering', while resources with a 'placing' effect – keeping speakers 'in place' – would be a feature of disempowerment. If the use of a particular form of English fails to turn you into an international businessman, but rather makes you more than ever the small-time shopkeeper from Magomeni, then the mapping of form over function needs to be looked into carefully. But the point is that such mappings occur locally, that the 'sociolinguistic system' referred to by Hymes cannot in any way be equated to some supposedly internationally valid system in which English is always empowering or disempowering, and similar simplicities are applied to indigenous languages – the sociolinguistic system consists of the local orders of indexicality. What is disempowering in the case of Tanzania is the whole historical process of being caught in a marginal position in the world-system. This whole process governs the value of the linguistic resources: it governs what people can do with them and what they do to people. In the case of Tanzania, inequality resides in the fact that the functions of linguistic resources controlled by speakers are primarily local, and this goes for local languages, Swahili and English alike. As soon as they get moved out of the local environment and get circulated translocally, they lose function at a rapid pace. The strong-weak state has left its mark.[1]

Discussion

Let me now try to move this discussion back to the issue of linguistic rights. I shall first summarize my case. I have tried to show that if we adopt an ethnographic viewpoint on the issue of language in society, we need to focus on how linguistic resources are actually employed, and under what conditions, in real societies. In order to arrive there, we can use a framework in which language use is seen as oriented towards multiple but stratified centres that construct and offer opportunities to reproduce indexicalities. Such indexicalities determine the 'social' in language use, and they are the basis of interpretive work. The way in which they are organized is the locus of inequality.

In order to understand real processes of inequality, the different processes need to be situated. In contemporary scholarship, no analysis of national phenomena can afford to overlook the global level which defines or constrains a lot of what can be done nationally. This is where we need a fresh look at the state as an actor in this field: even if the state appears to be weak, its position vis-à-vis global forces remains crucial, as does its position vis-à-vis grassroots and civil society processes. We must look, however, not exclusively at the state's concrete *performative actions* such as legislation, enforcement of regimes of language in education, bureaucracy, and so forth, but also at its role as a centre, a point of reference, contrast and comparison which often defines the value and relevance of actions undertaken by other actors. Looking at sociolinguistic phenomena from this angle might help us understand the real role and function of language practices for people – their value-attributions and their understandings of such practices. For if we believe we can do something about inequality, we need to know its locus, its real modus operandi, its structure and objects. And this, I would argue, requires an ethnographic outlook informed by history and general sociolinguistic insights.

Applying this, as in the case of Tanzania, may yield disturbingly complex and ambivalent, but solidly realistic results. In the Tanzanian case, I cannot be led to believe that English is only an agent of oppression or minorization. The varieties of English spread across society enter a local social-semiotic economy, and so offer opportunities for localizing transnational indexicalities to speakers, the effects of which are highly meaningful locally. The problem is: they are *only* meaningful locally, they do not count as 'English' as soon as translocal norms are imposed on them. The kinds of English we have seen in our discussion above (and in various examples in the previous chapters) are what we could call 'low-mobility' forms of English: they only count as English in that particular environment. So the story of the 'killer language' English becomes considerably more complicated (and interesting, I would suggest). There are very different Englishes at play, at very different scale-levels, and with very different effects and functions.

Neither can I be led to believe that Swahili, an indigenous language, has only led to progress and liberation for the Tanzanians. Again, it is not that simple. Swahili was, during its heyday as the national language of *Ujamaa* Tanzania, as effective an 'imperial' language as English, Russian or Mandarin Chinese. It was imposed as a monoglot standard with its own prestige varieties, and it was promoted together with strong encouragements to stop using other languages. The introduction of Swahili in primary education in the early 1960s may be seen, from one angle, as a liberating and revolutionary act which eroded the unquestioned hegemony of English in the country. Seen from another angle, of course, it meant the elimination of the hundred-plus other indigenous languages as media of formal instruction; and for those speaking these other languages the new medium of instruction was a *foreign* language – a foreign *prestige* language, a language of power and control – that needed to be acquired. (Let us not overlook the simple fact that a language is not less 'foreign' because it is one's neighbour's language.) If indigenous minority languages have disappeared in Tanzania since the 1960s, Swahili is most likely to be one of their killers, to adopt for a moment the LRP line of argument.

The point is, however, that single 'languages' attached to single collections of attributes, values and effects will never do as a framework for thinking about these issues. Ethnographically we will always see complex blending, mixing and reallocation processes, in which, as said at the outset, the differences between 'languages' are altogether just one factor. Inequality has to do with *modes of language use*, including judgments passed on such use, not with languages, and if we intend to do something about it, we need to develop an awareness that it is not necessarily the language you speak, but *how* you speak it, *when* you can speak it, and *to whom* that matters. It is a matter of *voice*, not of language.

7.3   Conclusions

I hope this long illustration clarifies the potential of the approach I have tried to sketch in this book, and persuades others to explore the opportunities it appears to offer. Such opportunities, I would venture, lie in several domains of sociolinguistic inquiry. As I said at the outset, sociolinguistics is traditionally more at ease while studying a village than while studying the world. Studying the world has become inevitable now, and what is required for that is a different sociolinguistics, one that has recast its foundations so as to fit the current phenomena and processes. Such phenomena and processes are messy, as we have seen, and many of the traditional concepts of sociolinguistics will have to be sacrificed in favour of more open and flexible ones, capable of capturing the unpredictability of sociolinguistic life in the age of globalization.

The main sacrifice for sociolinguistics is the old Saussurean synchrony: the idea that language phenomena can be examined without taking into account their spatial and temporal situatedness. There is no room for such a synchrony in the sociolinguistics of globalization that I have sketched here. I have argued that the observable sociolinguistic phenomena and processes – synchronic in traditional jargon – are in effect *synchronizations* of tremendously complicated series of historical and spatial processes. Every synchronic snapshot of sociolinguistic reality represents a moment in a process of temporal and spatial mobility, and we can understand this synchronized reality only when we consider the mobility dynamic in which they are encapsulated. It is the end of the Saussurean synchrony that makes this shift paradigmatic. It is a shift in the foundations of the study of language in society, not just in its methods or vocabulary. The fundamental image of language now shifts from a static, totalized and immobile one to a dynamic, fragmented and mobile one, and it is from this fundamental image that we now have to start working.

This work is only beginning, and this book has only just scratched the surface. I have tried to define the paradigmatic shift that we need to make, emphasizing the focus on mobile resources rather than on immobile languages. I have tried to develop a little vocabulary for it, with terms such as orders of indexicality, scale and polycentricity at its core. I have tried to show that we need to understand the sociolinguistic world as one in which language gets dislodged and its traditional functions distorted by processes of mobility. I have argued that we need to see the sociolinguistic world as a system of relatively autonomous local systems, each with their own historicity and patterns of experience and normative conduct. I have argued that sociolinguistic resources and repertoires, consequently, appear in a different shape and need to be understood as 'truncated' and 'unfinished'. This I explained by looking at the historicity of language phenomena, arguing that we need to look at synchronic realities as synchronized realities in the sense outlined above. And I finally tried to demonstrate how contemporary sociolinguistic realities of globalization articulate old and new patterns of inequality and so make language into a problem for many people. Globalization is something that has winners as well as losers, a top as well as a bottom, and centres as well as peripheries, and throughout the book I have often focused on the periphery as the locus from which we need to look at globalization. This, I believe, is essential: part of the shift we need to make is also a shift away from a metropolitan perspective on globalization, stressing the uniformity of such processes, towards a perspective that does justice to 'vernacular globalization', to the myriad ways in which global processes enter local conditions and circumstances and become a localized reality.

This would be especially beneficial for studies on the topic that defines sociolinguistic globalization, English in the world, as I have demonstrated in the previous section. I hope to have convincingly argued against the shortcomings of approaches that capture this phenomenon merely in terms of oppression and imperialism. Certainly there is oppression, and perhaps there is imperialism, but such patterns occur in certain segments of society only and so are locked into specific scale-levels. Elsewhere in society, realities may be profoundly different, and it is our task to take these realities into account as well. Sociolinguistics has everything to win by being comprehensive, nuanced and balanced in its accounts and judgments of language in society, and by providing the right diagnoses for social injustice and inequality. In times of globalization, this becomes an ever more pressing challenge because, as we saw in the previous chapter, there are people whose fate may depend on such diagnoses, accounts and judgments. The world is not a nice place for everyone, and sociolinguistics has the capacity to show, in great detail and with an unparalleled amount of precision, how language reflects the predicaments of people in a globalizing world. It has the capacity to read the infinitely big features of the world from infinitely small details of human communicative behaviour – at least, when it takes on the challenges outlined here.

Notes

2 A MESSY NEW MARKETPLACE

1. The reference date for the Internet data used in this section is 15 January 2008.
2. Observe also the indexical currency of authenticity expressed in 'thanks to God': Sanaz is Iranian, therefore he is Muslim, and Muslims use expressions like that.
3. It is interesting that none of the websites here mentioned offers 'plain speech', that most 'typical' Americanist symbolic speech economy embodied by public figures ranging from Joe McCarthy, Lyndon B. Johnson and Ronald Reagan to George W. Bush. See Silverstein (2003b) for a discussion on Bush's 'plain' rhetoric. The speech offered by these websites is clearly technical, high-brow and sophisticated, aimed at insertion in elite (not 'plain') networks.
4. Note the curious statement that American pronunciation 'is different from spelling'. Observe also that none of the websites, in addition, makes reference to *multilingualism* as an outcome of learning American accent. The fact that the typical customer would not be a 'native speaker' and that, logically, the learning experience ought to result in new multilingual repertoires is nowhere thematized. The vision articulated here is clearly monoglot: American accent is more than enough and the only language that really matters here (Silverstein 1996).

3 LOCALITY, THE PERIPHERY AND IMAGES OF THE WORLD

1. *Mzalendo*, the singular form of *wazalendo*, was also the name of a prominent government-sponsored newspaper in Ujamaa Tanzania.
2. One need just think of the particular ring to names such as Paris, the Kremlin, Tien an Men Square, the White House. The indexicalities tied to such places are often the basis for their metonymic usage in everyday or institutional speech. Thus 'Brussels' in Eurosceptics' discourse means more than 'the capital of Belgium'.
3. Fieldwork in Wesbank High was done in July–August 2004 and continued in July–August 2005 by teams of students from Ghent University. Nathalie Muyllaert and Marieke Huysmans are responsible for the data discussed here, and their input is gratefully acknowledged.

4 REPERTOIRES AND COMPETENCE

1. See for a basic survey of the terms of reference: http://en.wikipedia.org/wiki/ Common_European_Framework_of_Reference_for_Languages
2. The Almighty may even work in close concert with ICT technology. Here is a fragment from another message, not included in the corpus: 'I then came across your address on the Internet as I was browsing through a Christian site, and as a matter of fact, it is not only you or your ministry that I picked on the Christian site initially, but after my fervent prayer over it, then you were nominated through divine revelation from God so that was how I received such a divine revelation from the Lord, how I got your contact information, and I then decided to contact you for the fund to be used wisely for things that will glorify the name of God.'
3. Messages I received on other occasions were sent by the relatives of almost every dictator known to man: Mobutu Sese Seko, Marcos, Sani Abacha, Saddam Hussein, warlords from Liberia and Sierra Leone, and so forth.

5 LANGUAGE, GLOBALIZATION AND HISTORY

1. The various contributions in Blommaert (ed. 1999) used the 'debate' as a unit for historical-sociolinguistic analysis, because debates are historical moments in which identifiable actors engage in specific language-ideological practices, with (usually) clear outcomes and results.
2. It was also a distinctly elite event. Tickets were sold at 5,000 Yuan, an equivalent of 500 Euro and the average annual income of a farmer in China. The game was organized by Pine Valley Golf resort and Country Club, described on its own website as 'the most exclusive private club in China for business leaders and the elite, offering members and guest the highest international standards in products and services for their leisure as well as their business entertainment' (www.pinevalley.com.cn/en/ 00_01.asp). Naturally, this is quite ironic in light of the appeal towards a 'harmonious community' discussed below.
3. The following reflections are based on a fieldwork trip to Finnish Samiland in April 2008. I thank Sari Pietikainen and Rob Moore, my partners on this trip, for very valuable input.

6 OLD AND NEW INEQUALITIES

1. In the UK, the interview record is handwritten by the interviewer and is called 'verbatim account'. Regardless of the actual language of the interview, however, the record is in English (and thus reflects the institutional voice). It contains both the questions and the answers. In the first interview record of the 'screening interview' in November 2001, Joseph initialled all the answers written down by the interviewer as a token of agreement, though he later argued that the interviewer presented the initial-ling routine as just a matter of proving that the interview had effectively taken place. The first interview was conducted partly in Kinyarwanda, partly in Runyankole; the second one was conducted completely in English. In the second ('substantive') interview as well as in the official verdict letter, Joseph's nationality and his date of birth are qualified as 'disputed' or 'doubted'.

2. I am deeply grateful to the man I call Joseph Mutingira here, as well as to his legal counsel Anna, for allowing me to publish elements from his case. I came across these materials in the spring of 2006, when I was asked to provide an expert report for the appeal case, on the treatment of language in Joseph's application.

3. A very good source for this is Colette Braeckman's (1996) book *Terreur Africaine*.

4. Joseph's account of the lady's involvement is vague and evasive. It is not unthinkable that he deliberately tried to shield her from the probing eyes of the Home Office. It is a common problem for asylum applicants that they have to narrate the details of their escape, as this may endanger persons who assisted them and/or expose valuable networks of migration support. At the same time, vagueness and contradictions in this part of their story work heavily against them in the asylum procedure (see Maryns 2006 for examples and a detailed discussion of this problem).

5. If Joseph had been accepted as a minor, the application procedure and the legal framework in which he would have found himself would have been significantly different and far more lenient. The way in which Joseph was declared an adult is a gross violation of his rights, of course.

6. We see a form of governmentality here, in which 'order' (here: national order) is policed all the way down to the microscopic (or 'capillary') levels of pronunciation and writing. This form of policing, to Foucault, would fit in a system of security (Foucault 2007).

7. This makes the position of interpreters in asylum applications quite precarious. Cases have been reported in which (government-appointed) interpreters identified applicants' accents as being a 'rebel accent'.

8. Languages of that cluster in the Great Lakes region often carry the prefix 'Ru-', such as Runyoro, Ruhaya, Runyakitara, and so on, or the related 'Lu-' prefix such as in 'Luganda'.

9. The Home Office did not display much sensitivity to African language features in general in this case. Thus, the name of the nursery school in Kenya which Joseph mentions is systematically written as 'Kinyatta', whereas it is no rocket science to know that the school would very likely have been called *Kenyatta*, after Kenya's first president and independence hero.

7 REFLECTIONS

1. In that sense, the Tanzanian state played a role equivalent to the French state described by Bourdieu (1991), and Bourdieu's thesis that the state is the central actor in shaping the linguistic market remains valid, even for 'strong-weak' states such as Tanzania. The outcome, however, need not be a 'unified' linguistic market; it can be a highly diversified market. Remember also the discussion in chapter 6.

References

Agha, A. 2003. The social life of cultural value. *Language and Communication* 23: 231–273.

2005. Voice, footing, enregisterment. *Journal of Linguistic Anthropology* 15(1): 38–59.

2007. *Language and Social Relations.* Cambridge University Press.

Appadurai, A. 1990. Disjuncture and difference in the global cultural economy. *Theory, Culture and Society* 7: 295–310.

1996. *Modernity at Large.* Minneapolis: University of Minnesota Press.

Arrighi, G. 1997. Globalization, state sovereignty, and the 'endless accumulation of capital'. Paper, Conference on 'States and Sovereignty in the World Economy', University of California, Irvine, Feb. 21–23, 1997.

Bakhtin, M. 1986. *Speech Genres and Other Late Essays.* Austin: University of Texas Press.

Baron, N. 1998. Letters by phone or speech by other means: the linguistics of email. *Language and Communication* 18: 133–170.

Barthes, R. 1957. *Mythologies.* Paris: le Seuil.

Barton, D. 1994. *Literacy: An Introduction to the Ecology of Written Language.* Oxford: Blackwell.

Barton, D. and Hamilton, M. 1998. *Local Literacies: Reading and Writing in One Community.* London: Routledge.

Bauman, R. and Briggs, C. 2003. *Voices of Modernity.* Cambridge University Press.

Bauman, Z. 1991. *Modernity and Ambivalence.* Cambridge: Polity.

Bekker, I. 2003. Using historical data to explain language attitudes: a South African case study. *AILA Review* 16: 62–77.

Bernstein, B. 1971. *Class, Codes, and Control, Volume I.* London: Routledge and Kegan Paul.

Block, D. 2005. *Multilingual Identities in a Global City: London Stories.* London: Palgrave.

Block, D. and Cameron, D. (eds.) 2001. *Globalization and Language Teaching.* London: Routledge.

Blommaert, J. 1998. English in a popular Swahili novel. In Van der Auwera, J., Durieux, F. and Lejeune, L. (eds.), *English as a Human Language: to Honour Louis Goossens,* 22–31. Munich: LINCOM Europa.

1999a. The debate is open. In Blommaert, J. (ed.), *Language Ideological Debates,* 3–38. Berlin: Mouton de Gruyter.

1999b. *State Ideology and Language in Tanzania.* Cologne: Köppe.

2001a. Analysing narrative inequality: African asylum seekers' stories in Belgium. *Discourse and Society* 12: 413–449.

2001b. The Asmara Declaration as a sociolinguistic problem. *Journal of Sociolinguistics* 5(1): 131–142.

2005. *Discourse: A Critical Introduction*. Cambridge University Press.

2006. From fieldnotes to grammar: artefactual ideologies and the textual production of languages in Africa. In Sica, G. (ed.), *Advances in Language Studies*, 13–59. Milan: Polimetrica.

2008. *Grassroots Literacy: Writing, Identity and Voice in Africa*. London: Routledge.

(ed.) 1999. *Language Ideological Debates*. Berlin: Mouton de Gruyter.

Blommaert, J. and Verschueren, J. 1998. *Debating Diversity*. London: Routledge.

Blommaert, J., Creve, L. and Willaert, E. 2006. On being declared illiterate: language-ideological disqualification in Dutch classes for immigrants in Belgium. *Language and Communication* 26: 34–54.

Blommaert, J., Collins, J. and Slembrouck, S. 2005a. Spaces of multilingualism. *Language and Communication* 25: 197–216.

2005b. Polycentricity and interactional regimes in 'global neighborhoods'. *Ethnography* 6: 205–235.

Blommaert, J., Beyens, K., Meert, H., Hillewaert, S., Verfaillie, K., Stuyck, K. and Dewilde, A. 2005. *Grenzen aan de Solidariteit*. Ghent: Academia Press.

Bonfiglio, T. 2002. *Race and the Rise of Standard American*. Berlin: Mouton de Gruyter.

Bourdieu, P. 1984. *Distinction : A Social Critique of the Judgment of Taste*. Cambridge MA: Harvard University Press.

1990. *The Logic of Practice*. Cambridge: Polity.

1991. *Language and Symbolic Power*. Cambridge: Polity.

Braeckman, Colette 1996. *Terreur Africaine*. Paris: Fayard.

Braudel, F. 1949. *La Méditerranée et le Monde méditerranéen à l'Epoque de Philippe II*. Paris: Armand Collin.

1969. Histoire et sciences sociales: La longue durée. In *Ecrits sur l'Histoire*, 41–83. Paris: Gallimard.

Britain, D. and Cheshire, J. (eds.) 2003. *Social Dialectology: In Honour of Peter Trudgill*. Amsterdam: John Benjamins.

Brutt-Griffler, J. 2002. *World English: A Study of its Development*. Clevedon: Multilingual Matters.

Bubinas, K. 2005. Gandhi *Marg*: The social construction and production of an ethnic economy in Chicago. *City and Society* 17: 161–179.

Calvet, L.-J. 2006. *Towards an Ecology of World Languages*. Cambridge: Polity Press.

Castells, M. 1996. *The Rise of the Network Society*. London: Blackwell.

1997. *The Power of Identity*. London: Blackwell.

Clyne, M. 2003. *Dynamics of Language Contact*. Cambridge University Press.

Collins, J. and Blot, R. 2003. *Literacy and Literacies: Texts, Power and Identity*. Cambridge University Press.

Conley, J. and O'Barr, W. 1990. *Rules versus Relationships: The Ethnography of Legal Discourse*. Chicago: University of Chicago Press.

Coupland, N. (ed.) 2003. Sociolinguistics and Globalisation. Special issue, *Journal of Sociolinguistics* 7(4): 465–623.

Crang, M. 1999. Globalization as conceived, perceived and lived spaces. *Theory, Culture and Society* 16(1): 167–177.

Dyers, C. 2004a. Ten years of democracy: shifting identities among South African school children. *Per Linguam* 20: 22–35.

2004b. Intervention and language attitudes: the effects of a development programme on the language attitudes of three groups of primary school teachers. In Brock-Utne, B., Desai, Z. and Qorro, M. (eds.), *Researching the Language of Instruction in Tanzania and South Africa*, 202–220. Cape Town: African Minds.

2008. Truncated multilingualism or language shift? An examination of language use in intimate domains in a new non-racial working class township in South Africa. *Journal of Multilingual and Multicultural Development* 29: 110–126.

Eelen, G. 2000. *A Critique of Politeness Theories*. Manchester: St Jerome.

Elmes, S. 2005. *Talking for Britain: A Journey through the Nation's Dialects*. Harmondsworth: Penguin Books.

Errington, J. 2001. State speech for peripheral publics in Java. In Gal, S. and Woolard, K. (eds.), *Languages and Publics: The Making of Authority*, 103–118. Manchester: St Jerome.

Extra, G. and Verhoeven, L. 1998. *Bilingualism and Migration*. Berlin: Mouton de Gruyter.

Fabian, J. 1986. *Language and Colonial Power*. Cambridge University Press.

Fairclough, N. 1992. *Discourse and Social Change*. Cambridge: Polity.

2006. *Language and Globalization*. London: Routledge.

Fals Borda, O. 2000. Peoples' SpaceTimes in global processes: the response of the local. *Journal of World Systems Research* 6(3): 624–634.

Feld, S. and Basso, K. (eds.) 1996. *Senses of Place*. Santa Fe: SAR Press.

Ferguson, J. and Gupta, A. 2002. Spatializing states: toward an ethnography of neoliberal governmentality. *American Ethnologist* 29: 981–1002.

Foucault, M. 1984. [1971] The order of discourse. In Shapiro, M. (ed.), *Language and Politics*, 108–138. London: Basil Blackwell.

2002. [1969] *The Archaeology of Knowledge*. London: Routledge.

2003. *Abnormal*. New York: Picador.

2005. *The Hermeneutics of the Subject*. Basingstoke: Palgrave Macmillan.

2007. *Security, Territory, Population*. Basingstoke: Palgrave Macmillan.

Fraser, N. 1995. From redistribution to recognition: dilemmas of justice in a 'post-socialist' age. *New Left Review* 212: 68–93.

Fukuyama, F. 1992. *The End of History and the Last Man*. New York: Free Press.

Geertz, C. 2004. What is a state if it is not a sovereign? Reflections on politics in complicated places. *Current Anthropology* 45(5): 577–593.

Goffman, E. 1974. *Frame Analysis: An Essay on the Organization of Experience*. New York: Harper and Row.

1981. *Forms of Talk*. Philadelphia: University of Pennsylvania Press.

Goodwin, C. 2002. Time in action. *Current Anthropology* 43, supplement: 19–35.

Goody, J. 1968. Restricted literacy in Ghana. In Goody, J. (ed.), *Literacy in Traditional Societies*, 198–264. Cambridge University Press.

Gumperz, J. 1982. *Discourse Strategies*. Cambridge University Press.

Hanks, W. 1996. *Language and Communicative Practice*. Boulder: Westview.

2006. Context, communicative. In Brown, K. (ed.), *Encyclopaedia of Language and Linguistics*, 2nd edition, 115–128. Oxford: Elsevier.

Hannerz, U. 1991. Scenarios for peripheral cultures. In King, A. (ed.), 1991. *Culture, Globalization and the World-System*, 107–128. London: Macmillan.

Harris, R. 2006. *New Ethnicities and Language Use*. London: Palgrave.

Haviland, J. 2003. How to point in Zinacantan. In Sotaro K. (ed.), *Pointing: Where Language, Culture, and Cognition Meet*, 139–169. Mahwah NJ: Erlbaum.

Heller, M. 1999. *Linguistic Minorities in Late Modernity*. London: Longman.

2003. Globalization, the new economy, and the commodification of language and identity. *Journal of Sociolinguistics* 7(4): 473–492.

Heugh, K. 1999. Languages, development and reconstructing education in South Africa. *International Journal of Educational Development* 19: 301–313.

Hobsbawm, E. 1975. *The Age of Capital*. London: Weidenfeld and Nicholson.

1987. *The Age of Empire, 1875–1914*. London: Abacus.

2007. *Globalisation, Democracy and Terrorism*. London: Little, Brown.

Hymes, D. 1966. Two types of linguistic relativity (with examples from Amerindian ethnography). In Bright, W. (ed.), *Sociolinguistics: Proceedings of the UCLA Sociolinguistics Conference 1964*, 114–167. The Hague: Mouton.

1974. *Foundations in Sociolinguistics: An Ethnographic Approach*. Philadelphia: University of Pennsylvania Press.

1980. *Language in Education: Ethnolinguistic Essays*. Washington DC: Center for Applied Linguistics.

1996. *Ethnography, Linguistics, Narrative Inequality: Toward an Understanding of Voice*. London: Taylor and Francis.

1998. When is oral narrative poetry? Generative form and its pragmatic conditions. *Pragmatics* 8: 475–500.

Irvine, J. and Gal, S. 2000. Language ideology and linguistic differentiation. In Kroskrity, P. (ed.), *Regimes of Language*, 35–83. Santa Fe: SAR Press.

Jacquemet, M. 2000. Beyond the speech community. Paper, 7th International Pragmatics Conference, Budapest, July 2000.

2005. Transidiomatic practices: Language and power in the age of globalization. *Language and Communication* 25(3): 257–277.

Jaffe, A. 2000. Introduction: non-standard orthography and non-standard speech. *Journal of Sociolinguistics* 4(4): 497–513.

Johnstone, B. 2008. *Discourse Analysis*, 2nd edition. London: Blackwell.

Jonckers, G. and Newton, C. 2004. *The Cape Flats: An Urban Strategy for Poverty Alleviation*. Unpublished MA dissertation, St Lucas Institute Ghent.

Kapp, R. 2001. *The Politics of English: A Study of Classroom Discourses in a Township School*. Unpublished PhD dissertation, University of Cape Town.

Kress, G. and van Leeuwen, T. 1996. *Reading Images: The Grammar of Visual Design*. London: Routledge.

Kroskrity, P. (ed.) 2000. *Regimes of Language*. Santa Fe: SAR Press.

Labov, W. 1966. *The Social Stratification of English in New York City*. Washington DC: Center for Applied Linguistics.

1972. *Sociolinguistic Patterns*. Philadelphia: University of Pennsylvania Press.

Lefebvre, H. 2003. *Key Writings*. New York: Continuum.

Levinson, S. 1983. *Pragmatics*. Cambridge University Press.

Lewinson, A. 2003. Globalizing the nation: Dar es Salaam and national culture in Tanzanian cartoons. *City and Society* 15: 9–30.

Low, S. (ed.) 2001. Remapping the city: place, order and ideology. *Special issue of American Anthropologist* 103(1): 5–111.

Makoni, S. and Pennycook, A. (eds.) 2007. *Disinventing and Reconstituting Languages*. Clevedon: Multilingual Matters.

Malkki, L. 1995. *Purity and Exile: Violence, Memory, and National Cosmology among Hutu Refugees in Tanzania*. Chicago: University of Chicago Press.

Mamdani, M. 2000. The political diaspora in Uganda and the background to the RPF invasion. In Goyvaerts, D. (ed.), *Conflict and Ethnicity in Central Africa*, 305–353. Tokyo: Institute for the Study of Languages and Cultures of Asia and Africa (Tokyo University of Foreign Studies).

Mankekar, P. 2002. India shopping: Indian grocery stores and transnational configurations of belonging. *Ethnos* 67: 75–98.

Maryns, K. 2006. *The Asylum Speaker: Language in the Belgian Asylum Procedure*. Manchester: St Jerome.

Maryns, K. and Blommaert, J. 2001. Stylistic and thematic shifting as narrative resources: assessing asylum seekers' repertoires. *Multilingua* 20(1): 61–84.

2002. Pretextuality and pretextual gaps: on re/defining linguistic inequality. *Pragmatics* 12(1): 11–30.

May, S. 2001. *Language and Minority Rights: Ethnicity, Nationalism and the Politics of Language*. London: Longman.

Mazrui, A. 2004. *English in Africa after the Cold War*. Clevedon: Multilingual Matters.

Mbuguni, L. A. and Ruhumbika, G. 1974. TANU and National Culture. In Ruhumbika, G. (ed.), *Towards Ujamaa: Twenty Years of TANU Leadership*, 275–287. Kampala: East African Literature Bureau.

McKay, D. and Brady, C. 2005. Practices of place-making: globalisation and locality in the Philippines. *Asia Pacific Viewpoint* 46(2): 89–103.

Mekacha, R. 1993. *The Sociolinguistic Impact of Kiswahili on Ethnic Community Languages in Tanzania: A Case Study of Ekinata*. Bayreuth, Germany: Bayreuth African Studies.

Milroy, J. and Milroy, L. 1991. *Authority in Language: Investigating Language Prescription and Standardisation*. London: Routledge.

Msanjila, Y. 1998. *The Use of Kiswahili and its Implications for the Future of Ethnic Languages in Tanzania*. Unpublished PhD dissertation, University of Dar es Salaam, Tanzania.

2004. The future of the Kisafwa language: a case study of Ituha village in Tanzania. *Journal of Asian and African Studies* 68: 161–171.

Mufwene, S. 2002. Colonization, globalization and the plight of 'weak' languages. *Journal of Linguistics* 38: 375–395.

2005. *Créoles, Ecologie sociale, Evolution linguistique*. Paris: L'Harmattan.

2008. *Language Evolution: Contact, Competition and Change*. London: Continuum.

Mühlhäusler, P. 1996. *Linguistic Ecology: Language Change and Linguistic Imperialism in the Pacific Rim*. London: Routledge.

Nettle, D. and Romaine, S. 2000. *Vanishing Voices: The Extinction of the World's Languages*. Oxford University Press.

Othman, H. 1994. The intellectual and transformation in Southern Africa. *Dar es Salaam Alumni Newsletter* 1(1): 9–10.

Pennycook, A. 2007. *Global Englishes and Transcultural Flows*. London: Routledge.

Pietikäinen, S. 2008. Sami in the media. Questions of language vitality and cultural hybridisation. *Journal of Multicultural Discourses* 3: 1, 22–35.

Phillipson, R. 1992. *Linguistic Imperialism*. London: Oxford University Press.

Pratt, C. 1976. *The Critical Phase in Tanzania: Nyerere and the Emergence of a Socialist Strategy*. Cambridge University Press.

Prinsloo, M. and Breier, M. (eds.) 1996. *The Social Uses of Literacy: Theory and Practice in Contemporary South Africa*. Amsterdam: John Benjamins.

Rampton, B. 1995. *Crossing: Language and Ethnicity among Adolescents*. London: Longman.

1999. 'Deutsch' in Inner London and the animation of an instructed foreign language. *Journal of Sociolinguistics* 3(4): 480–504.

2001. Critique in interaction. *Critique of Anthropology* 21(1): 83–107.

2003. Hegemony, social class, and stylisation. *Pragmatics* 13(1): 49–83.

2006. *Language in Late Modernity: Interaction in an Urban School*. Cambridge University Press.

Richardson, E. 2007. *Hiphop Literacies*. London: Routledge.

Scollon, R. and Scollon, S. W. 2003. *Discourse in Place: Language in the Material World*. London: Routledge.

Shivji, I. 1996. *Intellectuals at the Hill: Essays and Talks 1969–1993*. Dar es Salaam: Dar es Salaam University Press.

Silverstein, M. 1996. Monoglot 'standard' in America: standardization and metaphors of linguistic hegemony. In Brenneis, D. and Macaulay, R. (eds.). *The Matrix of Language: Contemporary Linguistic Anthropology*, 284–306. Boulder: Westview Press.

1998. Contemporary transformations of local linguistic communities. *Annual Review of Anthropology* 27: 401–426.

2003a. Indexical order and the dialectics of sociolinguistic life. *Language and Communication* 23: 193–229.

2003b. *Talking Politics: The Substance of Style from Abe to 'W'*. Chicago: Prickly Paradigm Press.

2006a. Pragmatic indexing. In Brown, K. (ed.), *Encyclopaedia of Language and Linguistics*, 2ⁿᵈ Edition, Volume 6, 14–17. Amsterdam: Elsevier.

2006b. Old wine, new ethnographic lexicography. *Annual Review of Anthropology* 35: 481–496.

Silverstein, M. and Urban, G. (eds.) 1996. *Natural Histories of Discourse*. Chicago: University of Chicago Press.

Skutnabb-Kangas, T. 2000. *Linguistic Genocide in Education – Or Worldwide Diversity and Human Rights?* Mahwah NJ: Lawrence Erlbaum.

Skutnabb-Kangas, T. and Phillipson, R. 1995. Linguicide and linguicism. *Rolig Papir* 53, Roskilde Universitetscenter, Denmark, 83–91.

1999. Language ecology. In Verschueren, J. *et al.* (eds.) *Handbook of Pragmatics*, 1999. Installment 1–24. Amsterdam: John Benjamins.

Street, B. 1995. *Social Literacies: Critical Approaches to Literacy in Development, Ethnography, and Education*. London: Longman.

Stroud, C. 2001. African mother-tongue programmes and the politics of language: linguistic citizenship versus linguistic human rights. *Journal of Multilingual and Multicultural Development* 22(4): 339–355.

de Swaan, A. 2001. *Words of the World*. Cambridge: Polity Press.

Swyngedouw, E. 1996. Reconstructing citizenship, the re-scaling of the State and the new authoritarianism: closing the Belgian mines. *Urban Studies* 33(8): 1499–1521.

Thesen, L. and van Pletzen, E. (eds.) 2006. *Academic Literacy and the Languages of Change*. London: Continuum.

Uitermark, J. 2002. Re-scaling, 'scale fragmentation' and the regulation of antagonistic relationships. *Progress in Human Geography* 26(6): 743–765.

Verschueren, J. 1998. *Understanding Pragmatics*. London: Edward Arnold.

Vertovec, S. 2006. The emergence of super-diversity in Britain. Centre on Migration, Policy and Society, Working Paper 25 (Oxford University).

Vlassenroot, K. 2000. The promise of ethnic conflict: militarization and enclave-formation in South Kivu. In Goyvaerts, D. (ed.), *Conflict and Ethnicity in Central Africa*, 59–104. Tokyo: Institute for the Study of Languages and Cultures of Asia and Africa (Tokyo University of Foreign Studies).

Vlassenroot, K. and Raeymaekers, T. 2004. The politics of rebellion and intervention in Ituri: the emergence of a new political complex? *African Affairs* 103: 386–412.

Voloshinov, V. N. 1973. *Marxism and the Philosophy of Language*. Cambridge MA: Harvard University Press.

Wallerstein, I. 1983. *Historical Capitalism*. London: Verso.

1997. The time of space and the space of time: The future of social science. http://fbc.binghamton.edu/iwtynesi.htm

2000. *The Essential Immanuel Wallerstein*. New York: The New Press.

2001. *Unthinking Social Science*, 2nd edition. Philadelphia: Temple University Press.

2004. *World-Systems Analysis: An Introduction*. Durham NC: Duke University Press.

Webb, V. 1994. Revalorizing the autochthonous languages of Africa. In Pütz, M. (ed.), *Language Contact, Language Conflict*, 181–214. Amsterdam: John Benjamins.

Wong, C. H.-Y. and McDonogh, G. 2001. The mediated metropolis: anthropological issues in cities and mass communication. *American Anthropologist* 130(1): 96–111.

Index